SEXSCOPES

How to Seduce, Stimulate, and Satisfy Any Sign

STUART HAZLETON

A Fireside Book

Published by Simon & Schuster

New York   London   Toronto   Sydney

FIRESIDE
Rockefeller Center
1230 Avenue of the Americas
New York, NY 10020

FIRESIDE and colophon are registered trademarks
of Simon & Schuster, Inc.

Designed by Diane Hobbing

Manufactured in the United States of America
10   9   8
Library of Congress Cataloging-in-Publication Data
Hazleton, Stuart, 1968–
      Sexscopes : how to seduce, stimulate, and satisfy any sign / Stuart Hazleton.
          p.   cm.
      "A Fireside book."
      1. Astrology and sex.   I. Title.

    BF1729.S4 H39 2001
    133.5'83067–dc21

                                                    00-067188

    ISBN 0-7432-0300-3

Acknowledgments

I'd like to thank Marcela Landres, Frank Weimann, and Philip Metcalf for getting my writing into print, along with Christopher Poole, Julie Taylor, John Whitmore, Patty Moore, Kristi and Alice Hazleton for having faith in me and my ability.

I dedicate this book to my mom,
who introduced me to the wild,
wonderful world of astrology
and taught me that telling the truth
is always the best path to follow.

Contents

SEXSCOPES

Chapter 1

Why I Wrote This Book and How to Use It

When my fascination with astrology began, it blew my mind how on target the info it provided was. It was like I'd suddenly been handed a psychological road map explaining the motivation that drove my enemies, friends, and family. Within months, I realized why a certain Sagittarius in my life saw fooling around behind his spouse's back as A-OK and why an Aquarian bud was great at giving advice but when it came to putting her words into action, well, that was a totally different story.

Fast forward a few years and I got my first job writing astrolgy advice at Bolt, a website for older teenagers (www.bolt.com). My editor there was one of the coolest people I've ever met. Instead of trying to downplay my somewhat over-the-top writing style, she told me to run with it.

"If you want to write about a wet dream, do it," she said, and the sense of freedom she gave me opened my eyes further to what this too-cool tool could do for others. I could share what I knew in my voice, without trying to edit out all the controversial bits I'm notorious for. My philosophy, which is pretty damn liberal, came through full force. Bolt was happy and I was happy.

I wanted to do more though. I wanted to give sexual strategies that weren't really appropriate for the "Omigawd, did you watch *Buffy* last night?" age group. That's where *Cosmopolitan* stepped in. The staff there wasn't embarrassed by my trash-talk: They actually liked it. My own wet dream of saying whatever the hell I wanted to was coming true. As *Cosmo*'s astrologer, I could talk about bumping uglies, blow jobs, or whatever else popped into my bawdy brain. I still couldn't actually *say* blow job though, since I still had to mask my sexual stuff with *Golden Girls*-style innuendo. I didn't lose sleep over it though: Being *Cosmopolitan*'s astrologer gave me access to opportunities I'd been hoping for. Along with *Cosmopolitan*, *Cosmopolitan: All About Men*, and *CosmoGirl!*, I've also written about astrology for the Lifetime network.

One thing was still missing though. When I talk, whether it's to my spouse, best friend, or Joe Blow at the corner 7-Eleven, I can't help but communicate like a truck driver. Who knows: Maybe I share some DNA in common with Jamie Lee Curtis, but I figure why say "Yeah," when "Fuck, yeah!!!" feels so much easier slipping off my tongue. It's not that I'm thinking about sex 24/7, it's just that I've always been an earthy kind of guy. Meanwhile, when doing research for a *Cosmo* pull-out book, I realized that most books about sexual astrology are almost as exciting as reading the ingredients on a chewing gum wrapper. The info between the pages might be great but if it's written in a dull and dry manner, who the hell is going to read it? After weeks of complaining to my editor about the lack of pulse-pounding smutty astrology, she finally said, "Well, Stuart, why don't you get off your ass and write one yourself?" I took her advice, got off my ass, and wrote the book you're holding in your hot little hands.

Some words of warning: I believe in calling the shots as I see them and though many find this offensive, I've discovered that a lot of people talk the same way I do. In our country, it's cool to see someone's head chopped off in a *Friday the 13th* flick but forbidden to watch people bumping uglies. Why is this? I'm not sure but it's pretty damned ignorant: While almost everyone thinks about or engages in sex, unless you're a serial killer it's probably not all that important that you see someone's head severed from their bod. Don't get me wrong: I love horror flicks almost as much as I like sex. I just think that to allow seventeen-year-olds in to see *American Psycho* while the *Ellen* show is rated MA is amazingly lame. I mean, *Showgirls* sucked but the idea that jiggling tits or an erect dick is going to some-how corrupt America is so behind the times it's not even funny.

Astro 101

I wrote this book for everyday people, not the astrological elite. If you know what *adjunct, sextile,* and *cusp* mean put this book down because it's way too elemen-tal for you. But if you're wanting a quick, sexual analysis of any sign—whether you're aiming for an awesome one-night stand or a lifelong commitment—this is the book for you. With that in mind, there are still a few things that deserve ex-planations before you jump in.

First, what the hell *is* a Sun sign? It's easy to figure out once you understand how astrology works. Based on where the Sun was at the time you were born, you're one of twelve different zodiac signs. Each has its own basic psychology and sexuality and each is decidedly different from one sign to the next. Once you've figured out the birth date of the object of your affections, track down the corresponding chapter. Once you're there, I give you all the information you need to impress and understand them. I even elaborate on things further: Each Sun sign is broken down into three groups, called decanates. This can help to refine your sexual strategy even further. Instead of trying to be super specific—which isn't what astrology is all about—I work in generalities. To accompany the sexual secrets, I also add psychological information about each sign and decanate. It's hard to be 100 percent certain that your Pisces will be going down on you on the first date but after reading the lowdown I've dished out, at least you should have a damn good idea. I also give pointers on how to get what you want from your in-the-sack conquest, but don't worry: You won't have to read between the lines to know exactly what I'm saying.

A few other things worth mentioning are that each sign is from one of four groups. I don't make a big deal out of this, just casually mention it in passing during each chapter, but if you want a quick lesson, here it is.

There are four elements and each holds three signs from the zodiac. Fire signs (Aries, Leo, and Sagittarius) are go-getters who love to take action. Earth signs (Taurus, Virgo, and Capricorn) are sensible and practical. Air signs (Gemini, Libra, and Aquarius) tend to have their head in the clouds and love to talk. Water signs, meanwhile, (Cancer, Scorpio, and Pisces) are passionate with a strong sense of intuition.

Okay, lesson over—and that wasn't so difficult, was it? Now, get to work: Look up your lover—or lover to be—in the pages between this tome: Although my writing style might be soft, we want to make sure *something* gets hard.

The Nitty-Gritty

Okay, if you're aiming to get your rocks off tonight, I'd skip this part, but if you want to fully understand everything I'm going to explain in future chapters, skimming over this blueprint will help illustrate what every section details.

1. Sex Stats: These lists are detailed compilations of everything that could possibly warm the form of your intended sign from their favorite drink to their ultimate sexual position.
2. Do You Know What You're in For?: This is where I deliver the dirt on every sign.

Like Aries guys always seem to miss the toilet when they're pissing and if you're going to dump a Scorpio female, you'd better make damn sure you don't break the ties that bind in a public place. Get it? 'Nuff said.

3. Five Surefire Ways to Break the Ice: These are pickup lines that actually work. Forget lame intros like, "I wish you were a plastic horse outside Kmart so I could drop a quarter in you and ride you all night long," and use these sexual strategies instead.

4. Refining Your Sexual Strategy—The Subrulers: The plot of your intended amour thickens in this area as I break down each sign into three different sections. Depending on when the Capricorn in question was born, you might be faced with a *chica* who's 100 percent businesswoman or a girl who's got a wild streak a mile long.

5. Sexual Synergy: So how's the sex going to be between you and your intended? I tell it like it is in this section and explain if your coitus will be more fun than a trip to Disney World, just okay, or more boring than a *Who's the Boss?* marathon.

6. Exploring Their Erogenous Zone: Here's the skinny on the fastest way to get your lover's libido revving on all eight cylinders. Pisces like their feet tickled while Scorpio would rather you explore a more intimate region. Wanna know what it is? Turn the pages to find out.

7. Come Again? If you're like me, that Jacqueline Susanne novel *Once Is Not Enough* is written all over your face the minute you've gotten off. I've found begging for more usually doesn't work so these are my tips for getting your other half to gun for a round two without having to explicitly ask.

8. But Will It Last? If you're just looking to scope out a fast and furious fuck, forget this section—but if you want to know your odds at a long-term love affair or the big M, keep reading.

9. Celebs: Celebrities I've picked who exemplify the traits of their sign.

Chapter 2

ARIES
(March 20–April 19)

Sex Stats

Ruling planet: Mars, the fuck now/think later god of war, aggression, and *action*.

Signature symbol: The ram, headstrong and stubborn but sure-footed in sensual arenas.

Trademark color: Red—as in those cherry-colored edible undies Aries not-so-secretly wants you to slip into, it's also the shade associated with pedal-to-the-metal sexuality.

Favorite position: Always on top and *always* in charge.

Potent porn: Retro raunch like *The Story of O* for the straight and lesbian set since it's all about beautiful women, submission, and domination. If you're a gay guy, snag anything with Jeff Palmer: Not only is he a dominating prick—he's got one, too.

Ultimate outfit (male): A black leather ensemble that would put *Shaft* to shame or a good old cowboy look complete with shit-kicking steel-toed boots: Raunchy rams dress in excess for sexcess.

Ultimate outfit (female): A tight-fitting Donna Karan top paired with a black or blood-red leather mini that's shorter than Danny DeVito—all above spike heels so high they're practically lethal.

Mattress mambo music: Hardcore Prince like *Sexy MF* or head-banging music from Metallica to bang a different kind of head to.

Best sex toy: Handcuffs for you (since your Aries loves to take charge).

After-fuck finger food: Lay's Bar-b-que potato chips—but don't make the mistake of buying a low-fat variety: Aries needs those calories to recharge.

Do You Know What You're in For?

Aries is a fire sign and, as such, the object of your affection is almost always going to be hot under the collar about something. Mood swings will be fast and furious, since the sign of the ram can go from blissfully happy to totally pissed off in a matter of seconds. If you've ever seen a three year old throw a temper tantrum then you have some idea of what's in store for you. But like a three year old, Aries is always ready to tackle new challenges. Taureans like to find one thing they're good at it and stick with it for a lifetime but doing the same ol', same ol' bores the hell out of an Aries. Although one of the most energetic signs in the zodiac, this excess chutzpah doesn't always translate into becoming the next CEO of a Fortune 500 company. Why? Because rams are famed for leaping before they look, taking immediate, impulsive action but never thinking through what repercussions their conduct will bring. Whether you find this trait irritating or exciting depends upon you, but before you go for an Aries, realize that this balls-to-the-wall approach to life isn't just a phase. It's what Aries is all about and if you think you can change that equation, think again. Speaking of balls, whether you're aiming for a *chico* or *chica,* just like the AC/DC song goes, rams have the biggest balls of them all. Fear is for losers and an Aries takes pride in the fact that he or she never takes the easy way out. Courage is their keyword and if you win the heart of an Aries you'll get an excellent bodyguard in the bargain.

Their constant quest for action and adventure can lead to boredom in the bedroom though, so if you're only comfortable with the missionary position and blush when you glance at a copy of the *Kama Sutra* go for a less bawdy sign like Capricorn or Aquarius. If you like forceful personalities and enjoy pretending you're a human pretzel, guess what? You've just found paradise.

Aries Man

The Aries man is loud, domineering, abrasive—and oftentimes 100 percent stud. This is the kind of guy who won't put the toilet seat up before he pees no matter how much you might beg and plead. This scattershot approach applies to other aspects of his life as well. He's from the bump-and-grind school of lovemaking so if you're looking for long romantic dinners by candlelight take my advice and *keep looking.* He's the original five-minute man, so if you're turned on by ultra-macho grunt-and-groaning types you've just found your ticket to heaven. Meanwhile, odds are higher than Robert Downey, Jr., that he's into all the typically masculine pursuits like hunting and fishing, although he probably avoids activities like weight-lifting, which, to him, smack of male vanity. He thinks women have their place so if you're not content cooking his meals and washing out his skid-marked undies he's probably not your type. If you're a gay guy aiming for an Aries dude expect similar treatment. Look at it this way: He won't have a problem if you feel like accompanying him on one of his hunting trips as long as you remember to stay in the tent, keep your hands clean, and keep his dinner warm. Whether he's gay or straight he's definitely got a chauvinist pig thing goin' on so although he's allowed to burp and fart as much as he wants to and gain a Clinton-esque belly in midlife you better keep a close eye on your own appearance. He'll show his appreciation in a multitude of ways though, so if you're willing to play ball with an Aries expect to be put on a pedestal and treasured well into your old age.

He's got other great things going for him, too. He's not afraid to voice his opinion—even if no one else around him agrees with it. He's not afraid to try new things either, as he welcomes new challenges as a test of his manhood. He's not prone to cheat like, say, a Sagittarius, but if you don't live up to his expectations he won't feel guilty looking for sex outside your relationship. So what kind of sex does he like? Fast and furious, baby. This guy lives for blowjobs and the good news for those of you who don't like to head south is that he comes the same way he does everything else—*quickly*. When it comes to the smutty samba, what he lacks in expertise he makes up for with energy. Although you might associate his technique more with a jackhammer than a love machine, you'll never wonder if he's having a good time. Unlike an enigmatic Pisces or manipulative Gemini, you'll know exactly what he's thinking on the headboard-banging front—probably because he'll be yelling it in your ear.

Aries Woman

The Aries woman is an odd combo. She's got all the drive of her masculine counterpart but a lot of the time that drive is subverted in directions that become destructive. Why does she feel weird about being a tough female? Because in our somewhat fucked-up society a man who calls the shots is a stud while a woman who does exactly the same thing is a bitch. She doesn't think this double standard is fair but since she tends to get a lot of shit when she speaks her mind, she's a bit quieter than an Aries male. She's still one of the toughest cookies you'll ever have the pleasure—or displeasure—of bumping heads with though. Aries women are often excellent in business and can usually amass a great deal of money in their lives. The reason why? They keep a tighter control on their emotions and think things through more thoroughly than their dick-dangling brethren. When you combine an abundance of testosterone with a fire sign like Aries, you basically end up with an eternally pissed-off teenager, but when you opt for estrogen instead you get someone who isn't just strong—she's rational too. Think of Sigourney Weaver's character Ripley in the *Alien* saga if you want to get a handle on a true Aries female. She's tough as nails, willing to blast the fuck out of anything that stands in her way, but she'll always return to protect the people she loves.

Some words of warning: Whether you're looking for lesbian love or are straight as an arrow, an Aries woman's style between the sheets will take some getting used to. She views sex as more of a physical act than some sappy Danielle Steele romance. This chick reads Jackie Collins instead—if she reads at all—and like one of Ms. Collins's heroines, sometimes a fuck to her is just that. If you're a bored exec and want to find out what it's like to be treated like a piece of meat, go for a one-night stand with an Aries. She'll be gone before you wake up the next morning and the next time she sees you she just might have trouble remembering your name. If you've fallen head over heels however, her forthright honesty couldn't be better. *Faster, slower, harder,* are all words she's not afraid to say when you're bumping uglies and if you choose to ignore her advice, get ready for her to ignore *you.* She's got a touch of kink to her personality so don't get freaked out when she talks dirty or wants to free your inner schoolboy or girl by bending you over her knee. The real truth is that she's all woman—the only question is, are you man or woman enough to handle her?

Five Surefire Ways to Break the Ice with Aries

Aries Man
1. Start a conversation about the football game that was on TV last night (it doesn't matter whether you watched it or not).
2. Ask where the best fishing spot is.
3. Play the part of a helpless female or male—Aries dudes love to act tough—by telling him you just can't understand why your car won't start.
4. Praise his masculinity, as in, "*Wow,* that box you just lifted sure looked heavy!"
5. (For women only) Apply lots of makeup (preferably with a trowel), slip into your most feminine dress, and "drop" something as you walk past him.

Aries Woman

1. Tell an off-color, preferably raunchy joke.
2. Start a debate over anything from politics to the merits of the *Scream* trilogy.
3. Be argumentative: When an Aries woman was little she was the type who'd punch whoever she had a crush on.
4. Discuss your too-cool sports car (or how much you want one): the Aries woman loves sleek, shiny things and has always felt a serious need for speed.
5. Talk about your accomplishments. Whether you're male or female, an Aries woman wants someone powerful or someone who's about to become powerful.

Refining Your Sexual Strategy—The Subrulers

Mars: God of War (March 20—March 31)

When you're faced with someone whose ruler and subruler both happen to be the god of aggression, you get someone with some badass attitude problems. This person can be overly abrasive and combative but they've got good attributes that balance the bad ones. An Aries born during this time period will *always* choose movement over stagnation, so if you're pursuing a partner who's aggressive or proactive, this guy or girl is just what you're looking for.

If you're seeking an equal exchange—whether it's long term or just for five minutes—you'd best look elsewhere. Aries born under this subruler must be in charge 24/7: There is no such thing as compromise. They must control each and every situation down to the smallest detail or they feel powerless and become overwhelmed with anger. If you want someone who's ballsy enough to call *all* of the shots, go for this particular strain of Aries. Arguments actually end up being more rare with this decanate of Aries than with the other two: While the last two Aries view trade-offs as a last resort, Ariens whose subruler is the mean guy of the zodiac will never give in. Putting it bluntly, most signs will have a very difficult time getting along with someone whose parameters resemble those of a pit bull.

Sexually, this sign is an explosion waiting to happen. Bumping uglies will be wham-bam but can still be very rewarding—*if* you're positioning yourself for a passive role. He or she must dominate all things sexual so if you try calling the shots this Aries will say adios. The good news is that this partner's passion won't just end in the bedroom. He or she will do everything in their power to protect you, which in turn can sometimes end up making you look like an idiot. They'll bitch out your boss or break the balls of your most dreaded enemy. Aries sub-ruled by Mars are assault charges waiting to happen but if you want someone with drive and determination to spare, you just found your ticket.

The Sun: Change and Innovation (April 1–April 10)

Aries subruled by the Sun are loosened up by the great ball of fire our world rotates around. Far less extreme than Aries whose subruler is Mars, those born during this time period are less combative and more caring. Their dominating drive—courtesy of ruler Mars—is tempered by the Sun's readiness for change, fun and new adventures. This decanate is *extremely* sexual so get ready for aaaaahhhh-inspiring adventures that will leave you wondering whether you're going or coming (but don't worry too much: With this Aries in charge, it'll surely be the latter).

This type of Aries is more of a forward thinker than the other two. He or she is concerned with changing his or her surroundings, which can make for a very re-warding equation in the bedroom. While other Aries like fast and furious fucking, this decanate prefers a variety of styles, so get ready for some slow and easy sex action in addition to the usual five-minute quickie. Am I implying this Aries will be a sucker for romance? Not just no, but *no fucking way*. The real skinny is that this Aries will be up for more than just dominating you, which *will* translate into your getting sucked or eaten out once in a while.

In bed, this type of Aries will try out almost anything once, so don't feel shy about breaking out the whipped cream or handcuffs. Whether he or she ends up *enjoying* your sexual scenario is a whole different story however, but since this is Aries we're talking about, you needn't worry about them sexually suffering in si-lence. They'll be very up front about whatever they want from you fornication-ally, so take notes and get to work.

Jupiter: Fun and Games (April 11–April 19)

Jupiter is the god of mirth and mischief, which serves as a perfect counterbalance to Aries' usual badass attitude. This Aries is far more subdued than the first two but if you think this means he or she doesn't feel free to speak his/her mind, think again, because this sign loves to yak just as much as the other two. It's sim-ply that he or she won't be quite as much of a bastard or a bitch when it comes to getting their way. Jupiter is laid-back, expressive and all about having fun. This Aries likes to play games in bed but not the "I'm gonna withhold sex 'till you buy me something expensive" kind. Like the navy, this Aries doesn't view sex as just a job—it's an adventure. Although his or her sexual spectrum isn't always on the go, like an Aries whose subruler is the Sun, this sign is still all about gettin' some. This decrease in military-style attitude means you'll have more of an even exchange in the sack. This sign also loves to travel, so get ready to safari to the Sahara, get drunk in New Orleans, and dance the night away in Paris. As an added bonus, this sign is extremely lucky in life, so another place you can count on going is Vegas.

Bet on joining the mile-high club during one of these round-the-world jaunts. This Aries is up for almost anything and an awesome way to get this decanate to do *whatever* you want between the sheets is to pose your sexual request as a dare or a game. This Aries will rise to any challenge but isn't driven by a sense of anger or a love of change like the first two. He or she will fight because life is a game and the only way to win is by fighting. Be abrupt and to the point since sexual innuendo will slide in one ear of this sign and out the other.

"I'll betcha twenty bucks you can't blow me for two hours!" What sounds horribly embarrassing on paper won't seem nearly as extreme when you encounter this, the most open-minded of the three Aries. And once you've forked over that twenty and your sex spot is exhausted, you'll be glad you took a gamble on this wild and crazy sign.

Sexual Synergy

Aries and Aries: Unless you're snockered on schnapps, chances are lower than Rush Limbaugh's IQ that you'll ever bed another Aries. If you do, the sex will be amazing—at least for the first time. After that, sex will quickly become a competition to see who gets to play top dog. Pointless and problematic, you're far more interested in playing head games with each other than giving head. Look elsewhere.

Taurus and Aries: Rams like their lovers somewhat submissive while bulls get a kick out of a tough guy—or girl—attitude. Take the phone off the hook for the first few days of your coupling because you won't be getting out of bed anytime soon.

Gemini and Aries: When you mix air with fire sometimes you get an explosion and that's exactly what Aries can look forward to with this oh-so-sexy air sign. Aries' no guts/no glory bedroom behavior makes Gemini breathe a little faster while Gemini's playful nature in the sack is exactly what the ram requires. A porn flick waiting to happen.

Cancer and Aries: Aries will have fun making you feel like a cheap piece of meat but unless you're a glutton for punishment you won't enjoy the ride. Aries thinks you're a wuss and the first time this ram uses the bathroom without shutting the door you'll know you've died and gone straight to hell.

Leo and Aries: When a ram rocks your world your kingdom won't be the only thing that comes. Both of you view sex as a game—and a damn fun one at that. Competition is your only curse so skip the 68 (you do me and I'll owe you one) to go for a solid 69.

Virgo and Aries: In a word, "Yeeeuuucch!" Virgos are all about heated eye-contact and prudent passion while subtlety isn't exactly a strong suit for the sign of the ram. Aries' trademark five-minute quickies will lead to catty comments from Virgo like, "Let me know when you're finished," and "Is it in?"

Libra and Aries: Aries is the yin, to your, well, yang: The raunchy daydreams you're too shy to share with other signs will spill out easily to this talkative ram. Even better, Aries gets off on role-playing so he or she will take pleasure in making your fantasy come true right before you do.

Scorpio and Aries: When you put these hardcore signs together you get so much heat you better have the fire station's number handy. You'll have fun competing to see who can bring the other the most pleasure. Count on mind-blowing orgasms and exploration of sexual avenues you'll never want Mom to know about.

Sagittarius and Aries: Aries' approach to the wild thing is way too forceful for your naturally laid-back nature. Sagittarius wants to drip ice cream over each other's bods while Aries is from the "let's get it on *now*" school of bump and grind. Sagittarius thinks Aries is amazingly unskilled; Aries thinks Sagi's fascination with sexual experimentation is spooky.

Capricorn and Aries: At first, it will seem like you're having sex with a sibling: On some fronts you couldn't be more alike (ambition and drive) while on others you couldn't be more different (Cappy's quiet while the ram is louder than Mariah Carey). Trying to understand each other will heat the sex up gradually but if you're aiming for just a one-night stand, aim somewhere else.

Aquarius and Aries: Talking is something you both love to do but in the bedroom Aries will wonder "Where is the love?" unless Aquarius can shut up long enough to do it. The Aquarian who-gives-a-damn attitude is a big turn-on for Aries, who will eventually enjoy trying out the various sexual scenarios Aquarius envisions. Great sex, but it might take some pushes and shoves to get you there.

Pisces and Aries: Aries breaks out the big guns in the bedroom and passive Pisces can't get enough. Aries' blunt behavior may be a mild turn-off to Pisces but if Aries will put his or her social skills to work, Pisces won't complain too much. Aries likes to command and Pisces loves to serve, and once you start enacting this power play between the sheets you'll both be smiling. Sounds like passion paradise to me.

Exploring Their Erogenous Zone

Unless you're one of the sorry saps who think oral action is better left to porn stars, just about everyone likes getting head, right? For an Aries though, giving up what he or she wants doesn't necessarily involve waxing the beanpole or munching the bearded clam. Nope—Aries is interested in a different kind of head altogether, namely that big thing attached to their neck. Licking or nibbling a ram around the face and neck is an awesome intro to getting your female hot and bothered or your male to stand at immediate attention. Don't drool on them like a Great Dane though: Although Aries might be a bit sloppy in the sack, sometimes, *you* should be artful, with a strong emphasis on teasing titillation—not by leaving some Scooby Doo slobber trail down their cheek. If you want to seduce an Aries, running your fingers through his or her hair is an awesome starting point. Start out with slow, soft stroking as you stare into their eyes. Aries aren't big on kissing and other traditional signs of romance. They want to be turned on and one of the things that most excites them is a partner who can keep themselves under control. Am I saying you should play hard to get or be a prude? *Fuck, no.* But you should never act trashy or whorish—unless its a one-time fantasy that you both understand is a momentary game of fiction turned to friction. Aries are turned on by breeding—or at least the appearance of it—so acting like something that rolled out of a late-eighties Madonna video *isn't* a good idea. Keep this simple rule in mind: Show some class, give some sass, and they'll always come back for a piece of ass.

Come Again?

Aries Man

Aries dudes are about the easiest guys in the zodiac to manipulate into a pulse-pounding round two or three. How do you do it? Piecing the puzzle will be as easy as he is if you just learn to appeal to his manhood. Yup, this means you're going to have to free your inner helpless side—even if you don't have one. The cool thing is, since the Aries man already thinks he's God's gift, he'll usually fall for your line even if its just a bunch of BS. When the deed is done, catch your breath, wait a few seconds to a few minutes (Aries doesn't need much time to recharge) then say, "Wow—that was utterly *fantastic!*" Practice saying this in front of a mirror a few times in case you're afraid you'll crack up when faced with the real deal. Then act somewhat shy and clueless as you compliment him on anything from his control to his cock. Keep your Pollyanna performance in mind though, because if you're not acting somewhat innocent by blushing or appearing embarrassed, this technique will fail faster than Pat Buchanan on the campaign trail.

That said, if you find gunning your guy for more rounds is simple but keeping him from, um, shooting his wad in fifteen seconds is a bit more of a problem, realize that rams get right to the point. If you can teach him some things a bit less basic than his standard wham-bam-thank-you-ram technique you'll end up a much happier camper. Focus his attention more on foreplay and if he insists on getting right to business, send him south so you'll ultimately have as much fun as he does. Aries guys are pretty oral so probably all it will take is a gentle push and once he's down there you'll realize that Aries always aims to please.

Aries Woman

Rule number one—don't beg. Although the Aries man may be easier to resurrect than Jason in a *Friday the 13th* sequel, keep in mind that his female counterpart is harder to get into than the Viper Room on a Saturday night. It's that testosterone thing again. While a ram man often lets his little head do the thinking for his big one, the Aries woman is looking for quality instead of quantity. And just like buddying up to Johnny Depp would allow you free access to his club any time you felt like going, there's a secret to making a ram woman want to ram again. Putting it bluntly, you better be a damn good lover. If you're just into pleasuring yourself or fall prey to premature ejaculation, you can bet your ass she'll opt for a late-night rerun of *Seinfeld* instead of a rerun with you. Honesty is a key issue also, because Aries women hate being lied to. If you're fooling around behind her back or bullshitting her on an important issue, she'll sense it sooner rather than later and although she probably won't say no to your first sexual advance, she'll be doing so to get her own sexual rocks off and once she has, she'll seek entertainment elsewhere. The Aries woman likes to take charge so you can easily put yourself in a win/win situation by making her come more times than that pesky salesman who keeps showing up at your work—and then turning on the *Seinfeld* rerun yourself. In other words, if you drive her wild *and* let her assume the driver's seat, you won't need to ask for a round two because she will.

But Will It Last?

Aries and Aries: Yup, sparks will fly but not for very long in the bedroom. Both of you are used to getting what you want and won't take no for an answer. Plan on making war instead of love and your romance having a shorter shelf life than rump roast.

Taurus and Aries: You're slow and methodical, while Aries believes in acting today and analyzing tomorrow. The sex will be stellar—at first—but beyond the bedroom Aries thinks you're a stick-in-the-mud, while deep down you think Aries is the ultimate asshole.

Gemini and Aries: Your skillful use of words and ready wit freak Aries out and his or her semipossessive streak makes you feel both admired and desired. Totally raunchy dialogue is going to play a major role in your relationship so slip out of your clothes, slip your tongue into trash talk mode, and watch Aries' eyes widen.

Cancer and Aries: What begins with a bang ends with a whimper as you slowly come to terms with the fact that Aries couldn't be less your type. You want to play house while Aries is just a player. Compromise is key to your happiness, so when Aries orders you around you'll beat a hasty retreat.

Leo and Aries: All signals are go if you can learn to curb your competition with each other. Both of you like to call the shots but for entirely different reasons. Leo wants to be the star while Aries aims for the director's seat. When you learn to view this as an asset instead of a liability your love life with Aries will flourish.

Virgo and Aries: Can we say, "Match made in hell?" The only thing that will suck harder than your relationship will be your sex life. Even worse, those are the only things that'll *ever* get sucked since both of you are way too haughty to please the other first.

Libra and Aries: Aries' forceful approach to life comes into direct conflict with your peace-loving, playful nature. What Aries views as conversation you view as argumentation, so unless you're using the universal language of love, count on quarrels. One-night stand? Definitely. Emergency booty call? Maybe. Lasting love? Sorry, but there's no cigar, Monica.

Scorpio and Aries: You could have a spectacular lifelong romance with the sign of the ram—if you don't kill each other first. Face facts, Scorpio: You're the jealous type, so Aries' dive into a diversity of interests can fuel your insecure side. If you avoid jumping to conclusions this could be a glorious mating though—and the sex will be mind-blowing.

Sagittarius and Aries: Aries is willing to give you the long leash you want in life and your droll sense of humor presents a constant mental challenge that Aries truly loves. Your bond will be blissful unless you give into your penchant for screwing around. Heed this warning, Sagi: Cheat once and you'll lose this ram *forever.*

Capricorn and Aries: Rams are wild while goats live for order, but if you're willing to work hard at making your relationship work your love life stands a strong chance of success. Both of you are honest, hard workers who can't stand liars and cheats. Traits you find irritating early on will become endearing sooner than you think. Stick it out.

Aquarius and Aries: You like to theorize while Aries has to act, but in this coupling opposites can attract. Your radical views of the world keep Aries on his or her toes while the reality-based thinking of the ram is a perfect complement to your head-in-the-clouds way of thinking.

Pisces and Aries: Whether you're comfortable admitting it or not, there's a part of you that loves to be ordered around and that just happens to be one of the ram's fave activities. Aries protects you and your affectionate devotion makes the ram weak in the knees. Aries' boldness in bed and beyond brings out your best and you'll take to this ram's sexual prowess like a fish to water.

Aries Celebs: Tough Guys and Badass Girls

Holly Hunter	March 20
Spike Lee	March 20
Gary Oldman	March 21
Timothy Dalton	March 21
Reese Witherspoon	March 22
William Shatner	March 22
Chaka Khan	March 23
Mase	March 24
Sarah Jessica Parker	March 25
Elton John	March 25
Aretha Franklin	March 25
Mariah Carey	March 27
Quentin Tarantino	March 27
Reba McEntire	March 28
Jennifer Capriati	March 29
Lucy Lawless	March 29
Elle Macpherson	March 29
Celine Dion	March 30
Warren Beatty	March 30
Ewan McGregor	March 31
Al Gore	March 31
Christopher Walken	March 31
Debbie Reynolds	April 1
Jennie Garth	April 3
Eddie Murphy	April 3
Robert Downey, Jr.	April 4
Christine Lahti	April 4
Russell Crowe	April 7
Jackie Chan	April 7
Francis Ford Coppola	April 7
Patricia Arquette	April 8

Dennis Quaid	April 9
Hugh Hefner	April 9
Steven Seagal	April 10
Shannen Doherty	April 12
Claire Danes	April 12
Vince Gill	April 12
David Letterman	April 12
Rick Schroder	April 13
Sarah Michelle Gellar	April 14
Robert Carlyle	April 14
Emma Thompson	April 15
Martin Lawrence	April 16
Victoria Adams	April 17
Melissa Joan Hart	April 18
Conan O'Brien	April 18
Tim Curry	April 19
Ashley Judd	April 19

Chapter 3

TAURUS

(April 20–May 19)

Sex Stats

Ruling planet: Venus, the goddess in charge of love, beauty, and *sex*.

Signature symbol: The bull—earthy, stubborn, and perpetually horny.

Trademark color: Light blue to bring out the lighter sexual side of your oh-so-serious bull.

Favorite position: Missionary style, since Taurus believes in getting back to basics.

Potent porn: For the straight crowd, some by-the-numbers humping, preferably starring that too-cool queen of porn, Nina Hartley. For *chicas* who do *chicas*, check out *Girlfriends.* For gay guys, pop *Courting Libido* into your VCR, then talk about the first thing that pops up.

Ultimate outfit (male): A lumberjack-style shirt paired with basic blue jeans from Abercrombie & Fitch.

Ultimate outfit (female): A loose-fitting outfit by Versace to bring out her over-the-top love of luxury.

Mattress mambo music: Depending on the tastes of the bull whom you plan on mounting (or being mounted by), either heavy metal, a la Metallica, or classical music with a strong, thumping backbeat by one of the goodies but oldies like Grieg.

Best sex toy: An erotic massager; your Taurus will put those batteries to good use.

After-fuck finger food: Strawberries and whipped cream.

Do You Know What You're in For?

Unlike their namesake in the wild, bulls are usually somewhat shy and sweet. This only makes sense since they're ruled by Venus, goddess of love, beauty, and peace. Taurus also loves to buy beautiful things. If you think this is their only failing though, think again. In a word, bulls can give new meaning to the word *boredom*. They like life in the slow lane surrounded by all the stuff they've accumulated during their lifetime. If you're a sign who joneses for security like Virgo or Cancer, this can be an extremely attractive trait but if you're a talkative, wild sign like Sagittarius or Gemini the only thing you'll enjoy about bonding with a bull is helping to spend their usual overabundance of cash. Do you like to party into the wee hours of the morning? Have you harbored secret fantasies of threesomes with your future mate? Does talking dirty between the sheets turn you on as you figure out how many times you can scream the F-word during one lovemaking bout? If you answered yes to any or all of these questions, Taurus probably isn't your type. This doesn't mean bulls are boring in bed though—in fact, for many signs, sensual Taurus can go at it for hours and if anyone can hold off on the big O till you've hit yours, it's the oh-so benevolent bull.

Taurus is stubborn as hell and notorious for holding lifelong grudges. Screw a bull and you might find paradise but if you screw over a bull you've just made an enemy for life. Used to getting their way, bulls rarely change their mind-set— even when the facts disagree with their view of the world. Arguments can become explosive if Taurus feels his or her beloved security is being threatened or feels in danger of being exploited in love. Unlike a combative Scorpio though, Taurus usually fights fair when it comes to arguing. While a scorpion will want to discuss that affair you had seven years ago ad infinitum, Taurus will bring up a sore subject once before relegating it into "never to be discussed again" terrain. Does this mean your mating magnet has forgotten your past indiscretion? Hell, no: Every positive and negative thing you do is instantly filed into a Taurean's mental database. When your fact sheet starts to get too soiled you'll be tossed out like yesterday's garbage, so keep your nose clean if you feel like buddying up with a bull. Some words of caution on bumping and grinding behind the bull's back: She or he will *never* view you in the same light again, so either don't do it or make damn sure you don't ever get caught. Not only will Taurus find a sexual trespass unforgivable, she or he will get revenge sooner than you think.

Taurus Man

Taurus men come in two shapes and sizes—everyday dudes with a bit of pudge around their middles and studly jocks who are built like brick shithouses. Whether he appears like a fierce, worked-out Adonis or a fleshy Billy Joel, you can count on two things: He's amazingly strong for his size and his mental strength is just as powerful as his physical side. He uses his strong and steady cerebral skills for a variety of tasks and whatever he aims for he's likely to walk away a winner. Making money, accumulating power, and beefing up his business or stock portfolio are all ultra-important tasks for the sign of the bull. Sounds just like his female half, huh? Not quite: While the Taurus woman is looking for love, Taurus man is doing the same—but *only* after he's scored a multitude of sexual conquests to mull over in future masturbatory episodes. How do you tell if he plans on making you his steady Eddie or just another notch on his rearview mirror? Actually, it's simple since figuring out the motivation of a male bull is easier than I was in high school.

Although no pun is intended, the Taurus man isn't the type to beat around the bush—he'll zero in on what he wants and go for it in a combined burst of anticipation and perspiration. On your first date does he buy flowers or beg for a blow job? Is his fave topic a future family or favorite fuck style? A nice thing about Taurus is that he won't mislead you. While Pisces indulges in mind games and Cancer is harder to understand than Chinese math, a male bull will be very honest and open about what he's looking for. You might be his lifelong pursuit or a momentary diversion but a Taurus man will let you know which category you fall into *before* you bump uglies instead of three days after the fact.

Taurus Woman

Female bulls are stronger than nails but while the Aries woman wants her power to be a focal point of their relationship, the Taurus woman will only fall back on her skills of persuasion when the need arises. In other words, some Taurean women with oodles and oodles of cash might opt for sitting around the house eating bonbons (along with Pisces, a bull's weight can bounce up and down more than Pamela Anderson's boobs on a rerun of *Baywatch*). Stick the same chick into a different equation and you get far different results, however. Stuck in a trailer park with five bounced-check notices in her mailbox, a Taurus female will kick into immediate action.

Much like her sister earth sign, Virgo, love isn't a game for Taurus. If you tell her you're going to call the next day, *do it* or risk her wrath in the sack. She can become colder than a cadaver when faced with a person or situation she doesn't completely trust. Reading feedback from a female bull can become harder than Ricky Martin's abs since she's excellent at keeping her emotions in check. It's difficult for her to admit that she's fallen in love because it makes her feel vulnerable, so whatever you do, don't try to force an early admission of adoration. An interesting sidebar about earth signs is that they're, well, earthy, so if you get a bull to fall for you she'll do whatever you want in bed—as long as it's within certain parameters and you make sure you return the favor. Wanna get your balls nibbled while you mutter passages from your favorite Madonna tune? You got it. Looking for hours of lesbian lovemaking with a partner who lives for steamy eye contact? You've found what you're looking for. Think you can screw her best bud while she watches? Think again. Sex is a very personal issue for Taurean females and she doesn't want more than one witness to her lovemaking prowess. Are you rolling your eyes as you read this since she shared you with another last night? Guess what? Your girlfriend is going through an experimental phase and you're *not* the one with whom she plans on growing old with.

Five Surefire Ways to Break the Ice with Taurus

Taurus Man

1. Whether you're a gay guy or a woman with waves, ask him if he'd like to work-out with you at the gym—he loves to show off his physical side.
2. Have a mutual friend fix you up: This guy is shy!
3. Ask his advice on a financial problem.
4. Make heavy eye contact: The Taurus man is totally into long, loving stares.
5. Discuss something naughty because though he might not admit it, he loves keeping secrets.

Taurus Woman

1. Ask where she got that cool new outfit.
2. Compliment her on a physical feature as in, "Wow—your eyes are *amazing!*"
3. Ask her if she'd like to check out that posh, new restaurant with you but don't think hip—think luxurious.
4. Let her know you're attracted to her g-r-a-d-u-a-l-l-y—then let her make the first move.
5. Send a bottle of fine wine to her table, but if you can't afford the best don't go this route.

Refining Your Sexual Strategy—The Subrulers

Venus: Double the Love (April 20–April 30)

If you want to get inside this sign's pants fast, go buy them something expensive. Ruled *and* subruled by Venus, the goddess of beauty and love, they're so into objects that are lovely to look at they have a tendency to be more materialistic than the Donald. Venus also ups their odds for being a bit scatterbrained, so although you'll certainly encounter intelligent conversation from this totally noncontroversial sign, the topics they love to talk about seem to randomly hop from one arena to another with no logical steps in between. In other words, your bull will go from a debate over Burt Reynolds's newest hairpiece to that art museum they just stopped by without a pause for breath between. Actually, this can be quite refreshing, but if you're like Spock from *Star Trek* and like all of your conversations to have a logical beginning, middle, and end, this sign will drive you batshit long before you bed them.

In bed, this carefree attitude is a blast—but again, *only* if you're willing and able to roll with the punches. You might go from going down on the object of your affections to anal exploration to a quick-glance discussion of Letterman's low points before finishing off your other with a hand job. What you see is never exactly what you get when you bump heads (or something else) with this type of Taurus because like the James Bond flick of the same name, the world is not enough. Their mind must flit like a butterfly from one object to the next because they're terrified they won't be able to witness everything life has to offer.

Eventually, their all-encompassing quest for money and all things material might put you off but their carefree good nature in and out of bed makes them a ballistic bed partner for many signs.

Mercury: Brains with Beauty (May 1–May 10)

Taureans born with Mercury, god of intellect, as their subruler have a hell of a lot going for them. Their head honcho Venus makes them affable, fun, and all about beauty and love. Mercury tempers that *Pollyanna* approach with the mental chutzpah this sign needs to make ends meet. While a Taurus subruled by Venus will almost invariably opt for a wealthy mate, this type of Taurus is smart enough—and driven—enough to make their own money. Then again, Mercury might simply increase their odds for intelligently picking out the man or woman with the most money, so really it all depends on where their basic priorities lie.

In the bedroom, Mercury balances the naturally laid-back attitude of Venus with a little grit and grime, which can increase the hours you spend engaged in sex and the activities you indulge in. This sign will stay awake at night trying to think of new ways to pleasure the two of you, so when this type says, "Bedroom—now," ask no questions. Just head in that direction and get ready to have a mile-wide smile on your face in seconds. This proactive approach to fornication makes for some interesting sexual scenarios, so get ready to indulge in fantastical fun and games that can include almost everything but S&M (Taureans are almost never into receiving or causing pain).

Mercury increases the sexual synergy for another reason. He tunes in your Taurus to your wants and needs better than the other two decanates. This sign is excellent at reading feedback so don't worry about having to yell, "Less teeth!" or "Let's break in that dining room table right." This type of Taurus will already know what you're thinking about and be one or two steps ahead of the game. Less materialistic than the other two decanates, this sign is still into beautiful things. If you're aiming to get your guy or girl a gift, make it something beautiful, extravagant, and out of the norm. When they get it, you can bet on gettin' some, too.

Saturn: Drive and Devotion (May 11–May 19)

With the sixth planet pulling their behind-the-scenes strings, this bull has the biggest balls of them all. With Saturn as their subruler, this sign is determined, resolute, and all about getting ahead. Venus' tendency to be flighty and somewhat out of it mentally is weighed down heavily by Saturn's "gotta get there" motto. For this bull, life is a spreadsheet that's all about accomplishment, and if he or she doesn't reach the final chapter with every piece in the right place they'll have a tendency to think their life was a waste.

This serious side comes out in the bedroom, too. You'll need to loosen this sign up a bit to fully explore their sexuality (and trust me: Though it may take you a while to find it, it's there in a *big* way). As a side note, since this sign is far more stressed out than the other two types of Taurus, you'll need to give lots of extra tender loving care. Translation? You'll buoy this bull's somewhat sour view of life if you're willing to give them hours and hours of oral affection. Sex is a release for this tense type of Taurus and if you're willing to go the extra mile to make them smile you've just found an ultimate protector. This sign is great at making money but unlike the first two types, she or he is *extremely* resolute about sticking by those he or she loves, so don't worry about this bull ever leaving you unless you've done something to deserve it.

Just because this bull needs to receive more than he or she gives doesn't mean you'll have an uninteresting sex life. If you're a giving sign like Libra or Pisces, you can't find a better choice than this hard-working hero or heroine. You'll have to go the extra mile in the bedroom, but once you're outside it, this sign will do whatever it takes to keep you happy. When sex is one-on-one—in other words, when your bull is giving back the pleasure you're giving—this type of Taurus has amazing staying power, so count on your girlfriend being totally into Tantric-style lovemaking or your boyfriend being able to withhold his big O until you've experienced several. This Taurus is an excellent lover, but if he or she isn't in love with you don't expect anything out of the ordinary. If an everyday affair is your goal, expect some cool gifts from this money-matters sign, but don't expect 'em to lick your ass or anything else decidedly different in the sexual arena. This Taurus finds giving extremely difficult—if just because of the fact that to them, giving by definition puts them into a vulnerable position they simply can't stand. If you just want a good blow job or someone who's all about pleasing your pussy, this sign couldn't be less your type—although if you get off on giving the above-mentioned oral acrobatics, you've found paradise. If a long-term lover is what you're in the market for who will *never* let you down, you have a rough road in front of you, but one that ultimately leads to everlasting love.

Sexual Synergy

Aries and Taurus: Aries is always on the go; Taurus is usually looking for a way to slow down. If you're thinking this leads to stagnation in the sack though, think again. Taurus freaks out on Aries' ultralust when it comes to bonding in the bedroom—just don't forget to hang up that "Don't Disturb" sign.

Taurus and Taurus: Since both of you are slow to reach your boiling points you might end up discussing sticky philosophical subjects instead of gettin' nekkid. Have you ever witnessed two tortoises going after it? Kinda scary, huh? Okay—enough said.

Gemini and Taurus: If you're looking for an awesome one-night stand, stop, because you just found up to eight hours of happiness. Taurus loves to do it while Gemini loves to talk about it, but when you combine the two you get a lot of loving—and if boredom does rear its treacherous head, Gem can always find a different use for those loose lips.

Cancer and Taurus: Nope—you're not going to talk dirty and neither one of you will scream when you hit the big O (at least until you've figured out each other's erogenous zones). But the simple truth is that sex between the signs of bull and crab is stellar. You're both into the slow-and-easy approach but your differences make the bedsheets *sizzle*.

Leo and Taurus: Leo is into being worshipped in the sack, seeing him or herself as the porno version of Superman or Wonder Woman. Taurus is *soooo* not into that though, and whether you're faced with a male or female bull, count on their un-willingness to take the Clark Kent role. Unfortunately, what comes in with a whimper goes out the same.

Virgo and Taurus: You'll never win an award for most spontaneous couple but in reality neither of you give a shit about other people's opinions. This will be a slow burn as the two of you gradually explore each other's secret moan zones. This is homework both of you will *fully* enjoy, so throw down this book and get to work.

Libra and Taurus: Since Venus rules both of you, you share an easy approach to lovemaking. While Taurus is forthright and determined, Libra is playful and eas-ily amused. A great combo for sex? You bet—but probably not for very long, so enjoy the getting while it's still good.

Scorpio and Taurus: Arguments will come soon after you do, so count on this being a short-lived affair. You're both so highly sexed, addiction to the mattress mambo will set in fast, but unless you can stay locked in the bedroom problems *are* on the horizon.

Sagittarius and Taurus: Sagittarius is totally uninhibited when it comes to banging in the bedroom and sensual Taurus finds this a major turn-on. Sagi's rov-ing eye is where the fun ends unfortunately; so count on future lovemaking ses-sions to be far less fantastic. If you've caught a buzz from booze though—and remembered your rubbers—this could be a *mucho* fun one-night stand, so don't say nay if you're looking for short-lived ecstasy.

Capricorn and Taurus: Like Taurus, Capricorn likes love slow and steady, so when you mate a goat with a bull you get marvelous bed buddies. Both of you are intensely sexual and see boning home as an important way of communicating.

Neither are into games but Capricorn's dry sense of humor and smoldering sensuality butter the bull in all the right ways. The only downside? You're going to be *very* sore in the morning.

Aquarius and Taurus: Aquarius wants to talk about love in the abstract; Taurus is jonesing for an awesome blow job. Sound like a lethal love connection? You got it: Odds for an awesome climax between a water bearer and bull are about as high as a successful Jenny McCarthy sitcom, so make like Nancy Reagan and just say no.

Pisces and Taurus: So what if there won't be fireworks? At least neither of you will fall asleep: Pisces likes Taurus' dependability and duration in the sack, while the vivid imagination fishies are famous for keeps the bull coming back for more. Not exactly a forecast for fornicational bliss but combining an earth sign with his or her watery counterpart *doesn't* equal mud.

Exploring Their Erogenous Zone

Remember when you were a kid and *Sesame Street* would explain letters by naming things they started with? You know, like, S stands for sassy, short, and sweet? Well, now you're an adult, but to keep a bull in bliss it's the same scenario, just on an R-rated level. Your letter to remember is N and the words it stands for are *neck, nape,* and *nuzzle.* That's right; whether you're aiming for *l'amour* with a *femme* or *homme* bull, the body part you aim for first is the neck.

First though, get ready for a quick psychology lesson. Bulls live for subtlety—they like taking their love lives slow and easy and overly aggressive signs are a major turn-off, so instead of zooming in on a bull's neck like the Starship *Enterprise* honing in on a landing beacon, make your caresses down a bull's throat and the base of their skull seem almost accidental. Light, feathery caresses up and down the neck followed by gentle licks—no biting!!!—will make a female writhe with delight and a male stand at attention within seconds. Eventually, all of this oral affection will lead to more erotic escapades but even when you're caught in the throws of the big O you can do a lot worse than trading kisses with gentle nuzzling up and down the neck of your loved one. In other words, this isn't just a trick for fabulous foreplay. Keep your mate's neck in mind during your whole love-making process for a truly mind-bending experience. If you're bonding with a male bull, all this attention might make him come too quickly the first few rounds but once he gets used to your skill in the sack, his ability will accelerate accordingly. Females don't have this problem however, and the more orgasms you can let her indulge in, the faster she'll become putty in your hands.

Come Again?

Taurus Man

Getting a bull to bond a second time is much easier said than done. The basic problem you face is Taurus' innate stubbornness: If he's not in the mood for a second shot almost *nothing* is going to change his mind. That's not to say it's impossible, however: Getting this earth sign to go again might be harder than a teen at a porno flick, but it can be done. The key is to make your bull *think* he's the one initiating things and that you'll be going along for the ride just to make him happy. If you can pull the wool over your bull bed buddy's eyes adeptly enough he'll be ready to bone home whenever you're ready, so follow these tried-and-true techniques to make him rise to the occasion.

Lesson number one: Bulls are *very* visual. Since he's ruled by Venus, the goddess of love and beauty, he's thrilled by all the sexy images you can beam into his brain. Forget slutty—after all you're not dealing with Gemini or Sagittarius—as you go for a sexy, luxurious look instead. In other words, drop that stained red G-string of yours in the garbage to slip into a cream-colored teddy that leaves something to the imagination. Alternately, if you're gay and want to get your bull's lovegun ready for round two, don't wear a thong—unless you've got a better butt than Antonio Sabato, Jr. Wear a Ralph Lauren–style top that's open to give a pumped-up view of your pecs along with some classy boxer shorts. Taurus can't stand aggression so whether you're gay or straight, opt for a classy, well-tailored look even if you're just going to take it off again.

Lesson number two: Make sure your breath smells better than the rose garden in the backyard of your bull's house and make sure your pits, pussy, or pubes (depending on your gender) are totally clean. If you're moving in for the sexual kill with the sign of the bull and he smells something he'd rather not, his eros will turn icky instead of erect, so show him your respect by being as clean as he is.

Now that you've had a crash course in increasing your bed ability with the sign of the bull, here's how to really up the odds for action. Let's say you've just finished fucking. His natural tendency is going to be to go right to sleep—along with Leo, Taurus loves driving to dreamland after dumping his load. How do you keep him from falling asleep? Appeal to his second favorite appetite: food. There are two ways to accomplish this. Go with something light and airy like angel food cake served on separate plates. Exchange stares as you're eating—having made sure in advance that the TV set is off (throw a Taurus a remote and you'll never regain his attention). Lean close to him as you're both satisfying your initial appetites and play with his neck and upper shoulder area. Nothing too suffocating, just a stray glance of your hand here and there. If you've opted for a heavier food—like ice cream—make sure to share it on one plate instead of two and only bring a little: Too much will put him to sleep. Take turns spoon-feeding yourself and your bull—before too long, your bull should be ready to sample some of that chocolate almond straight from your lips instead of having to deal with a spoon. Once you've crossed this hurdle, make like a baby bird and take turns sampling the tastes of each other's mouths. Again, stroke his upper torso and neck while you're packing on the calories to really turn up the heat. At this point, your bull's dick should be *almost* as hard as his all-or-nothing attitude, so reach down between his legs and get what's coming to you.

Taurus Woman

Getting a Taurus female into bed a second time is much easier than doing the same to her male counterpart: Taurus females are less lazy and stubborn and they view sexuality as more of a give-and-take proposition than their pump-and-dump brethren. Before going any further, read the two cardinal rules listed above about scoring with male Taurus: If your breath and bod don't smell sweet, you'll be left alone to beat your meat.

Keeping cleanliness in mind, you've only got three more things to remember: Romance, romance, and more romance. Prop pillows all around the object of your affection and expound on everything you adore about her. Is her hair beautiful? Do her lovemaking skills leave you breathless? Are her boobs to die for? (Taurean females usually are pretty top heavy so this compliment should be a no-brainer.) Anything positive and loving you can say that will reaffirm her feelings of safety and security will increase her odds to get wet, so list all her positive points as s-l-o-w-l-y as you can. Detailing her attributes as if you're reading from a dictionary will be a major turn-off for this heart-felt sign. If you're not feeling truly complimentary, then keep quiet, concentrating on loving licks from the nape of her neck to her breasts and back again. If your mate is straight, letting her know you're hard as a rock will hold special appeal but instead of guiding her hand down your leg to say, "Check this out, mama," score a more subtle approach as you gently brush her thigh with your man meat as you're doing the lickin' thang.

If your lover's lesbian, shoot for a similar scenario—sans dick—as you gently rub your lower torso against her legs as you're licking her uppermost regions. Taurean women take another's arousal as a major turn-on, so don't be shy about letting her know your attraction for her is sincere and secure.

In the world according to Taurus women, life is a romance novel and the more you can do to indulge her in that fantasy, the more nooky you can negotiate. Cinammon-scented candles, sea-salted bubble baths, and caviar (if you can afford it) are all ways to get this bull's blood pumping to all the right places. Once you've regaled her with romance she'll give in to any amorous affections and though her second sexual act might be a bit more by the numbers than the first, it will still hold just as much meaning—and be a hell of a lot of fun to boot.

But Will It Last?

Aries and Taurus: Fabulous fucks don't always equal great relationships. Even though the bull might curl your toes momentarily, drag his or her ass out of the bedroom and you'll wonder what you've gotten yourself into. As a fire sign, you're always intent on getting some action—both in the bedroom and beyond. That's the last thing Taurus will ever deliver, though, so blast past this bull.

Taurus and Taurus: One bull mounting another might be interesting as Animal Planet fodder, but in the real world two bulls bonding is, in a word, *boring*. After seventeen not-so-scintillating sexual sessions, all in the basic missionary position, you'll be left with two important questions: 1. Will I ever get off? and 2. Will this fucker ever get off me?

Gemini and Taurus: Your idea of excitement is dancing till dawn; Taurus gets a major charge out of finding the perfect laundry detergent. Why such a problematic prognosis? You're entirely different animals, for one thing: Your fast-paced wit makes you more akin to a butterfly than a bull, and if you've ever seen a Monarch land atop an ox's back, you'll notice one thing, it won't stay there for long.

Cancer and Taurus: When you're horny as hell but too shy to admit it, this bull will drag your ass to the bedroom without saying a word. When you're feeling lonely, count on Taurus to stick by your side—even if that means calling in sick to work or keeping watch over you till the wee hours of the morning. This is the sign that can morph your nervousness to nirvana, crabby, so grab this bull by the horns and never let go.

Leo and Taurus: You're the star of the hit show *My Life*, but Taurus is unwilling to buy a ticket! For you, life is a grand adventure, but Taurus thinks you're just grandiose since the sign of the bull innately distrusts drama junkies. A so-so sex life leads to an even crappier coupling, so keep in mind that if you opt for a bull you'll be left with bullshit.

Virgo and Taurus: You're way too embarrassed to admit you want a bed partner who fucks like a rabbit—but combine that hidden desire with a bull's dependability and you get an excited, trustworthy lover who's not afraid to help you explore your steamy side. You're a bit of a prude but don't worry: Taurus will pull the shades down before getting to work. Once you start exploring the other assets Taurus has to offer you'll discover—EEK!!!—you're falling in love *big time*.

Libra and Taurus: Maybe things wouldn't be quite so bad if Taurus didn't insist on being so goddamned serious all the time. You need a light-hearted mate who knows how to relax and that's simply *not* what the bull is all about. Meanwhile, your easy approach to life makes the second sign of the zodiac think you're up to something. Making this love connection last will take a lot of work, Libra—are you up to the challenge?

Scorpio and Taurus: You'll need a fire extinguisher handy for the ever-increasing heat of your sexcapades but stop bumping uglies for a second and you'll realize this slow-and-studied earth sign irritates the hell out of you. You're both unbelievably stubborn and competitive. You know that sibling you've always shared that blazing rivalry with? Multiply that by ten, then imagine having sex with 'em. *Yeeeeuch!*

Sagittarius and Taurus: Taurus isn't the most possessive sign in the zodiac—that honor is reserved for Scorpio—but the sign of the bull comes pretty damn close. The long leash you covet from life will be quickly reigned in by this controlling type, which, in turn, will bring your straying side out faster than you can spit out the word *divorce*. The two of you will drive each other crazy, which leaves only one real question: Who will drive the other there *first?*

Capricorn and Taurus: When you were a kid you told yourself love could wait so you never made contact with that wide-eyed, quiet stud or siren you couldn't take your eyes off. Well guess what, goatface? Here's your second chance for an amazing merger that *The Wall Street Journal* won't be discussing between its illustrious pages. Somewhere between stock options and mutual funds, buy this bull as well and you'll be *very* glad you did.

Aquarius and Taurus You want to talk about the closest presidential race in recent history; Taurus makes cracks like, "If you wanna lick Bush, you don't know Dick." You're fascinated by the nuts and bolts of our daily existence; Taurus just wants you to play with his nuts. All this talk about bush, dick, and nuts has Taurus so horny she's off in your bathroom masturbating while you still want to talk. No dice, Aqua.

Pisces and Taurus This bull puts you in the swim in many important ways, fishy. Taurus is the solid sexual scenario you're striving for in the bedroom and beyond. Taurus will temper your wild ways, ground any crazy ideas you might concoct, and still want to bedroom bop once dusk delivers its monochromatic rays. Though the bull's monochromatic *ways* might get on your oh-so-inventive nerves every once in awhile, this will be a slow burn you'll fully enjoy. Reel this one in, Pisces.

Taurus Celebs: Stubborn, Sweet, and Sexy

Joey Lawrence	April 20
Carmen Electra	April 20
Jessica Lange	April 20
Andie MacDowell	April 21
Tony Danza	April 21
Jack Nicholson	April 22
Aaron Spelling	April 22
Scott Bairstow	April 23
Valerie Bertinelli	April 23
Craig Sheffer	April 23
Barbra Streisand	April 24
Shirley MacLaine	April 24

Renee Zellwegger	April 25
Hank Azaria	April 25
Al Pacino	April 25
Tionne "T-Boz" Watkins	April 26
Jay Leno	April 28
Ann-Margaret	April 28
Andre Agassi	April 29
Uma Thurman	April 29
Michelle Pfeiffer	April 29
Jerry Seinfeld	April 29
Kirsten Dunst	April 30
James Brown	May 3
George Clooney	May 6
Traci Lords	May 7
Enrique Iglesias	May 8
Melissa Gilbert	May 8
Steve Yzerman	May 9
Billy Joel	May 9
Candice Bergen	May 9
James L. Brooks	May 9
Bono	May 10
Natasha Richardson	May 11
Emilio Estevez	May 12
Dennis Rodman	May 13
Stevie Wonder	May 13
Bea Arthur	May 13
Harvey Keitel	May 13
Cate Blanchett	May 14
George Lucas	May 14
Robert Zemeckis	May 14
David Charvet	May 15
Madeline Albright	May 15
Tori Spelling	May 16
David Boreanaz	May 16
Tracey Gold	May 16
Pierce Brosnan	May 16

Janet Jackson	May 16
Debra Winger	May 16
Trent Reznor	May 17
Bob Saget	May 17
Chow Yun-Fat	May 18
George Strait	May 18
Reggie Jackson	May 18
Grace Jones	May 19
Pete Townshend	May 19
Nora Ephron	May 19

Chapter 4

GEMINI
(May 20–June 20)

Sex Stats

Ruling planet: Mercury, the swiftest god in the skies, who also happens to be in charge of ultra-extreme raunchy talk.

Signature symbol: Twins, so get ready to double up on bedroom fun.

Trademark color: Yellow, as in bananas, and—yup—golden showers.

Favorite position: The fabulous fun of 69ing, since either of you can always come up for air if you need to.

Potent porn: Since Gemini likes mind fucks almost as much as the real thing, go for trippy titillation, like *Nightwalk* for gay guys or *Bad Girls* for the straight set. Lesbian lovers should aim for *No Man's Land*.

Ultimate outfit (male): Vibrantly bright, nylon jogging shorts and a jock.

Ultimate outfit (female): A skimpy, sexy jog bra paired with Joe Boxers.

Mattress mambo music: Any of Madonna's spicier stuff like *Justify My Love* or *Erotica*.

Best sex toy: Any illustrated book detailing the world of kinky sex—your Gemini is sure to pick up some wild, new ideas.

After-fuck finger food: A veggie platter with balsamic vinegar dip since Geminis love to eat light.

Do You Know What You're in For?

Jumbo shrimp. Oklahoma celebrities. An empathetic Dr. Laura Schlessinger. What do these seemingly at-odd terms have in common? They're all paradoxes and, as such, harder than hell to understand. But if you can grasp the concept that all these things *can* actually coexist (okay, okay, so maybe the Oklahoma celebrity thing is pushing it), then maybe you can get a handle on Gemini, the most confusing sign in the zodiac. Geminis are mutable air signs, which means your heart's desire is going to have his or her head stuck permanently in the clouds and can change opinions faster than Courtney Love changes her hairstyle. One minute, a Gem is more charming than Cary Grant on his best day, while the next, that same Gemini will be pitching a fit far more in line with one of the bad boys of Motley Crue. Keep in mind that Gemini's mood swings bear little in common with those of, say, Aries: When an Aries is pissed, the sign of the ram slips into infant mode, where lashing out becomes the end-all, be-all of the moment. Gemini is much more sophisticated and while Aries will volley any and every insult your way in the hope that one or two might stick, Gemini has thought out his plan of attack long before the need has arisen. Why? Because like Virgo, Gemini is ruled by Mercury, the god in charge of lightning-fast wit. Virgos and Geminis go through different scenarios in their head long before they've taken place in real life so when you're trapped in a verbal argument with either, get ready to fight someone who's *very* willing to play dirty. Want an example? Irritate an Aries and you get an explosion: His face turns bright red as he screams, "I can't stand you!!!" The next morning (though he might have trouble admitting it) he'll be sorry since he didn't really mean what he said. Gems are a whole new ball game, however. Inflame this air sign and you'll get something she's been holding close to her chest that she definitely *does* mean and will cut you to the quick. Let's suppose you've somehow embarrassed her in front of your mutual circle of friends—a major no-no for either Gemini or Virgo. While Aries' anger would become instantly apparent, Gemini keeps her cool. She'd probably lean over to you and pleasantly whisper something in your ear. To your pals, all would appear hunky dory. But you'd be on the losing end of her offensive and whatever she says will strike close to your heart.

"You know that awesome orgasm you gave me last night?" she might coyly ask as you bubbled over with pride before acknowledging her comment. "Well, I faked it," she'd add coldly, as, all the while, she'd still *appear* super sweet to anyone who wasn't within earshot. And what's the best way to avoid her righteous wrath? Simple: Don't piss her off. Dating a loving, happy Gem is like dating a diamond. No matter how well you think you might know her or him, there's always going to be a new facet you can explore tomorrow; a new way of thinking you haven't been exposed to as of yet, or a sexual position or act that only a Gemini would try or imagine. Let's put it this way—bond with a Gemini and you'll *never* be bored.

Gemini Man

The Gemini guy is bright-eyed, mischievous, and often rather slight in build. His mind leaps from one subject to the next so quickly you'll probably have difficulty keeping up but if you like to talk, you've just found an awesome partner with whom to exchange ideas. Although he may not appear it, he's an extremely sexual creature; while a Scorpio is always ready for spit-swapping, the Gemini guy has got to be in the mood. Like Virgo, he's constantly wrestling with concepts, but while Virgo is obsessed with certain chosen subjects, whether sex, horror flicks, or Hindu spirituality, Gemini's mind flits from one subject to the next with the attention span of a butterfly. If all the signs were bound for college, Gemini would opt for a liberal arts major. He wants to think/try/experience everything at least once. He's the type to climb a mountain just because it's there, while Taurus would do the same to prove his manhood. This can create catastrophe when it comes to bedroom bonding since status quo is anathema to this spirited sign. Let your imagination run riot if you want to retain your romance. Not only should you be open to his novel sexual shenanigans, you should come up with a few of your own. While Capricorn likes to dominate and Pisces loves to be possessed, Gemini wants to keep his partnership on an equal footing, so if you begin to lag behind him intellectually, spiritually, or sexually, your relationship will surely suffer.

The Gemini guy's favorite form of communication is brainstorming, so don't be afraid to roll with the punches by saying whatever is on your mind. In fact, Gemini will be angry if you don't say what's running through your mind. Running is an important concept that shouldn't be glossed over: Not only is his ruler, Mercury, head honcho of ideas, the first planet is also in charge of *speed* and although Sandra Bullock isn't involved in this go-round, keep in mind the image she helped to represent in the first flick of the same name. If your mental engines fall below sixty mph *at any time,* your relationship is going to explode. The last thing you should do is to panic, however. Enjoy the ride instead, since that's exactly what a Gemini guy plans on doing. If you're naturally shy about sharing ideas and are looking for a partner who is going to dig deep below the surface, run, don't walk, from a relationship with the third sign in the zodiac: You're asking for trouble and he'll be only too happy to oblige.

Gemini Woman

Usually, each sign's female half is a bit more grounded than her male counterpart, but, as is the case with Gemini in general, rules are meant to be broken. If anything, her mind moves faster than her brother's for one important reason. While our society does its best to mold minorities into what it *thinks* they should be, the Gemini woman has bypassed the societal stigma of what a woman should be because her dramas, for the most part, are internal. Think about it: When a female Aries tries to dominate she's told to act like a lady. A Sagittarian female who sleeps around (just like her masculine counterpart,) is called a slut while he gets the far more complimentary S word of stud. The Gemini woman escapes this dilemma, however, by "spinning" the situation. She's so skilled at manipulating public perception, she knows when to keep her manic mouth shut to make the most of a circumstance frowned on by society. If you diss a Cancer female she'll withdraw, and if you attack a Virgo female, odds are she'll return the offensive immediately. Gemini bides her time, however. If she works for a chauvinist pig boss, she'll grin at his inept behavior as the word *bastard* plays in silent mental accompaniment to her manufactured smile. She'll play the game until she's advanced far enough up the food chain to fire his sorry ass—and she'll do so without a second of hesitation. She'd never reveal her true reason either. Instead, she'd invent a logically sound reason why that sad sack of shit is better off flipping burgers at McDonald's. And she'd do all this with a smile on her face. These skillful manipulations translate into other arenas as well, so if you're ever sued by a Gemini, you'd better get your checkbook ready: Whether you're in the right or wrong, Gemini will likely turn the public tide of opinion in her direction.

She's an amazing bed partner—willing to go from trashy truck driver talk to regular romance in the blink of an eye. Anything new and different pleases her, so if you're into something out of the norm like sex toys, kink, or S&M, feel free to share your fantasies with her. She may only indulge your eccentricity once but you'll certainly enjoy the experience. If you plan on doing a female Gemini, plan on doing it anywhere and everywhere. Soon after you join the mile-high club, she'll have you in the back bathroom stall of that sleazy restaurant on Sunset Boulevard, only to be followed a few days later with a five-minute quickie in your basic missionary-style position. Being open to change isn't good enough for this chatty *chica:* You must encourage it every step of the way.

Five Surefire Ways to Break the Ice with Gemini

Gemini Man

1. Use dry, cutting-edge humor somewhere between Kevin Williamson's writing style and *Monty Python*-esque outrage.
2. Gossip: Gemini guys love to dish.
3. Give a gift that stimulates his cerebrum like a puzzle, video game, or surrealist painting.
4. Be prim and proper 99 percent of the time, then let a *really* raunchy comment fly by, but *only* do this if you can make it look effortless.
5. Give him a goose: Gemini guys groove when the object of their affection makes the first physical move.

Gemini Woman

1. Discuss something controversial to society, whether it's *Will and Grace* or segregation laws from before the 1960s.
2. Indulge in delicious, witty wordplay, like George Carlin's, "Why is it okay to prick your finger but everyone freaks when you finger your prick?"
3. Ask what she thought of the latest art-house flick that made the rounds in your neck of the woods (if you're trapped in Bum Fuck, Egypt, ask what she thought of *The Blair Witch Project*).
4. Make a wager, as in, "Okay, if I'm right about Snare a Mare coming in first in this race, I get to take you out to dinner."
5. Belittle a hypocritical public figure.

Refining Your Sexual Strategy—The Subrulers

Mercury: Face to Face with Brainiac (May 20–May 31)

When Geminis share Mercury, god of intellect, as both their ruler and subruler, you'll be faced with some traits typically associated with their sister sign of Virgo. This sign is more tense than the other two types of Gemini and can't help but sweat the small stuff. Amazingly intelligent, this Gemini's mind is constantly trying to make sense of the cyclone of new and old ideas whirling around inside of his or her brain. Relaxation is an idea for other signs, because Geminis born under this decanate can never truly take time out.

In bed, these factors can make for fabulous fornication though, because this sign takes sex just as seriously as they take everything else. Sex is like a fascinating algebra problem that they can never quite figure out—but they sure as hell keep trying!

Since this Gemini believes in leaving no stone uncovered, bet on him or her discovering most of your moan zones within the first few weeks of dating. A few words of warning: If you're as easy to read as an open book and more innocent than Dorothy Gale from Kansas, this relationship won't last long, so get your rocks off and then get out. If you've got as many mental facets as Gemini does, however, he or she will stick around a lot longer as they try to decipher your each and every hidden desire.

If any type of sign is guaranteed to get you off, it's this brilliant sign who believes in anything but by-the-numbers sex. From butt fucking to beau sucking, from muff diving to pile driving, this sign is up for anything, so get ready to get off.

The downside to this sign is that he or she can get more testy than Charlie Sheen on a bad day. If you're not logical and witty they'll use and abuse you before they lose you. If you can keep up with this marvelously mental sign—both in and out of bed—then you'll discover you had hidden sexual facets you never knew existed. You might not even know they're there but Geminis born with Mercury as their subruler will get to them before you can and get you off almost before you even get started.

Venus: Seriously Social and Searingly Sexual (June 1– June 10)

If loners turn you on, forget Geminis born with Venus as their subruler. This type is the Marcia Brady of the zodiac: Forever surrounded by a bunch of adoring pals. There will always be someone secretly crushing on this extrovert, so even when you're committed, pulling for the party circuit with your people pleaser can leave you feeling insecure, unloved, and unwanted. In other words, you better have a lot of charm and finesse to compete with this sign's all-encompassing charisma or you'll be spending lots of your free time in psychotherapy sessions. Since this sign always has others hitting on him or her, cheating can often rear its ugly head during both the early and later stages of the dating game. Since the deadlock of wedlock doesn't change this sign's social circle, you'll always need to worry about one other big D—and I don't mean Dallas.

One-night stands are stellar with this wild child as is any type of sexual experimentation. Three-ways, foot fetishes, and role-playing are all part of this sign's sexual repertoire, so get ready to try things you won't feel free to discuss poolside with your pals. Let Gemini know you're open to these ideas and he or she will take you on sexual adventures so extreme you'll be exhausted while your Gem adopts the role of the Energizer bunny—going and going and going . . .

This sign isn't the type to go down on you for hours and hours. Sex is an experience that is active, passive, and *everything* in between. Yeah, he'll eat you out but he'll expect you to do the same for him the next morning—or even a few minutes later. The charisma that makes this Gemini strain so exciting is also great at breaking the ties that bind. If you're looking for amazing sexual experiences, stop—but be aware that your Gemini is probably getting some on the side as well.

Uranus: The Unruly Intellectual (June 11–June 20)

Uranus is the planet that always keeps you guessing. When you aim for a job promotion and end up getting fired, only to slide into a higher salary at a different firm days later, Uranus has had a hand in what's happened. Uranus is everything you can't count on and nothing that you expect. When you give a highly mental sign such an unstable subruler almost anything can happen, so don't waste time trying to figure him or her out—roll with the punches instead and see what happens as the excitement builds.

This type of Gemini walks to his or her own drumbeat. While the other two strains of Gemini care what other people think, this sign could give a shit: He or she is all about voicing an opinion and if you happen to disagree, well then, fuck you. It's not that disagreement unleashes an inner wrath from this type of Gemini, it's simply that with wild-child Uranus shining on their scene, they could really give a damn whether you agree or not.

If you've got a forceful personality and are cool with agreeing to disagree though, this is a great sign to date, fornicate, or impregnate depending on your long-range goals. One thing that separates this Gem from the other two is that although they all love to argue, the first two do so more as a mental exercise. This Gemini backs up everything she or he does with strongly held personal convictions. Though those convictions can change at a moment's notice that doesn't lessen their strength over Gemini's basic psychological makeup. The world be damned: This sign is going to do what they want.

This characteristic strengthens any minority born under these ten days. Who gives a fuck if some segments of society whisper the word *colored* under their breath like it's akin to having cancer, or a born-again Bible-thumper thinks hell is made for fags. Geminis who have Uranus backing them have the spirit to forge past stupid societal constructs. If you're part of a minority and happen to be half of a dating duet with this not-so-shy sign, you'll never have to worry about riding on the back of the bus. This Gemini was sent here to change the world and that's all that he or she's about.

This subspecies of Gemini will rock your sexual world as well. The only rules are that there are no rules, so get ready for almost anything. If you can't keep up with Gemini's many fetishes—from half-hour hand jobs to filming themselves so they can watch their fornicational style on the big screen as they're screwing—Gemini will soon stop your dating game. If you enjoy rolling with the punches and are game for new adventures, then this is the strain to swoop for: They have everything you're looking for and more.

Sexual Synergy

Aries and Gemini: Such a hot combo you scorch each other sexually. Gem loves to talk while Aries loves action, but combining these traits makes for some mind-melding sexual acts. This is one arena where Aries feels comfortable having someone else call the shots, so plan on loosening your libido once you lose your clothes.

Taurus and Gemini: Slow and steady plus flighty and frantic equal odd bedfellows. The first time you'll think you've died and gone to heaven. The second go-round will see you feeling a lot less heavenly and by round three—if you get that far—you'll just *wish* you were dead.

Gemini and Gemini: Remember that goofy song from childhood where the refrain ran, "'Abba dabba dabba dabba dabba dabba dabba,' said the monkey to the chimp. 'Abba dabba dabba dabba dabba dabba dabba,' said the chimpie to the monk." Got the picture? You'll have more fun talking than torquing, so aim for something with an emphasis on the platonic rather than pumping.

Cancer and Gemini: Cancer reads romance novels, while Gemini indulges in the more hardcore aspects of life. Cancer is clingy and all about commitment; Gemini is all about expanding horizons. Gem might have fun manipulating the sign of the crab into anything from absolute oral affection to dressing up as a cheer-leader (as Cancer blushes with embarrassment). When Gem gets tired of fun and games Cancer will wreak revenge. *Not* good as bed partners—or almost anything else.

Leo and Gemini: Sex will be scintillating since both of you enjoy egging the other on to new heights of sexual satisfaction. Leo's tendency to call the between-the-sack shots will eventually irritate Gemini, but if you can find a satisfactory com-promise (taking turns, maybe?) sex between the lion and the twins will be a threesome you'll thoroughly enjoy.

Virgo and Gemini: Run, don't walk from this oh-so-scary sexual encounter. Since you both share the same ruler but have *totally* different takes on your exis-tence, count on your coupling to be creepier than sex with a sibling. You'll be awesome allies but boring bed buddies. Yuck.

Libra and Gemini: Both of you are air signs and this makes for a great combo in bed and beyond. Libra's playful approach to lovemaking is the perfect comple-ment to Gemini's love of raunchy talk and role-playing. Head for the bedroom and *stay there.*

Scorpio and Gemini: Minds won't be the only things that get blown in this ex-plosive love connection. Scorpio's hot and heavy view of the bump and grind meshes well with Gemini's anything-goes attitude. Lock your doors and bar your windows, because God forbid the neighbors figure out what you wild signs are up to behind closed doors.

Sagittarius and Gemini: Both of you love to talk but by the time you hit the bedroom that's where any hopes of oral activity end. You're both restless and used to having your own way and when you combine the two you're left with bed-room boredom, *not* bliss.

Capricorn and Gemini: Bedroom ballistics rate low when you mate an ambitious earth sign with a talkative air sign. Sex is a game for Gemini while Capricorn aims for "all work and no play." In time, you might discover an unhappy medium, but when the truth comes out you'd both rather watch *Ally McBeal* than head for bed.

Aquarius and Gemini: You're both as wild and crazy as Steve Martin in his younger years, so break out the handcuffs, silk scarves, and/or whatever floats your boat. No matter what sex act Gemini devises, Aquarius will be good to go, so slap on that rubber and get to work.

Pisces and Gemini: Your first fornication will be fab and oh-so fun, but once you make the major mistake of getting to know each other the sex act becomes about as scintillating as Britney Spears's views on politics. Translation? A first fuck is fine but then back out *fast*.

Exploring Their Erogenous Zone

For sharp-witted Geminis, life is a hands-on experience, so it only makes sense that their erogenous zones are their arms and hands. Remember how Gomez could always freak out Morticia on *The Addams Family* just by running light kisses up and down her arms? Well, put yourself in the role of Gomez because your Gemini has a hell of a lot in common with Morticia.

Since Gemini is such a fickle creature you should never start off by going directly for the kill. He or she will know exactly what you're up to and become instantly bored, so instead start off with some light, everyday kisses on your Gemini's lips. Exchange some kinky glances while you're doing so, letting your air sign know there's more to come. After a few kisses, "fortuitously" begin your attack. Kiss up and down each of your Gemini's arms, squeezing in a few licks and nibbles to stack the deck even more in your favor. Since you're not dealing with a cautious Cancer or prim-and-proper Virgo, be aware that your bites can border on boldness but stop short of drawing blood. If you get one or two yelps out of your Gem, then you know you're doing *something* right. Once you've got your air sign's blood boiling, move in on their fingertips, making erotic eye contact as you run your tongue over every digit. Now is the time for more nibbling, as you gently bite fingertips and the area between the fingers. Again, mix in lots of licks but skimp on leaving spit behind—it'll gross your Gemini out big time.

Now's the time to pull out your final—and truly killer—move. Start sucking on each finger, moving it in and out of your mouth as slowly as you would a lollipop. If your aim is wooing a woman, this will leave her groaning with desire, while if hardening a hunk is your goal, you just got what you're looking for. Geminis are ultra-oral creatures so watching you swallow their extremities will remind them that there are lots of other areas you could be licking as well. Slowly kiss, lick, nip, and nibble each fingertip as, all the while, you're using your hands to play with their free one. Now that your Gem is more hot and bothered than a Republican at a sex club, move their fingertips away from your mouth to more enticing areas. Whether this area happens to be your private parts, theirs, or another enticing area of your bod is up to you, but remember that if you coat their fingertip with a slight slathering of spit, it will increase the tactile sensation both of you receive. Now you know how to get a Gemini's juices flowing: Keeping their hands happy keeps them happily hedonistic for you.

Come Again?

Gemini Man

Getting a Gemini guy's love gun up and running for an awesome second sex act is easy—as long as you know the rules. Forget about playing with him under the covers (pretty much all you'd need to do with sexual Scorpio) or even parading around nude in front of him (works every time with Sagittarius). There's an excellent reason for this: The Gemini-guy's sexuality is based in his mind *not* his manpole.

So how do you handle this up-ending of the usual sexual equation? It's easy: Start talking so filthy your mom would wash your mouth out with soap. This isn't the time for flowery Taurean romance: "Gosh, you're beautiful," or a Leo-inspired lie: "That was the best sex I've ever had in my life." Pretend you're in a XXX-rated flick as you talk about everything you've done, everything you're going to do, and everything you've *ever* wanted to indulge in.

"Man, that first fuck left me bow-legged," you should mutter between clenched teeth before adding, "but I sure as hell wanna stick it in me again." If reading this makes you blush, you're probably better off with someone other than Gemini, who enjoys indulging in raunchier rhetoric than Eminem or Dr. Dre on their worst days. Want some more examples? "I can't get enough of your cock—lemme just look at it for a minute," and "Woah, I'm so fucking sore I can barely walk!" In other words, the nastier you can make your dialogue, the harder your hunk will get.

Since his imagination is almost overwhelming, this is a great time to let loose with some free-flowing fantasies. While you should never discuss crushes on others with most of the other signs (this would spell the final fuck if you were dating a Cancer), Gemini gets off on discovering your deepest and darkest fantasies. If you've always ached to orgy or wanted to have someone eat you out while locking lips with another, your Gemini dude wants to know every last dirty detail. Running wild with your sexual daydreams will loosen your own libido, which is an added bonus. While you've got to bend over to bed some signs a second time, with Gemini, getting him back to the bone-home stage is half the fun. Give free reign to your hedonistic hallucinations and before you know it, Gemini will be bouncing off the walls—and right into the sexual spot you want him in.

Gemini Woman

Gemini woman is just like her bro: hedonistic, unhampered by hang-ups, and horny as hell. And like her bro, a direct approach is a dumb one. Grabbing her tits and saying, "Let's get it on, pretty mama," is basically buying yourself a ticket to a night spent on the couch. Drill these sexual skills into your brain to make sure you never head for slumberland with blue balls or a mirthless monkey.

If you're a guy, you probably assume you need to abandon the locker room banter when you're lazing with your lady, but with the Gemini woman this is a notorious no-no. On the other hand, if you're a *chica* and Mom raised you to be a proper little lady, it's time to say, "What the fuck, Mom? I'm gonna have fun!" Translation? Everything you've ever been taught about women should be thrown out the door when it comes to dealing with a Gemini female. This girl has a very healthy appetite for hedonism, head, and humping, so when something dirty pops into your noggin, don't just blush—*say it.*

Talking like a trucker (or Jamie Lee Curtis, same difference) appeals to the Gemini woman for a number of reasons. First of all, she thinks societal rules are for the birds, so when you're willing to break those rules in front of her, she'll likely worship more than just the ground you're walking on. For another thing, her amazingly imaginative brain will instantly turn your wordplay into an ultra-erotic image that will titillate her inside and out. "We've never gone around the world on the staircase," might inspire a slap from a more stick-in-the-mud sign, but for Gemini, she'll immediately imagine the fun to be had with your idea. Tell her about that raunchy dream you had last night that involved her and two other females (hell, with Gemini, your dream could probably include one of each sex!)

Once you've indulged her in aural ecstasies, get ready to indulge in the real thing. There's almost nothing hotter than a sexually excited Gemini woman (although Scorpio would of course be some serious competition). Once you're facing the real deal and bumping uglies—or whatever sexual situation you've opted for—keep the dirty talk up and running. The more filthy your talk can get, the more likely your lady will get wet. Keep that inane rhyme in mind and she'll blow more than just your brain.

But Will It Last?

Aries and Gemini: Get ready to call the preacher because this is an awesome match (of course if you're gay, you'd best head for Vermont). Two signs who aren't afraid to say what's on their minds, your arguments will be hell—but if you can find a way to share your opinions without increasing your anger, these twins will find *lots* to do with their ram.

Taurus and Gemini: Your first weeks as a couple will be interesting since Taurus' quiet nature will bring out the best Gemini has to offer. As time passes, however, the bull's love of hearth and home will irritate extroverted Gemini. Maybe you'll make it as friends, but as long-term lovers? Guess again.

Gemini and Gemini: What happens when you combine the two signs that are famous for talk, talk, and more talk? Yup, you got it: Unless you're aiming for gossipy gab well into your nineties, you'll never reach the happy couple status. My advice? Fuck 'em and dump 'em.

Cancer and Gemini: Cancer wants security, hearth, and home. Gemini loves to flirt, party, and travel. Sound like a match made in hell? You're right on target: Gemini fuels Cancer's natural insecurity while the crab thinks the twins are sickeningly superficial.

Leo and Gemini: You're great in bed, you both love to talk, and Gemini doesn't mind sharing the spotlight with the somewhat self-centered lion. Leo loves your sparkling charm since its the perfect counterpart for his center of attention M.O. One lion plus two twins equals a tantalizing three-way, so grab this cat fast.

Virgo and Gemini: You share the same ruler, which means both of you are majorly mental but the similarity ends there. Geminis like to gossip while Virgo thinks dissing is despicable. Virgo's analytical approach to life makes Gemini think he's dating Spock from *Star Trek*. You'll be lucky to just make it as friends.

Libra and Gemini: Bad news and good news here. Take the bad first: You both love to spend money so brace yourself for future bankruptcy. The good news? You love each other so much you can't take your eyes off each other. Libras and Gems believe life is for the taking, so between the two of you there should never be a dull moment. Just *please* try shopping at discount stores once in a while.

Scorpio and Gemini: Although sex will be hotter than an A-bomb, those same sexual sparks will create a fire that causes more damage and distress than desire. Gemini is social and able to change their mind in a minute. Scorpio likes privacy over parties and can't stand Gemini's casual attitude. Screw your minds out on the first date but on the second say you've got to stay home to fluff the pillows.

Sagittarius and Gemini: Sex will be somewhat exciting but once you leave the bedroom problems will pop up faster than another boy band CD. Neither is very demonstrative with their affections and when Gemini starts critiquing Sagi's sexual skills, the affair will end on a *very* sour note.

Capricorn and Gemini: While Gemini's motto is "What the hell?" Capricorn's is "What the hell are you *thinking*?" When you put a wild child with a Fortune 500 type you get a parent/child relationship and unless you're into the Mommy/Daddy dance with a very twisted perspective, you'll groan *not* moan.

Aquarius and Gemini: Intellectual, innovative, and all-around fun. Which sign am I describing? Both—which will equal bedroom bliss *and* a love that can last a lifetime. You both think life is to be enjoyed and although Aquarius' tendency to think about life only in theory might create sticking points, they'll be easy to gloss over—and the making up will be well worth it.

Pisces and Gemini: You'll feel so passionate for each other you'll wonder if you're a Jackie Collins novel come to glorious life. But just like one of Jackie's heros or heroines, you'll face a myriad of soap opera-style problems. Gemini likes freedom and new challenges; Pisces likes the tried and true. A first date could spell ultimately unattainable affection, so just saying no to that first date is your best bet to keep your sanity.

Gemini Celebs: Multiple Personalities

Bronson Pinchot	May 20
Cher	May 20
Fairuza Balk	May 20
Mr. T	May 21
Naomi Campbell	May 22
Morrissey	May 22
Jewel	May 23
Drew Carey	May 23
Joan Collins	May 23
Priscilla Presley	May 24
Tommy Chong	May 24
Patti LaBelle	May 24
Lauryn Hill	May 25
Anne Heche	May 25
Mike Myers	May 25
Lenny Kravitz	May 26
Stevie Nicks	May 26
Todd Bridges	May 27
Lisa "Left Eye" Lopes	May 27
Gladys Knight	May 28
Melissa Etheridge	May 29
Annette Benning	May 29
LaToya Jackson	May 29
Wynonna Judd	May 30
Brooke Shields	May 31
Gregory Harrison	May 31
Alanis Morissette	June 1
Johnny Weismuller	June 2
Stacy Keach	June 2
Tony Curtis	June 3
Angelina Jolie	June 4
Noah Wyle	June 4
Michelle Phillips	June 4

Mark Wahlberg	June 5
Sandra Bernhard	June 6
Prince	June 7
Liam Neeson	June 7
Joan Rivers	June 8
Natalie Portman	June 9
Johnny Depp	June 9
Michael J. Fox	June 9
Tara Lipinsky	June 10
Leelee Sobieski	June 10
Elizabeth Hurley	June 10
Joshua Jackson	June 11
Joe Montana	June 11
Adrienne Barbeau	June 11
Marv Albert	June 12
Ally Sheedy	June 13
Tim Allen	June 13
Steffi Graf	June 14
Yasmine Bleeth	June 14
Donald Trump	June 14
Marla Gibbs	June 14
Courteney Cox Arquette	June 15
Helen Hunt	June 15
Tupac Shakur	June 16
Venus Williams	June 17
Dan Jansen	June 17
Carol Kane	June 18
Roger Ebert	June 18
Paul McCartney	June 18
Paula Abdul	June 19
Phylicia Rashad	June 19
Nicole Kidman	June 20
Lionel Richie	June 20

Chapter 5

CANCER
(June 21–July 21)

Sex Stats

Ruling planet: The Moon, which isn't a planet at all but the satellite responsible for this water sign's myriad of mood swings.

Signature symbol: The crab, with a rock-hard shell but nothing but sweet meat underneath.

Trademark color: Silver, a shade reminiscent of Cancer's shimmering sexuality.

Favorite position: Doggie style makes your crab feel safe, secure and oh-so sexual.

Potent porn: *Buffed and Sucked* for gay guys, *Strip Search* for the straight set and *Girlfriends* for lesbian lovers.

Ultimate outfit (male): A plush, white, oversized robe from a swank hotel like the Plaza.

Ultimate outfit (female): Satin pajamas like the ones Hugh Hefner seems to live in.

Mattress mambo music: Twang-free country ballads from singers like the Dixie Chicks to "Unchained Melody" by the Righteous Brothers.

Best sex toy: A drink or joint that will relax your overly cautious crab.

After-fuck finger food: What else? Seafood—from, yup, crabmeat to lobster dipped in salty, melted butter.

Do You Know What You're in For?

In a word, Cancers are *confusing*. Though highly compassionate, Cancer women can come across as total bitches while Cancer males are outside blowing the heads off the coolest animals nature has to offer. Why the paradox? It's simple, really: While critical Virgos can be prima donnas and over-the-top Aries loves to hunt, Cancer's fucked-up features *might* be a mere façade. Symbolized by the crab, Cancer spends life building an elaborate defense system that can be just as hard to penetrate as any shell. Cancers are afraid to let the world bear witness to their hearts of gold, because they fear if they do, friends and enemies alike will discover their hidden weakness: Whether they're full of bravado or totally detached, they don't want you to know they care—even though they care a great deal.

In spite of efforts to keep the world at bay through a myriad of defensive maneuvers, Cancers are easily wounded. While Gemini will throw off a criticism and Leo thinks any critique thrown his or her way is off base since she's perfect, Cancer will internalize any and all negative comments until a boiling point is reached. Boil a crab and you've got dinner at a fancy restaurant; boil a Cancer and you've just created a powder keg that could blow up today, tomorrow, or twenty years from now. Cancer is embarrassed by his or her need for love and affection but if you screw the fourth sign in the zodiac you'll encounter another key tenet the sign of the crab is known for: revenge. This is a trait shared in common with Scorpio, but while scorpions are ruled by passion, Cancers are driven by a strong sense of one-upsmanship. If you tangle with a Cancer get ready for almost anything to happen: Since this sign isn't as blinded by emotion as Scorpio, a Cancer can ultimately end up a far more lethal enemy, so whatever you do, don't fuck with the crab.

Even when you're nice to Cancer expect the inevitable. Ruled by the Moon, Cancer's conflicting emotions reflect the ocean's tides. One minute your Cancer will be sweet as can be while the next, that same old crab will be sulking about something of which you're totally unaware. Communication with crabs is difficult but key to making a successful relationship or forging a temporary love connection. As a cardinal water sign, Cancer is an uneasy combination of forward thinking and introspection. Making the equation even more difficult to understand, Cancer is often victim to good old Catholic-style guilt. This can drive your crab to do seemingly unexplainable activities. Driven by a conscience that conflicts with many of society's rules, Cancer is above all concerned with protection: Protection of those the crab loves and protection of *self*.

Cancer Man

Cancer guys are usually set to a slow boil since they're always pissed off about something. Why were you ten minutes late to dinner last night? What's the deal with you parading around in that ultrarevealing outfit? Were you just checking out another guy? Be prepared to field questions like these on a daily basis from Cancer and if your answers aren't up to snuff, be prepared to deal with your crab's wrath. While Aries gets pissed before getting over what made them angry in the first place, Cancer isn't nearly as predictable. He may be angry at you about something that took place ten minutes ago—or ten years. Deciphering his thoughts is almost impossible since his defense system is so elaborate. So what should you do? Be very open and honest and do everything in your power to stroke his sense of security. A secure Cancer presents a far different picture than one who is unsure of you and your feelings.

If you're just gunning for sex, Cancer man is much easier to deal with. While Cancer females usually are on the lookout for relationships, male Cancers are happy to separate the sex act from their emotions: Its just another way to protect themselves. Cancer's myriad neuroses can actually make for an awesome one-night stand: You get the wild bonding Cancers crave without having to deal with the emotional fallout the next morning. When I say crabs are into wild lovemaking, don't expect the scorching sexuality of Scorpio or the easy fun and games of Sagittarius. Cancer craves attention, whether he happens to be on the giving or receiving end. Whether you're a straight *chica* eyeing the sign of the crab or a gay guy, this boosts your odds of getting or giving eye-opening oral sex into the stratosphere. Fucking is a far different arena, however, and unless the Cancer guy loves your ass—or is intent on proving his in-the-sack prowess—count on fornication to be an exercise in getting himself off. Again, this is all about protection. While Gemini feels comfortable with a temporary bond, Cancer is afraid the connection might make him vulnerable to future pain. He'll avoid this at all costs so prepare for some so-so sex. However, if you're looking for someone to momentarily dominate you in the bedroom, Cancer will step up to the challenge happily. Being in charge of a temporary liaison makes Cancer feel dominant—a position he *must* be in to take advantage of the situation—and you.

So what's it like if you're totally honest with the fourth sign in the zodiac, are gunning for forever, and he lets his guard down? In a word, it's heaven: When a Cancer guy decides he's in this with you for the long haul, he'll do whatever it takes to keep you happy in and out of the bedroom. Virgos love the release sex gives them, Libras live for the partnership, but Cancer *needs* sex: It makes him feel complete and each time you bump uglies with him you'll be reinforcing the bonds that make your relationship work. Be forewarned that though this is the ultimate combo, with a Cancer man it will take more work than Calista Flockhart trying to gain weight. If things do go wrong, divorce or breaking up will be absolute hell for the Cancer man. Utterly nostalgic, he's unwilling to completely let go of anything with which he's ever come in contact. Although you might never speak to him again, he'll always think of you and will constantly obsess about what went wrong.

Cancer Woman

Cancer women are much easier to get a handle on than their masculine counterparts. As usual, the difference for this has more to do with societal reasons than ones from the zodiac. In America, it's cool for a girl to be ultra-emotional but guys are supposed to keep their feelings in check. This creates an uneasy duality in Cancer men that female Cancers don't have to deal with. Cancer women, in many ways, are in tune with the idyllic fifties picture of the way life is supposed to be. Although career may be extremely important to her, staying close to the homefront and a tightly knit family are even more so.

Figuring out Cancer females in the bedroom is almost like an algebra problem. Once you plug in all the different factors, finding answers is faster than Usher on a first date. The question is: Have you discovered all the factors? If you haven't, you're screwed—but not by the Cancer you're coveting. Here's a crash course on key things to look for. Is she twenty-five years old or more? If so, she's definitely *not* into casual sex, with one exception. If she's buzzed on booze—or almost anything else—Cancer women might momentarily dispense with their innate shy nature and try you on for size. Are you her one and only or is she screwing around on her other to be with you? If you fall into the latter category, realize this: the Cancer woman is using you to avenge some real or imagined mistake her mate made. Whether you like it or not, your position in her life is transitory. Once she's accomplished her objective—making her mate feel absolute crap—you'll be tossed in a pile with yesterday's garbage, so unless you get off on being treated like shit, use the rhythm method and pull out *now*.

The last question you should consider is this: Is the Cancer of your affections in love with you? If she is, and you're willing and able to go the extra mile with careful, constant communication and never fooling around, she'll take you around the world when you bounce into bed—both figuratively and *literally*. Sometimes, Cancer women will choose partners they're not all that enticed by just because no one else is around. If you're exactly what she wants though, she'll do anything in her power to keep you and keep you happy. Yup, you'll always wonder where her mood will jump next but if you remain true, in every sense of the word, a Cancer woman will probably make an ideal mate.

Five Surefire Ways to Break the Ice with Cancer

Cancer Man
1. Give a *direct,* understated compliment as in, "You know, I've always thought you were a really handsome guy."
2. Ask one of his friends what cologne or perfume turns him on the most, spray some on, and then walk past: sweet smells freak out this cool customer.
3. Whether you're a Baby Boomer or part of Generation X or Y, discuss something from the past, since this guy lives for nostalgia. Still clueless? Try this: "Remember when *Gilligan's Island* would be on every day after school got out?"
4. Ask him where he likes to water-ski or swim.
5. Tell him what a great listener he is.

Cancer Woman
1. Talk about kids—yours, hers, or just rug rats in general.
2. Ask her out to an opera or other classy musical event (in other words, *not* Nine Inch Nails, okay?).
3. Mention a cause you back (preferably something concerning animals or children).
4. Mention a personal problem (unless its a raging case of VD).
5. To totally freak her ass out, give her a serenade outside her bedroom window: She'll act embarrassed but secretly she'll love it even if you're off-key.

Refining Your Sexual Strategy—The Subrulers

The Moon: Moody Blues (June 21–June 30)
The Moon is all about mystery, romance, and seething unrest underneath a seemingly placid exterior. It moves in cycles, going slowly from one extreme to the other, but like the ocean's tides there is a method to this madness. With the Moon as both ruler and subruler of this subspecies of Cancer, be prepared for someone extremely emotional, but as I mentioned, there is a pattern to your Cancer although it may take you months or even years to discover it.

Whether male or female, this type of Cancer didn't just write the book on PMS, they own the entire fucking company. Mood swings will be fast, furious, and sometimes even frightening as your Cancer faces the myriad fears his or her life presents. Much like Jamie Lee Curtis's battle against her big bro in the *Halloween* flicks, this type of Cancer is all about meeting their destiny. This idea frightens them—whether they're meant to be the next Vincent van Gogh or Vince Gill, it's tough to face your worst fear so keep this in mind when you have to deal with their many downward-spiraling mood swings.

In bed, this sign is passive/aggressive. If he wants you to blow him, he won't ask. He'll sit there sulking instead, with his hands locked behind his head as he sneaks nervous glances toward his crotch. If she wants you to bend her over and spank her—a secret desire this sign hates to have known—you'll hear a lot of anxiety-ridden sighs and notice her irritation but have no idea what she's freaking on. The key to solving this sexual suckiness is communication and with this kind of Cancer, you'll need to keep all the aural doors open *all of the time.* With such a strong tendency to withdraw, you might experience awesome sex the first night and a whole lotta nothing the next, so unless you're a *very* communicative sign like Sagittarius, figuring this person out might ultimately be more trouble than it's worth.

Surprisingly, as far as one-night stands go this sign can be sexually spectacular: Without the onus of a commitment, this crab will feel more free to open up sexually, though you'll probably be forced to opt for more conventional forms of sexuality. If you want a fearsome four-way or want to play out that rape fantasy you've been to afraid to talk about, don't make the mistake of telling this sign what's on your mind.

Pluto: Deepest End of the Ocean (July 1–July 11)

Pluto is the god in charge of death and rebirth. If you're familiar with the story of the phoenix, you know that every time something dies it gives life to something new. Combined with the romanticism and sensitivity of the Moon, this strain of Cancer is one of the most fascinating areas in the zodiac. The ocean of the object of your affections is so deep, you'll probably never reach the end of it, but you'll be fascinated in spite of yourself.

This type of Cancer would run into a burning building to rescue the house mouse trapped inside—and if he or she ever caught the arsonist to blame, that fire starter would get the shit beaten out of him on a figurative and literal level. This Cancer is less concerned with him or herself than the other two subspecies. Cancers born during this time period share some personality traits with Pisces since they're concerned with otherworldly ideas, spirituality, and/or the occult.

The ultimate dream lover, it's as if this Cancer can read every sexual thought that sizzles to the surface of your brain. Existence for this sign is surreal and somewhat larger than life, so prepare for a drama queen or king. While Leo likes center stage because that's where he or she wants to be, Cancer doesn't enjoy seizing the spotlight but on occasion, this type feels they must. If this kind of Cancer feels strongly enough about something, they'll speak their mind (a *very* rare trait for the sign of the crab).

This sign is extremely sentimental so if the thought of seeing a guy cry grosses you out, pass this one up (or better yet, *grow* up). Life is always somewhat sad and sepia-toned for this ultrasensitive type: He or she is fully aware of the idea of rebirth and renewal but the pain that is part and parcel of this process is terribly upsetting to this sign. Be careful not to let this sign withdraw too far into their shell because once they make a mental break with you, they'll never completely return. Intuition is so strong in this sign their BS detectors don't even need to be turned on to catch you in a lie. It's as if they have a guardian angel who's whispering secrets into their ears. This is their blessing and their curse. If you can get this sign to trust you, you'll have the world at your feet but don't waste time playing games: This Cancer will know what you're up to and they won't be above gunning for revenge.

Neptune: The Romantic Dreamer (July 12–July 21)

Neptune sees over our subconscious, rules our dreams, and manipulates our everyday fantasies. When that sexy secretary walks past and you think about bending her over there and then—but know you never will—Neptune is grinning down at your hard-on. The same goes for when you face a reoccurring dream about that *chica* who already has a girlfriend. Neptune helps us to explore things, ideas, and people we would never normally encounter, so when you let this concept conspire with the Moon's innate sensuality, you get a shy, quiet type who has loads to give but is insecure about sharing it.

This person is extremely artistic—whether they know it or not. You'll either be dating a full-blown songwriter or a number cruncher who loves to doodle imaginative drawings in her spiral notepad. Like many artistic types, this type of Cancer is extremely volatile, both in and out of the bedroom.

Sex with a person born during these ten days is a supremely satisfying experience. All water signs are pretty oral creatures, but this sign is especially drawn to head-onistic pleasure. If you're opposed to the number 69, sex with someone else is your better bet. For this kind of Cancer, going down isn't just a sexual experience—it's spiritual as well, so get ready for plenty of loving licks from this strong, loyal, and protective type. Often prone toward depression and despair, sex is the perfect antidote for this secretive sign: It makes them feel loved and in play with the world's forward movement. Sex silences their preoccupation with death—from your first date onward they'll worry about losing you—because it reminds them that first and foremost, we were put here to live. Open this Cancer's eyes to the brighter side of the world and you'll have a lover who will never leave you, a friend who will listen to all your dreams and desires, and an unbelievably tough cookie who will share the weight of the world with you. Life and love with this kind of Cancer is a dream, with all the good and bad elements that that implies.

Sexual Synergy

Aries and Cancer: Aries' idea of a libidinous lovemaking session lasts all of five minutes, so just about the time Cancer's had *almost* enough foreplay, Aries is headed for slumberville. If snoozing next to a never-satisfied sex partner is your idea of fun, snag the crab, but if you want someone who can float *your* boat, pass on this overly romanced water sign.

Taurus and Cancer: Taurus' slow-and-steady approach to the mattress mambo needs just the spice Cancer can willingly supply. You're both possessive and think cheating is better left to more superficial signs like Gemini and Sagittarius. Yup, the sex might seem surreally slow to some signs but by your fifth big O in one night, you'll say, "Screw what the other signs think."

Gemini and Cancer: Sex will be scintillating but only as a competition or power play. Gemini excites Cancer with the "anything goes" attitude for which this air sign is famous, but by the next morning when his roving eye becomes apparent, Gemini will be the only thing that's got to go.

Cancer and Cancer: You have so much in common you might as well be twins. You're both clingy, sensitive, and ultra-easy to wound. Mounting a mirror image might appeal to some signs but for you, two Cancers are one too many. First-time sex might singe your soul but by the second round you'll think sexuality sucks.

Leo and Cancer: Leo's sunny attitude in the sack keeps Cancer guessing, but since Leo sticks by those he or she loves the crab won't need to worry about a Sagittarian-style stray. Cancer shows Leo love and radiates the possessive nature kitty cats desire. Meanwhile, Leo presents Cancer with a myriad sexual situations—and positions! Paradise found.

Virgo and Cancer: Virgo will do anything to please his partner (unless a one-night stand is the objective), while Cancer loves being doted on. From blow jobs to bed-bouncing to late-night bonds in the bathtub, this combo of earth and water signs *doesn't* equal mud.

Libra and Cancer: Libra can't stand Cancer's mood swings in bed or beyond. Cancer thinks Libra is a lackadaisical lover more interested in pleasing himself or herself than the crab conquest at hand. This is one of the worst combos in the zodiac and if you're willing to die trying to make things work out, ask Mom to send lilies.

Scorpio and Cancer: Morph these water signs and you get three Fs: tons of fun and fabulous fucking. Scorpio's more than happy to give whatever Cancer yearns for between the sheets—from five hours of hedonistic head to humps and grinds that will leave the crab begging for more.

Sagittarius and Cancer: Sexcapades will be odd adventures for these two. In the long term, odds are awful, but if you're only aiming for a few fucks or a one-night stand, Sagittarius will be turned on by Cancer's sweet bedroom behavior, while Cancer will be ultra-excited by Sagittarius' anything-goes attitude. Have fun on your first date, because the next one won't be nearly as much fun.

Capricorn and Cancer: Expect sexual sparks from the minute the crab makes first contact with this goal-oriented goat. Cancer likes strong authority figures and that just happens to be Cappy's favorite M.O. These sparks *won't* lead to fire, however, so have fun while you can.

Aquarius and Cancer: Sex will be so-so—if the two of you can even make it as far as the bedroom. The problem is that you couldn't have less in common. Aquarius views sex as entertainment while Cancer sees the sex act as an all-important union. Sound like a heartache waiting to happen? You got it, so make the right move and move past this unsettling union.

Pisces and Cancer: Both of you are affectionate, giving signs and this results in some unbelievably erotic lovemaking sessions. Since both of you are water signs, trust is an all-important issue that will keep your bed bonds solid. Don't be afraid to exchange fantasies with each other, since you're both ruled by an imaginative eros.

Exploring Their Erogenous Zone

Want to know the secret for getting through your crab's shell *fast?* In spite of your love magnet's myriad mood swings, each crab has a very susceptible spot. Although it's the same region for guys and girls, your approach should be different since the subject matter at hand isn't exactly the same. What am I babbling about? In two words, boobs and pecs, the two erotic areas that will leave you with a soft-shelled crab instead of the usual hard-to-break exterior.

Let's start with the female side of things. The Cancer woman is all about romance, so grabbing her tits the same way you'd test a melon at FoodMart isn't the best way to get this ingenue in the sack. Instead, concentrate on kissing initially, brushing up against her breasts as you do so, almost as an afterthought. Go for slow, gentle strokes instead of squeezes or a push/pull motion and you're on the right track. Licking her nipple through her clothing is an awesome way to bring out the wild woman in your Cancer *chica*. Like Virgo, she almost views sex as dirty, but since ultimately this is part of the turn-on, anything you can do to encourage this attitude will increase the wetness factor of the female at hand. Once you've got her riled up with lots of foreplay, slowly unbutton her blouse as if you were opening an ultra-expensive Christmas present. While ripping off a woman's top might appeal to a wild Gemini or a savage Scorpio, it's a great way to receive a solid slap from a Cancer woman. Once her top is off, trace her breasts—*lightly*—through her bra. Again, you should be doing this as if you're dealing with a fragile piece of art, not an anyday piece of ass. This should inspire a few groans on her part, which is your clue to lose her bra. Once undone, take a good look at what she has to offer: Diving right in will offend Cancer female *big time*. Bend, to slowly run your hands over her divine upper area, before replacing your fingertips with your tongue. Subtlety is key for the first few seconds, but after she's writhing with delight feel free to add some mandatory nips and nibbles.

Now, on to the testosterone side of things. Say you're faced with a Cancer male wearing a tight-fitting Polo-style shirt. If he's built like the bomb, take a good, long, sober stare at his torso: The Cancer man appreciates appreciation. Once you've done this, your moves are similar to what you'd do with a Cancer woman, but with some important changes. First off, forget about kissing him. Go right for his goods, trailing your fingers over his proud pectoral region like you're blind and trying to read the best book you've ever come across. Don't waste too much time finessing your Cancer male: Go in for the kill after just a few strokes. Grab both pecs and squeeze hard—as all the while you're making erotic and intimate eye contact. Letting out a few breaths of passion at this point will let the Cancer man know that the ball—or balls as may be the case—is about to come into play. Now, yank his shirt off. This is in direct contradiction to what you'd do with a Moon-child *chica:* What she finds unforgivable, *he* finds amazingly erotic. Once you've got his shirt halfway off, bend down to take some bites from his bod. This will freak Cancer man out for more than one reason. First, with his T-shirt still obscuring his views and trapping his arms, he'll feel powerless and in *your* control—a big turn-on for the Cancer man. Second, aggressively gnawing on his nipples lets him know you're not exactly aiming for by-the-numbers sex. Cancer man will often opt for the basic missionary style—but only because he thinks he should. If you can loosen him up with lots of pectoral play, you'll get this studly sex object to bounce off the rafters—and do *anything* in his power to keep you happy.

Come Again?

Cancer Man
Getting the Cancer man to gun for a second shot takes a lot of finesse and an ever-changing strategy. Keep in mind his basic psychology: Cancers love to sulk and often end up using sex—namely the withholding of it—as a weapon. Therefore, you shouldn't think you're going to get him going again without a little work on your part. It might piss Cancer guys off to hear this, but the best approach to make his little head rear again is to treat the dude in question like a high school girlfriend. In other words, you better be ready for *loads* of foreplay. Don't let him think this is a prelude to another lovemaking session. Instead, play it cool by acting as if you simply can't get enough of his awesome—or not so awesome, as the case may be—bod. As stated earlier, pay close attention to his chest: He loves having it licked, nipped, and nibbled but there's a lot more to the picture than just pectoral pinching. The Cancer guy is one of the most oral signs in the zodiac, which means licking him all over will almost always insure *something* pops up. If he's clean as a whistle, don't head for his whistle just yet. Manipulating his man-

thing should only be used during the final stages. Instead, delicately lick up and down his entire body—from his toes to his tush to his top. Roll him over as you clean him up, so you can gain access to every secret sexual spot Cancer man would rather you didn't know about. Lightly lick his pecs, then run kisses down his treasure trail—making sure you avoid his dick except for maybe a few reckless rubs. Then flip your crab onto his belly and give him the same treatment from behind. Starting at the top of his neck, slowly trail kisses and licks down his entire back and around his ass (how far you go in this arena, I'll leave up to your own discretion). Then, lick the hair on the back of his upper thighs, teasingly working your way down to his calves. Don't be afraid to be a bit brutal. While the Cancer woman finds pain just that, for the Cancer man, kink is all part of his raunch repertoire. Pull some of his hair with your teeth and nip at his ankles. As the pièce de résistance—assuming he's just taken a shower of course—end your oral journey on his toes. If your Cancer man isn't standing at attention by now and ready to roll, you're faced with two alternatives: Either you're not exactly his cup of tea—or he's dead.

Cancer Woman

The Cancer woman is a lot like her male counterpart—just minus the sado-masochistic streak. Your bedpartner wants to bond and if you can reinforce her ideas about your relationship, she'll become putty in your hands. Concentrate on two arenas to get things off to a great start: compliments and kissing. Whispering, "You're so beautiful," as you lick the inside of her ear—but skipping the snail trail of slobber, please—will relax her usually rigid bedroom demeanor. Gentle close-mouthed kisses all around her face—from her ears to her eyelids—will get her all aflutter for an awesome second sex act.

Now, stack the deck further in your favor by heading south. Circle her breast with your tongue as if you're licking honey off of an apple as you get closer and closer to her Achilles' heel of hedonism: her nipples. Once you get there, chew, lick, bite, and nibble—basically everything you'd do if you were eating a Mars bar except there's no swallowing involved. One sex act that will drive a Cancer woman wild with desire is to nibble on one nipple as you flick the other with your fingertips. This is one area where subtlety doesn't pay off: Your finger flicks should be just as forceful as your tongue action on the other side. If the workout isn't the same for each you won't be receiving the payload you're looking for.

Okay, so now she's moaning and groaning and thinking you're the closest thing to Harrison Ford or Anne Heche she's ever come up against. Your next step?

Make like an old-time explorer and head even farther south: Muff diving on this oh-so sexy water sign will put her in a whole new world of sexual passion. A few words of warning: Cancer women are often scared off by their own sexuality so don't be freaked out if she says she's uncomfortable with your making like a koala and heading Down Under. In a word, that's bullshit. This water sign is *extremely* oral—whether she wants to admit it or not, so try to let her see that there's nothing dirty about directly pleasuring another person's sex part. As long as you make her feel safe and secure she'll let you head in to her no-man's-land—and once you're there a second sex act will be well on the way.

As you're lapping between her legs, concentrate on artistry not aggression. Trace your name with your tongue throughout her nether region or alternate hot breaths blown against her private parts with loving licks that get deeper with every passing minute. Okay, so now your usually stiff and stodgy sex partner is a whole lot more like Silly Putty. You can figure out what to do next, can't you?

But Will It Last?

Aries and Cancer: The same Arien traits that so excite the crab behind closed doors will ultimately spell doom for the relationship. Aries' aggressive, argumentative nature makes Cancer feel burnt out while the ram's roving eye brings out all the insecurites for which crabs are famous. Long-term love is about as likely as Ralph Nader bagging the presidency.

Taurus and Cancer: Both of you love security and sex and when you combine these two traits you get a very romantic relationship. Taurus loves to do sweet little things to prove his or her affection like sending flowers, and this is an awesome way to keep the sign of the crab smiling. Definitely a match made in heaven.

Gemini and Cancer: So what if the fucking is fantastic? Out of bed you'll barely be able to stand each other. Gemini's basically fickle nature will irritate the oh-so serious crab and Cancer's quest for security grates on Gemini's nerves. Gem only views this clingy characteristic as bordering on the obsessive. Maybe there's a way to work things out, but you'll probably end up saying, "No, way!"

Cancer and Cancer: You have way too much in common to spend your life with another crab. You're both experts at hitting below the belt, so if you opt for an existence together get ready to make war, *not* love. Both of you need loads of attention, but neither is willing to give what the other desires. Pair two crabs and you've got a lethal alliance.

Leo and Cancer: Once Cancer can get used to Leo's over-the-top attitude, all signals are definitely go in this awesome mix. Cancer's intuition enables him or her to say all the right things to compliment proud but needy Leo, while Leo will do anything to protect the easily wounded sign of the crab.

Virgo and Cancer: Maybe this isn't the ultimate love connection, but you can certainly make it work if you're willing to go the extra mile. Virgo's fussy behavior will throw Cancer off until the crab realizes Virgo isn't infuriated by the crab, but rather by life in general. Virgo's analytical approach to life is just what over-emotional Cancer needs. Not a perfect pairing but pretty damn close.

Libra and Cancer: Welcome to hell. Libra's flighty, fickle approach to life leaves Cancer aghast, while the crab's needy nature leaves Libra looking for the easiest escape. When Cancer heads home for a quiet evening only to find Libra has planned an impromptu get-together for thirty of his/her closest friends, the end is near. Don't make the mistake of aiming for this union.

Scorpio and Cancer: While other signs are turned off by Cancer's possessiveness, the sign of the scorpion thinks it's a total turn-on. Cancer is so naturally loyal, Scorpio's anger and avarice are kept permanently at bay. Who cares if monogamy isn't the rule on soap operas? For the two of you, sticking together will be easy—and you'll be glad you did.

Sagittarius and Cancer: As friends, you're the perfect foils for each other, but as lovers there's a lot left to be desired. Sagittarius lives for freedom—and loves to cheat—which certainly doesn't sit well with the security-coveting crab. Conversations will be fascinating but when you face cold, hard reality you'll wish you were with someone else.

Capricorn and Cancer: You can make it as a couple but it will be anything but a perfect pairing. Capricorn views life as a business strategy and though he or she will bend over backward to keep your intimacy intact, the crab will eventually get tired of discussing boardrooms instead of bedrooms. If you're aiming for a marriage of convenience, this is your best bet, but if you're looking for love, keep on looking.

Aquarius and Cancer: Aquarius' detached—some might even say cold—approach to life repulses sweet-natured Cancer. Aquarius is all about theories, ideas, and the future while crabs would rather retreat into treasured memories and nostalgia. Aquarius' cutting humor does anything but crack up the crab. Expect a lot of hurt and even more misunderstandings.

Pisces and Cancer: Both of you are affectionate, sweet romantics. Pisces supplies an abundance of imagination while Cancer takes care of the mundane aspects of day-to-day life, like making sure the checkbook is balanced and that the mortgage gets paid before the due date. Combining this realist with the ultimate in imagination is an awesome coupling.

Cancer Celebs: Taking the Indirect Approach

Prince William	June 21
Juliette Lewis	June 21
Carson Daly	June 22
Cyndi Lauper	June 22
Meryl Streep	June 22
Bob Fosse	June 23
Jeff Beck	June 24
George Michael	June 25
Derek Jeter	June 26
Chris O'Donnell	June 26
Ross Perot	June 27
John Cusack	June 28
John Elway	June 28
Kathy Bates	June 28
Mel Brooks	June 28
Gary Busey	June 29
Mike Tyson	June 30
Liv Tyler	July 1
Pamela Anderson	July 1
Princess Diana	July 1
Deborah Harry	July 1
Tom Cruise	July 3

Geraldo Rivera	July 4
Huey Lewis	July 5
George W. Bush	July 6
Sylvester Stallone	July 6
Della Reese	July 6
Michelle Kwan	July 7
Cree Summer	July 7
Kevin Bacon	July 8
Anjelica Huston	July 8
Fred Savage	July 9
Courtney Love	July 9
Tom Hanks	July 9
O. J. Simpson	July 9
Lisa Rinna	July 11
Giorgio Armani	July 11
Kristi Yamaguchi	July 12
Cheryl Ladd	July 12
Richard Simmons	July 12
Bill Cosby	July 12
Cheech Marin	July 13
Harrison Ford	July 13
Patrick Stewart	July 13
Brian Austin Green	July 15
Jesse Ventura	July 15
Corey Feldman	July 16
David Hasselhoff	July 17
Diahann Carroll	July 17
Paul Verhoeven	July 18
Anthony Edwards	July 19
Carlos Santana	July 20
Josh Hartnett	July 21
Robin Williams	July 21

Chapter 6
LEO
(July 22–August 22)

Sex Stats

Ruling planet: The Sun, which isn't a planet at all, but a star. It adds vibrancy and intensity to Leo's sizzling sexuality and just like Leo's opinion of him or herself, it also happens to be the center of our solar system.

Signature symbol: The lion, king—or queen, as the case may be—of all beasts and ultimate master of the universe. This translates into Leo's cool confidence in between the sheets.

Trademark color: Gold, a color that's warm and uplifting—just like Leo.

Favorite position: Receiving oral affections from you, since Leo is all about getting serviced.

Potent porn: If you're straight, *Palace of Pleasure* will make your cat feel like royalty. If you're a female on the prowl for the same, get your hands on a copy of *Nasty Girls.* Gay guy? Snag *Flex T.V.*

Ultimate outfit (male): A flamboyantly colored ensemble most other male signs wouldn't be caught dead in. Think Duran Duran in the mid-eighties.

Ultimate outfit (female): An attention-grabbing look from an independent designer like Vera Wang.

Mattress mambo music: Any light, classical music that will leave the attention directed at your Leo. Think Mozart—not Bach.

Best sex toy: A camera that will throw your lion into fornicational focus or a game of strip poker that will get your cat purring.

After-fuck finger food: Ice cream will make your Leo feel deliciously decadent and don't worry about your lion packing on the pounds, since this speedy sign never seems to gain weight.

Do You Know What You're in For?

Leo rules. Whether the sign of the lion rules a brilliant career, a financial empire, or just a circle of friends, the fifth sign in the zodiac *must* be in charge. For some signs, Leo's naturally dominant personality is just what the doctor ordered, but if you're turned off by the idea of having to constantly praise your mate or want the spotlight centered on you, Leo probably isn't your type. Leos want to be stars and if they happen to be lucky enough to have Bill Clinton's or Madonna's chutzpah, they'll leap into their role with gusto. Problems occur when Leo can't reach the place he or she wants to be. Whether they suffer from two left feet, little business sense, or are just lazy as hell (a major problem for many Leos) since they must be top dog, their brain will rearrange reality to fit their needs. Whether a giant success or a total failure, Leo will see him or herself in the first category—even if the facts totally dispute his or her invented reality.

As a partner *d'amour*, Leo is excellent, but only if you're the type who believes in satisfying your own needs. Leo is all about getting off and if you share this viewpoint, lasso your lion and hop into bed now—but if you need major mental or physical stroking to enjoy the big O, the sign of the lion *won't* leave you sighin'. Leo thinks everyone else is like he or she is and thinking from another person's viewpoint is next to impossible for the fifth sign in the zodiac.

If you're getting the feeling that Leos are cold or callous, think again: Leos are great philanthropists and often donate a lot of their time and money to various charities once they reach the top of their profession. It's simply that Leo is so focused on him or herself and fulfilling their own needs that your concerns will often come in a distant second. It's not that Leo doesn't care, it's just that the lion figures everyone should deal with their own problems. This sounds great on paper and is something every psychiatrist worth her salt would echo, but in real life you better have a strong sense of yourself and a fully developed ego if you don't want the lion to puncture yours with one of his catty claws.

As fixed fire signs, Leos are very driven and active. While Virgo forces him or herself to get ahead because life is all about reaching the next level and Gemini achieves so he can blow some occasional dough, Leo enjoys the work in and of itself. If you're aiming for love and marriage, keep in mind that Leo has already been married once—to her career. If you're fixated on a few days of illicit lust with no strings attached, uncork the champagne: Leo is exactly what you're looking for.

Leo Man

Leo guys are blustery, full of themselves, and loads of fun to hang around. Everyone should have at least one Leo in their lives, just in case their TV set breaks down: Leo guys *love* to entertain and though their swelled heads might grate on your nerves every now and again, their base sense of fun and happiness will almost always put a smile on your face. Libra sees the glass as half full, Cancer sees it as half empty, while Leo thinks, "That's all the milk I wanted anyway." An eternal optimist, Leo can always make the best out of a bad situation—even if he's only changed his version of reality to accommodate the situation he faces.

Since Leo loves to be worshipped, get ready for constant head requests. He enjoys getting blown for more reasons than just the physical. He likes the feeling of having power over someone else and craves one-on-one attention where he can just kick back and bask in your affection. While Sagittarius is prone to stray because it sounds like fun, Leo men will sometime look to others for love just to reinforce their idea that they're basically, well, godlike. In other words, if you're unwilling to treat him like the next Tom Cruise in bed, he'll find someone who will. If you can give Leo everything he's looking for, however, he'll be an honest partner and won't screw around even when an occasional argument occurs.

Leo guys aren't as wildly imaginative in bed as, say, a Scorpio, but they're always ready to try something new. From drizzling champagne down his bod for you to lick off to tying you up before he has his way with you, almost nothing is too extreme for Leo. The one thing he's not really enthralled with is role-playing. It makes sense, after all: Since Leo thinks he's perfect already, why in hell would he pretend to be anyone else?

Subtlety isn't the way to communicate with the Leo man since irony and sarcasm aren't concepts with which he can readily identify. Be ready to scream out, "Not there—*here!*" and "Go down on me, now!" Many of the cues you might have discovered that work with other signs won't work with Leo. From facial expressions to muffled moans, Leo's not so great about reading between the lines, so instead concentrate on keeping the lines of communication as open as they can possibly be.

Leo Woman

Leo women are like the cast of *Charlie's Angels* brought to life. Fun, funny, and almost always spectacularly charismatic, Leo women are an awesome choice as friends or lovers. A bit less narcissistic than her male equivalent, Leo women don't need the constant compliments that Leo men crave—although she certainly wants more than any other female sign in the zodiac. Just like lion guys, deep down she not-so-secretly believes she's the absolute shit, but she's not as intent on smearing your face in her success.

Lionesses are more receptive in the sack than lions, as they view sex more as give and take while Leo guys fixate far more on the latter. She also is a stronger believer in sexual experimentation than her brother. "If it feels good, do it," the Leo woman would say. "And how do you know if it feels good unless you're willing to try it?" Translation? Break out the whips, handcuffs, silk scarves, and X-rated videos: Even if she doesn't end up liking 'em she'll try them all on for size at least once. Her sexuality is more well rounded than that of a male Leo, so although she might beg you to orally explore her nether regions, she'll be happy to exchange the favor once you're through (once you've given her time to recharge her sexual batteries with a break).

She's looking for fun both in and out of the bedroom, so if you shun the social scene or can't stand anything but the missionary position you're better off finding a quiet Cancer or shy Virgo. Not quite as communicative as witty Gemini, Leo women still thrive on the exchange of ideas. Who cares if she always thinks her ideas are the best? For her, being number one isn't just a goal, it's all important, so she *has* to think that her way is the best way.

What are some major no-no's with the sign of the lion? First off, never take the indirect approach. Even if gentle sarcasm or irony is your objective, the plastic grin she'll give in reward is no indicator of what she's truly thinking. Deep down, any attack—no matter how small—is a sign of your disloyalty and ultimately, if you attack too often, she'll start looking for another kitty cat with whom to play. Listing her flaws is another giganto mistake: Pointing out her failings is the equivalent of cutting off a lion's mane (and if you've ever seen a shaved pussy, you know it's not exactly a pretty sight). Last, end any—and all—arguments by letting her win. Although this might sound shallow, it's not. Lions can't back down during the heat of battle. If you're willing to take on the onus of bad boy or girl till the next morning, you'll allow Leo to think through her mistakes on her own. In other words, forget forcing anything with a Leo woman. She'll have life on her terms—or not at all.

Five Surefire Ways to Break the Ice with Leo

Leo Man

1. Compliment him on *anything*.
2. Make him the center of your attention—Leo will do the rest.
3. Be openly in awe of everything he does (this is best for one-night stands since doing this long-term can get pretty unnerving).
4. Ask about any competition he recently won.
5. Tell him that he's so much larger than life, he should be in Hollywood.

Leo Woman

1. Tell her she has beautiful hair.
2. Take her to a major opening or event (from a movie premiere to first night at the opera).
3. Buy her the most expensive drink or dinner you can afford.
4. Ask her about her friends (a Leo woman is sure to have a lot).
5. Be honest about your attraction since any praise heightens your chances for lassoing this lionness.

Refining Your Sexual Strategy—The Subrulers

The Sun: Too Much of a Good Thing? (July 22–August 1)

The Sun brings out the big shot in all of us. It makes us proud of who and what we are, happy with what we do, and okay with what the world has to offer. In astrology, the Sun is all about ego. It represents our conscious will and the power that we hold inside ourselves. Sounds good so far, huh? The bad side is that when someone is ruled and subruled by the Sun you occasionally get to add some sucky suffixes to the end of their ego, as in ego*maniac* and ego*tistical*. Here's the good news: Supposing you eventually permanently pair off with this sign, you'll never have to spend a penny on psychological counseling! Whether or not they're a winner or a loser, they'll *think* they're the best, which can either infuriate or excite you, depending on the way you look at your lioness or lion.

Sex, or worshipping at the shrine of Leo—same difference—is quite an interesting proposition. People born during this eleven-day period can be excellent at *amour*—or all about pleasing themselves. This all depends on the fifth sign's view of the world. Does he or she view him/herself as the lead actor in an interactive drama or the superstar who has surrounded him or herself with groupies? One thing you *can* count on: You'll find out on the first date.

Either way you look at the equation, this sign is selfish. Period. You'll either be the costar or a contributor but you will never be the main event. This assumption of "I'm number one," can result in odd romantic raunchery. Deep in the throes of passion, you might sometimes wonder if your alley cat is even aware you exist. Try this test: Next time you're fucking face-to-face take a good look at 'em. Do they return your look of desire or are their eyes glazed over in a kind of eternal, "I am God of all I survey" expression? Even if your feline falls into the latter category, there's no cause for alarm: Some signs get off on this from a partner. If you want someone who is aware of your sexual needs, however, good luck trying this type of Leo on for size. Either he or she *will* be the best sex partner you've ever pursued and you'll be glad you caught that cat or they'll *think* they're the best sexual liaison you've ever lingered with, in case you might be better off making a date with your five digits: At least they won't demand praise when they've finished pleasuring you.

Jupiter: Big, Buff, and Ballsy (August 2–August 12)

If Mercury was the brain that sat in the front row of algebra class and Venus was the Britney Spears lookalike everyone and their dog had a crush on, big-daddy Jupiter would be the class clown. He's the one sitting in the back row, cracking everyone up, and throwing the spitballs at Teach when no one is looking. Don't confuse him with the bully who sat beside him: Jupiter is always a nice guy. He might not stick with things for very long and he might not be the brightest light on the block, but he's an awesome ally and a downright delightful dude.

Pairing Jupiter with the ego-loving Sun is almost a too-good-to-be-true combination. While the Sun emphasizes the self as in, "I want," Jupiter counterbalances that egoism with generosity and good nature. Often, this subspecies will come across as just as bold and brash as Leos born in the first decanate, but while those really think they're the end-all, be-all, for the second set of Leos this overwhelming pride is more of a defensive nature. They want to take the world and all it has to offer and the fastest way they can accomplish this is by keeping their surprisingly fragile ego intact.

In bed this sign is giving and expressive, so don't just expect her to fuck like a wildcat—she'll also be making catcalls as she does so. Fun and fun-loving, this sign is all about enjoyment, but don't think that means he's going to lick your balls for hours on end as you kick back and contemplate his head-giving skills:

This *is* still Leo we're talking about, remember? While the first decanate borders on total self-absorption, however, this cat is quick to keep his partner happy if only because a beaming bed buddy is an excellent reflection on Leo. Think of a roman emperor and you've got this sexual predator pegged.

Give him or her a shitload of grapes, a divine lair to display their lovemaking prowess, and a happy, willing sexual partner and you've got a happy cat. You'll be happy, too, because this lion knows all the sexual tricks to keep you sighin'. He or she has to because, after all, Leo is the best, remember?

Mars: One Pissed-Off, Purposeful Cat (August 13– August 22)

When aggressive Mars pulls Leo's strings you get major changes in temperament. More of a prima donna than Madonna, people born under this sign go through short bursts of furious action followed by long periods of laziness. If this sounds like your pet tabby, you're absolutely right: People born during these ten days might seem to spend the day lazing around but by the time night falls, they always seem to get that mouse.

If you happen to be the mouse they're chasing, there's cause for celebration. Mars isn't all about being bad, which is the feeling many astrology tomes send off. Mars is action and often when that action gets deflected or thwarted in some way, anger is the result. This means you're faced with a very driven person prone to major outbursts when they don't get their way. Whether this ends up being childlike or child*ish* depends on your attitude and the cat at hand.

Leo is a fire sign to begin with, so when you combine that with the explosive action of Mars you get a bedroom bombshell. Girls and guys alike born during this time period can go at it ad infinitum. I'm not implying they're the type to hold back their orgasms so they can get you off. What I *do* mean is that they can come more times than the swimsuit season rolls around. Just when you think it's safe to get out of bed, *there they go again.* So does this excess in quantity equal less quality? Hell, no: This cat is a class act in the sack and knows all the right strings to pull you in to get you off. The fact that they can get off again and again is an amazing bonus. Forget about arguing over who has to sleep on the wet spot: If you take this lion as your lover you've just turned your bunk into a waterbed— whether it really is or not.

To some signs this excess sexuality is a turn-off. If you're a Cancer who wants one long, loving exchange, punctuated by dreamy glances, aim for a Leo born during a different time period. If wild sex totally floats your boat, however, you've just gotten in line for the biggest, baddest roller coaster Six Flags ever built. Don't make the mistake of thinking this quantity of cum somehow spells a decrease in romance or affection: It simply ain't so. The real truth is that between the Sun's energy and Mars' action, sexual synergy is an unbroken circle that can continually be tapped into. One warning: Your kitty cat *will* expect lots of sex. Pleasuring himself or herself solo is totally cool but they'll want to do it with you as often as possible. If you have a tendency to use sex as a weapon or tool to gain what you want, avoid this overly affectionate sign: You'll just end up hurting them. For this kind of Leo, sex is as simple as a handshake but that *doesn't* mean it loses any of its significance. Each position or pump begun anew has special meaning for this go-getter. Sex isn't just about romance or getting off to this special subsign. It's about being best friends with your bed buddy and getting to know every little detail about them. If you love this cat but aren't quite as stir-ringly sexual, don't worry: she or he won't mind if you just let your fingers do the walking sometimes and she'll/he'll get off on you nipping his nibbles as he jerks off toward load number four. Maybe all this sizzling sexuality sounds almost per-verse, as if you're going to walk into a sequel to that creepy *Blue Velvet* flick. This couldn't be further from the truth. Leos born under this decanate are some of the happiest signs in the zodiac and they see free-and-easy sexual expression as part of that exhilarating package. If you disagree, look past this Leo.

Sexual Synergy

Aries and Leo: You'd better call the fire department because when you combine these two explosive fire signs, you get so much sexual energy you might burn the house down. Leave the slow, passionate kisses to signs like Scorpio and Virgo: Aries and Leo would much rather swing from chandeliers. Fights will be formida-ble but fucking will be *fantastic*.

Taurus and Leo: Leo has got to be the boss but obstinate Taurus thinks that "I'm the king" attitude is just a bunch of bull. When the sign of the lion orders the bull to head down under, Taurus will most likely start laughing and bound from the bedroom faster than you can say "lethal love connection."

Gemini and Leo: Share a few drinks together and you'll be lucky if you can wait to get home to bump uglies. That's okay though: Since both of you have an exhi-bitionist side, letting your fingers do the walking in the darkened corner of your favorite bar will put a smile on both of your faces. Both of you have one rule about sex that will keep both of you coming back for more: there are *no* rules.

Cancer and Leo: Your odds for headboard-banging hedonism are about fifty/fifty when you pair the sign of the crab with the sign of the lion. Leo likes Cancer's constant attention but Leo's anything-goes attitude and need to be worshipped in the sack grate on Cancer's nerves. Probably not a good long-term option but an awesome emergency booty call.

Leo and Leo: Whether your coupling is king/queen, queen/queen or king/king, you're going to experience problems. Namely, who's going to call the shots? Get ready for childlike antics with a decidedly adult twist, like when Leo number one says, "Lick between my pecs," and Leo number two grimaces, saying, "Hell, no—you lick between *my* pecs." Maybe a good coupling for a drunken one-nighter but when you wake up the next morning, don't waste time leaving a note.

Virgo and Leo: Leo loves Virgo's mind but in bed Leo lives by the motto "A mind is a terrible thing to waste." See, the problem is that even when a Virgo is searingly sexual for their sign, that's still far too tame for the over-the-top tastes of a loving lion. Some of Leo's odder sexual requests will leave Virgo blushing, while others will make Virgo run to the bathroom to barf.

Libra and Leo: Libra views love as a mental exchange and all-exciting act while Leo has the more down to earth view of, "Hey baby, let's get off." Surprisingly though, if you work on your communication skills this can be a partnership to be proud of. Libra will have to be more open—and less diplomatic—than the norm, but if that feat can be achieved you'll both be happy. When all-knowing Leo licks your leg in the wrong spot, gently—but firmly—force his head where you *really* want it to go.

Scorpio and Leo: There'll be loads of sexual attraction between the two of you, but it will be more of the O.J. variety than the tried-and-true romantic model. Problems arise from Leo's natural extroverted nature, which makes Scorpio furious with jealousy. The resulting story is standard soap: Leo falls in love with Scorpio, Leo looks around, Scorpio cheats for revenge—whether it's deserved or not—and the rest, as well as their relationship, is history.

Sagittarius and Leo: You're both fun-loving, totally nonjealous types. Leo likes sex acts that are wild but Sagittarius can open whole new vistas for the lion—from dildos to dialogues about sex that will leave the kitty cat breathless and begging for the real deal. Make sure to close the curtains because you sure as hell don't want the neighbors knowing what you're up to.

Capricorn and Leo: Both like to call the shots. Leo likes sex to be spontaneous, hot, nasty, and uninhibited. Capricorn wants by-the-numbers sex—and a hell of a lot of it. Almost like pairing a businessman with a babe from *Baywatch*, this combo might work in the world of fiction but when faced with real world problems you'll just get friction.

Aquarius and Leo: The cool detachment Aquarians are known for intrigues the sign of the lion. Leo wants to get under an Aquarian's skin—both figuratively and *literally*—but problems pop up when Leo realizes Aquarius' penchant for pensiveness isn't an act but the real deal. Have fun for the first few screws, because all will go downhill from there.

Pisces and Leo: Leo takes the world by force while Pisces would much rather dream of a better place. Pisces thinks Leo's bravado is brainless while Leo thinks Pisces is the ultimate pansy. Unless you're buzzed on some strong substance, this mating will be almost as much fun as a rerun of *Saved by the Bell*.

Exploring Their Erogenous Zone

Remember the old adage about the way to a man—or woman's—heart is through her stomach? Well, forget that bullshit with the sign of the lion because it's the opposite side you're aiming for. That's right: A Leo's moan zone is his or her back, from the base of his/her neck to the top of his/her ass. This leaves a lot of room for play, so let me give you some pointers to get your lion sighin' for a roll in the hay.

Meet Leo's psychological demands first. Always listen to whatever story issues from your cat's mouth about all the awe-inspiring adventures they experienced that day. (And don't worry that this doesn't apply to all Leos—if your lion had a dull day, he or she will simply make something up.) Once you've indulged your lover in the mandatory *ooohhs* and *aaahhs* about what a fascinating person they are, ask 'em to roll over: You've got something fun in store.

Now, faced with your lion flat on his or her tummy, you're ready to rock. Start off with a gentle back scratch that runs from the top of his or her ass to the base of the skull. I'm not talking about tender tickles here (since you're not pumping a Pisces) or a tantalizing tease (reserve those fun and games for Gemini and Sagittarius). Instead, concentrate on a *real* back scratch, because if there's one thing cats love, it's getting scratched. Indulge your admirer in this cat-scratch fever for only a minute or so: If you do it for too long, you'll put your leonine lover to sleep. Now, grab that scented love oil off your bedroom stand and squirt some slowly along his back in a serpentine spray. (Don't use flavored love oil for this—it doesn't work as well for a massage, not to mention the fact it will make your bedsheets really gross when she or he eventually rolls over.) Use a gentle motion for the first few seconds, quickly supplanted by deep body rubs that really work out the back muscles of the cat at hand. If you sense your feline is in danger of falling asleep, reach between their legs occasionally to give their love canal—or muscle—an extra knead now and again. That should keep their eyes wide open and their mind intent on what's at hand (namely, *you*). Keep massaging until all of the oil has soaked into their back and then move back to what's between their legs. Leos love being in charge but sexually, at least, they find putting themselves in a subservient position can be extremely exciting. Therefore, even when your lion is more than ready to roll over, don't let them. Remember that *you're* the one calling the shots because by maintaining this sexual control you'll make Leo's eros shoot through the roof. Once your guy is hard as a rock or your girl's making like she's Niagara Falls, flip your feline over, for fabulous fornication is close at hand.

Come Again?

Leo Man

Number one thing to keep in mind: Lions are lazy, so always give your dude his due as far as sexual recovery time goes. Chat about how fabulous he is, how good he made you feel, and how you simply can't get enough of him. When talk turns away from sexual, slowly turn it back. While Gemini and Sagittarius indulge their sense of humor between sex acts and Virgo and Cancer might want to discuss something as mundane as gardening, if you take Leo's mind off lovemaking, it's more difficult to get him back on track than for Celine Dion to release anything but a ballad.

Now, as you're discussing all things sexual, lazily stroke your hand up and down his bod, paying special attention to each and every body part. If you've ever watched a pride of lions grooming each other on the Discovery Channel you'll know what you need to do. Make your lovemaking advances seem almost lazy and accidental. When you roll over, "accidentally" let your hand fall on his crotch. As you're bending down to retrieve your underwear from the bottom of the bed, sneak in a few kisses down his treasure trail. Think about L-words, like *leisurely, loving,* and *low-key.* Your lion is tired and re-revving his sexual energy will result in a different kind of sex. If your first round had you or him banging the headboard, count on a far more subdued round two. Your man cat will be far more intrigued with romantic gestures than in the first instance, like kissing, whispering your affection for each other, and a slow, sexual style. If your first go was rough and tumble, the Leo man will be in the mood for something far more subdued but just as sexual.

So what should you aim for? Almost anything oral, since this won't involve much movement on the part of your fatigued feline. 69ing is sublime because not only will your cat be rarin' to go, he'll also be able to rest his head on your leg. Prepare for a total change in attitude from your cat as his testosterone takes a backseat to bonding. If penetration is your aim, it doesn't matter if you're a top man wanting to mount your mate or a woman wanting your lion's dandy: Either way *you'll* have to be the one who gets on top and you'll have to be willing to do most of the work. The upside of this is you'll get to see a whole new side of your lion. He'll be sweeter and a lot more affectionate than he normally is, so enjoy this sidetrip into his subconscious—both of you will be glad you took the ride.

Leo Woman

Usually, it's harder to gain additional access to females than males, but Leos live by their own rules and the Leo woman is no exception. When you watch lions in the wild you'll notice that females do most of the work while the big-maned males lie around sunning and scratching their balls. These characteristics are reflected in the zodiac: Leo women will take a far more active role in another romp than their male parallel. The question is, how do you get her there?

You've probably heard before that flattery will get you everywhere. While Virgo would question the sincerity of your compliments and Scorpio might wonder what you're really after, this rule is the end-all, be-all motto to remember when it comes to dealing with Leo women. A few words of warning though: She's not as easy to fool as her male brother, so don't bury her with BS. If you tell a pencil-dicked Leo, "I've never seen a cock so big," he'll grin and believe you. Tell a small-breasted Leo female her tits are as amazing as Pamela Anderson's and she'll promptly roll over and go to sleep if she doesn't take things a step farther by heading for the couch. Make sure your flattery is sincere, and since Leo females usually have so many amazing attributes you shouldn't have to make something up to float her boat. What's the best compliment you can give a lioness? Something that concerns her hair—a hot topic for all Leos but especially important for the female side of the breed.

"Gee, your hair smells terrific," might also be an old ad slogan but it will increase your chances for bedability with this buff broad into the stratosphere. Run your fingers through her hair as you stare deeply into her eyes. Licking is an awesome libido loosener, just as it is with male cats. Tongue her from stem to stern and you'll get your kitty cat purring *fast.* As an interesting side note, you can tell your femme's having a fatally good time if you look down to see her flexing her feet the same way a cat would. When other signs get fabulously fucked, they clench their toes—when Leos indulge in the same, they flex their feet in and out. If you see this happening, *whatever* you're doing, keep it up: She's obviously enjoying your each and every move.

If you feel the foreplay is leading to a siesta instead of sex, slip your fingers inside her as you're licking her bod. Not only will this open her eyes, it will open her mind to what's on yours. Once you've finessed your feline to this point, all systems are go. She'll be a very active sexual partner and romance may or may not come into play. Follow her lead as to whether she wants a five-minute quickie or an earth-shattering orgasm: When it comes to second rounds, Leo women like getting their way—just as they do in almost *everything* else.

But Will It Last?

Aries and Leo: Both of your egos are bigger than Jim Belushi's butt, which will create a myriad of misadventures—but they're nothing you can't work through if you're willing to give this love connection everything you've got. Both of you want to take center stage, but if you learn to share the spotlight or take turns feeling its glare, you'll have found a partnership that will keep the lion smilin' and the ram roarin'.

Taurus and Leo: Bulls save bucks: Lions love spending 'em. Taurus likes a lover who doesn't look at others and thinks Leo's roving eye equals infidelity (even though it doesn't). Both are fixed signs, which means they're unwilling to give an inch. If you make the mistake of marriage, make damn sure you sign a prenup.

Gemini and Leo: You're both a party waiting to happen. Gemini is fun, spirited, and the perfect party host. Leo is wild, extroverted, and the perfect party entertainment. Sound like a meaningful merger? You bet—but only if Gemini can fight their natural tendency to fool around. Screw around on a lion and you'll ruin his or her world, so keep your pants zipped unless your leonine lover is the one doing the pulling.

Cancer and Leo: Both of you believe in true love but you have varied definitions on what true love means. For Leo, love is a parade—something to be celebrated in parties and public alike. For Cancer, romance is far more personal. The idea of exposing their inner soul to anyone other than their mate is anathema to the sign of the crab. Compromise is key to making this perilous passion work. If Leo takes two steps back while Cancer steps forward, you'll be a totally content couple.

Leo and Leo: Okay, so you already know that each of you likes to call the sexual shots. The need for dominance doesn't end there though: You'll fight about everything, from who has to clean the pool to who gets to decide where you head on your next vacation. Be willing to back down occasionally and you'll be stunned at how happy you can be together, but if you *must* have your way, realize this is a one-way street to nowhere.

Virgo and Leo: Virgo gets pissed at Leo's constant need for praise and affection. The earth sign thinks the sign of the lion has a lot of growing up to do and since Virgos are notorious for being know-it-all types, Leo can expect a lot of lecturing before the final ballistic breakup. Hard work can change almost anything, but this coupling is doomed from day one.

Libra and Leo: Libra loves beauty and so is fascinated by Leo's natural people-pleasing skills. Libra is somewhat indecisive on major issues but that fickle factor floats Leo's boat, since the lion loves to be in charge. Spending might get out of hand since both signs live for luxury and aren't exactly brilliant at making ends meet. Whether you end up bankrupt or a billionaire, you'll be happy you hooked up with this sign.

Scorpio and Leo: When Leo jokes about eyeing someone new, Scorpio will grab an ice pick a la Sharon Stone in *Basic Instinct* and go to work. Why such an extreme response? Scorpio isn't exactly known for a great sense of humor and what Leo sees as gentle pillow talk, Scorpio views as grounds for divorce. Take my advice and break things off before someone gets hurt.

Sagittarius and Leo: The king of the zodiac has just found his or her joker. Leo loves being the center of attention and Sagittarius is more than happy to kick back and enjoy the show. The downside? Sagittarians love to stray, so Leo better make sure his or her show is worth the price of the ticket or Sagi will find another to fill the bill.

Capricorn and Leo: Capricorn feels like Leo's parent and while that may be a momentary turn-on for the goat who rules the business world, Leo won't appreciate being dropped off at the adult equivalent of a day-care center. Goat guys and girls have a natural distrust—and distaste—for the sign of the lion, viewing them as frivolous, flighty, and fickle. The only thing that will suck harder than your relationship will be the sex, so don't try to force a creepy coupling between a goat and a lion.

Aquarius and Leo: Aquarius is independent, with their heads trapped high above ours somewhere in the solar system. Leo is totally down to earth and all too preoccupied with what others think. When Leo takes center stage at a soiree or other social function, Aquarius will likely head for the punch bowl to ignore the show. Instant irritation ensues with these two, so don't aim for a mating that lasts more than a month or so.

Pisces and Leo: Pisces can take almost any comment the wrong way since the sign of the fish is known for having rather thin skin. Leo's got a bigger mouth than Mick Jagger and is infamous for spouting off anything that occurs to him or her. Pisces wants a dependable partner who is fascinated with the fish; Leo wants the world as his lover and that's far too threatening for easily intimidated Pisces. Remember that cats only like fish when they're served for dinner.

Leo Celebs: In the Spotlight

Don Henley	July 22
Danny Glover	July 22
Monica Lewinsky	July 23
Woody Harrelson	July 23
Anna Paquin	July 24
Jennifer Lopez	July 24
Lynda Carter	July 24
Matt LeBlanc	July 25
Brad Renfro	July 25
Estelle Getty	July 25
Sandra Bullock	July 26
Kevin Spacey	July 26
Mick Jagger	July 26
Betty Thomas	July 27
Peggy Fleming	July 27
Tempestt Bledsoe	August 1
Coolio	August 1
Jerry Garcia	August 1
Edward Furlong	August 2
Judge Lance Ito	August 2
Martha Stewart	August 3
Martin Sheen	August 3
Billy Bob Thornton	August 4
Jeff Gordon	August 4
Patrick Ewing	August 5
Loni Anderson	August 5
Geri Halliwell	August 6
Charlize Theron	August 7
David Duchovny	August 7
Dustin Hoffman	August 8
Gillian Anderson	August 9
Melanie Griffith	August 9
Whitney Houston	August 9
Deion Sanders	August 9

Antonio Banderas	August 10
Rosanna Arquette	August 10
Pete Sampras	August 12
Dominique Swain	August 12
Halle Berry	August 14
Steve Martin	August 14
"Magic" Johnson	August 14
Ben Affleck	August 15
Angela Bassett	August 16
Madonna	August 16
James Cameron	August 16
Sean Penn	August 17
Robert DeNiro	August 17
Mae West	August 17
Patrick Swayze	August 18
Christian Slater	August 18
John Stamos	August 19
Bill Clinton	August 19
Robert Plant	August 20
Tori Amos	August 22
Valerie Harper	August 22

Chapter 7

VIRGO

(August 23–September 21)

Sex Stats

Ruling planet: Mercury, the god in charge of intellect and speed, but don't worry: Virgo takes his or her time in the sack.

Signature symbol: The Virgin, innocent, wide-eyed, and fascinated with what the world has to offer. Learn to play off this naivete by being a bad boy or girl and watch your Virgo grin from ear to ear.

Trademark color: Navy and khaki, two colors that symbolize the tried and true, class, and subtle refinement.

Favorite position: Almost any variant of bumping uglies as long as it involves eye contact.

Potent porn: *I Love Lesbians* for, yup, you guessed it—the lesbian set. *Smartass* for people who prefer the opposite sex, and *Lucky Stiff* for wide-eyed gay guys.

Ultimate outfit (male): Ralph Lauren all the way. This guy is all about being polished and perfect.

Ultimate outfit (female): Tailored tops and pleated pants from Ralph Lauren to Lacoste.

Mattress mambo music: Virgo is easily distracted, so turn off the radio and make your own sweet music.

Best sex toy: Write down five wild sex acts and fold 'em up in a hat. Have your Virgo pick one and then do what you're told—the spontaneous sexuality will freak Virgo out *big time*.

After-fuck finger food: Something healthy but high class, like Perrier and carrot sticks.

Do You Know What You're in For?

Virgo strives for perfection in a never-ending quest to reach the top. Whether she wants to become a movie star or he wants to become top dog at the local Wal-Mart, Virgo will do whatever it takes to get there. In matters of love and lovemaking, this overbearing need to be the best can become very problematic. Virgos are hypercritical—both of themselves and those around them. When a good-looking Virgo stares into a mirror he isn't gloating: He's looking for flaws. Teeth? They could be a little bit whiter. Bod? Better pump those weights some more over the weekend. Virgo lives to *improve* the things around him or her, so if you happen to be in his/her field of vision get ready for a lot of unsolicited advice.

Ruled by Mercury, the guy in charge of speed and wit, Virgo's mind is a constant whirlwind of self-doubt, Anthony Robbins–style motivation, and shoulds. Scorpio's keyword is *should* also, but while the scorpion is motivated by guilt, as in, "I should help my mom or I'm going to regret it," Virgo's *shoulds* are even more insidious. "I should help Mom because it's the right thing to do." Virgo is constantly bowing to this internal pressure and in certain instances it can lead to a pressure cooker-style situation. If Virgo buys into society's rules, he will *never* win: I should have a nicer car than the people next door. I should make more money than anyone around me. I should, I should, I should. As tired as you might get reading the same word over and over again, try to realize how Virgo feels. She or he hears these words every day and no matter how hard she/he tries to shut them up, they're always there.

If Virgo can come to the realization he is only in a competition with himself, he faces a far more relaxed equation. He'll still be high-strung and he'll probably always second-guess himself, but he's brilliant when it comes to seeing through smoke and mirrors. While Pisces escapes into the world of drugs and Leo thinks the world revolves around him, Virgo is deeply immersed in reality. "If you can't be realistic," Virgo would say, "then what's the point?" While other signs might pat themselves on the back for a halfhearted attempt, for Virgo it's all or nothing. She's a winner or a loser—there is no in-between.

When it comes to sexuality, Virgos aren't service-oriented. In other words, if you're a female looking for a girlfriend who's willing to go down on you for hours, you'd be better off with a Libra or Pisces. It's not that Virgos disdain the idea of giving head or anything like that, they don't—but unless they're super-attracted to you or deeply in love, Virgo finds the idea of offering oral gratification embarrassing and somewhat demeaning. When a Virgo smokes a joint or downs a couple of shots, these rules don't apply, however. Why is that? Because even at sixty years old, Virgo is still kind of embarrassed by the idea of sex. This is the sixth-grade girl who blushed every time the word *sex* was mentioned and the guy who got so tongue-tied when trying to ask you out that he finally ended up walking away without saying a word. As earth signs, Virgos love sex—you just need to break 'em in a bit before they'll *fully* enjoy it.

Virgo Man

Once this guy breaks through his shyness you'll find you have a very courageous stud on your hands but for Virgo, breaking through the wall he's built around himself can sometimes take a lifetime if he manages to do it *at all.* Once he does, he's a sexual dynamo. Scorpio gets off on giving others the big O: For him it's a sign of his power over his other half. Virgo is a power player also, but for him sex is more of a two-way street. Part of him wants to please his partner while another part is all intent on pleasuring himself. Some words of warning: If Virgo asks you to perform services he's not willing to return—from head marathons to hedonistic massage— don't walk, *run* for the hills. That is, unless your sexual bent is to be used and discarded like old Kleenex. In other words, this guy can be a sexual user and abuser.

For Virgo, life is a series of contracts and if your relationship doesn't have clearly defined boundaries, he'll do whatever the hell he wants to behind your back. His neurotic streak can be a major turn-off if he questions his ability in the sack. "Is my dick big enough?" and "Does my butt feel firm?" are both questions a self-doubting Virgo might ask when he's pounding away between the sheets: not exactly enticing pillow talk. According to most beauty rags, "Do I look fat?" is a number one sexual turn-off. Whether his partner is male or female, Virgo wonders things like this. Life is a competition and when he sees air-brushed pics of Brad Pitt on the cover of a magazine, he starts to fear he might be losing that competition. Stroke your Virgo's ego and he'll stroke you. Do this by complimenting his assets, but while you can lie your ass off in bed to a Leo, Virgo will instantly see through any BS, so make sure that no matter what you say it's truly from the heart. When his critical nature starts to rear its ugly head, nix it *quick*. "Wow, that scar on your arm is *really* getting more noticeable," would be acceptable dinner conversation. How should you respond? "Well, honey, it's barely noticeable next to your needle-size penis." Virgo will be shocked and upset that you've brought this to his attention, but when you explain the method behind your madness—that you don't like him putting you down—then he'll learn to keep his razor-tipped lingual lash to himself.

Virgo Woman

The Virgo woman is more of a prude than her bro, since she views sexuality as more of a sacred act. Virgo women think Virgo males who use others merely to get themselves off are sleazy, cheap, and nasty. While both sexes view the Mommy/Daddy dance as an extremely personal exchange, a Virgo female doesn't feel afraid to stick to her views. While Virgo males have fantasies of being love 'em and leave 'em types, Virgo females fantasize about a love she'll never leave. Virgo women take forever to reach their boiling point but when they do, you'll soon realize you've unleashed a sexual cyclone. Virgo women like sex a lot, which translates into a quest for quality *and* quantity. She's up for almost anything on the headboard-banging front as long as you approach it as partners. If you're itching to explore everything your sexuality has to offer with a female Virgo by your side, keep in mind that her feelings are easily hurt, and once she turns away from you she'll never feel the same way again. Lies are extremely damaging to a Virgo's psyche, so if you're from the ostrich school of "Let's stick our heads in the sand and talk about this tomorrow," you'll be much happier with a Pisces or Sagittarius.

The Virgo woman isn't just looking for love and sex. She's looking for a partner, and although Virgo females can be fabulous affairs, the breakup will be hell. Getting her into your sexual fantasy world can be as easy as asking but be fully prepared to hear "fuck, no!" to some of your wilder proposals. In time, she may change her mind, but if you do anything to try to speed that process, she'll dig in her heels just to spite you. If she feels used in any way, get ready for the silent treatment. Virgo females love communicating so cutting off her conversation will only come as a last resort—and as her ultimate revenge. As a perfectionist, her sexual skills are very important to her. Don't make the Virgoan mistake of giving advice that's unasked for, however: Yelling, "Less teeth, babe" while she's downing your dick is an excellent way to get it bitten off. Instead, keep your mouth shut. Pleasing you will become one of her top priorities if she thinks there is any possibility of your becoming "the one." She'll ask the questions herself. In fact, she'll ask so many questions, from "more suction?" to "faster or slower?" you'll wonder if you've become a teacher without an accreditation course. Once the questions stop, however, lie back and enjoy all she has to offer. Her crystal-clear thinking and brilliant mind have catalogued each and every one of your fetishes and preferences and she'll enjoy bringing you to explosive orgasms whenever you're ready. Buy Pisces chicks chocolates and Gemini babes books to show you care, but with Virgo, all you need to say is, "Hey! Wanna fuck?" The direct approach is always the best and once you've solidified your position as her personal love magnet, she'll view sex as a never-ending adventure.

Five Surefire Ways to Break the Ice with Virgo

Virgo Man
1. Ask how his career is going.
2. Talk about a problem: He'll give you his advice whether you want it or not.
3. Find out where he works out and what he does to keep his body buff.
4. Discover what kind of health foods he's into.
5. Talk about body maintenance (from trips to the dentist to plastic surgery).

Virgo Woman
1. Ask her where the best shopping deals are.
2. Discuss any kind of financial discipline you've forced on yourself (from cutting up your credit cards to opening up a 401K).
3. Invite her on a sunbathing safari: Virgos love the sun.
4. Find out what her favorite book is.
5. Buy her something useful, from a belt to a blender.

Refining Your Sexual Strategy—The Subrulers

Mercury: Two Brains Are Better Than One (August 23–September 1)
Remember the dweeb that the class asshole constantly put down? The supersmart guy or girl who always had their nose buried in a book and sat solo at all the school dances? Well, that person grew up and now they own Microsoft. While other signs were caught up in who Muffy fucked last weekend and who Buffy's going out with tonight, Virgos born under the first decanate were actually paying attention to what the teacher said. When Mercury, the big cheese of all things intellectual, isn't just your ruler but your subruler as well, you get someone with an excellent memory and a brain that can assimilate data in seconds. Does this sound like you're going to be sleeping with a computer instead of someone made from flesh and blood? You're half-right: This overly analytical sign is amazing

when faced with facts but sometimes not-so-hot when it comes to dealing with feelings. If you work at getting through this sign's all-logic, no-emotion exterior, you'll probably be pleased with the results. But if you're looking for a rough-and-tumble dude who pops back a beer before letting a ballistic belch fly or a chick so covered in makeup she'll smear lipstick around your dick when she's heading south, you're barking up the wrong subsign.

If you're wanting an ultradevoted sign who'll put in overtime understanding your sexuality though, this guy or girl has got what it takes. Though not exactly the type to take their pants off at the wilder parties you might venture toward, this subspecies will occasionally let their hair down. As time passes and you get to know the sexual ins and outs of this ultra-intelligent lover, you'll wonder why you originally saw them as somewhat cold. The uncaring exterior is all an act because this Virgo is more frightened by his or her emotions than the other two decanates (and this is a big deal, since virtually *all* Virgos hate showing feeling). Why? Because they're afraid if they let their guard down for one second, you'll walk all over them. (Plus there's the fact that most Virgos have a hellish time in high school, which doesn't exactly equate with an extroverted nature in adulthood.)

The upside to all this seriousness is that Virgo is just as earnest when it comes to intercourse. The same attributes that make this sign a money-making adult make him or her a master in the sack. Don't start expecting someone all-consumed by their own passion, however. If you want that, you'd better find a Sagittarius or Leo. Virgo will watch you closely when you're making love: Just like they paid attention in junior high, they want to know if they're pushing the correct sexual buttons in *you*—and Virgo isn't the type to just take your words for things. Once he or she figures out all the right moves, your Virgo will calm down a bit, but if you're wanting someone calm and carefree, this shy earth sign couldn't be less your type.

Saturn: Purpose and Passion (September 2–September 12)

Imagine Saturn as a drill sergeant barking out orders and you've got a pretty good picture of what the sixth planet is all about. This planet is what drives you to accomplish, whether it's to lift that heavy weight you can barely manage or work twelve-hour workdays so you can be a millionaire five years after graduating high school. Signs born under this eleven-day period start thinking about where they want to be at thirty-five when they're about seven years old, which can make for some pretty serious types. They must reach the top of their field or they become consumed with self-loathing. Even as an old man or woman, this sign views the world with the wonder and awe of a child, but when they are children they have the focus of an adult. Their focus is the future and they'll wrestle with it as hard as Hercules would to achieve their goal. For Virgos stuck in this subsign only first place will do: Coming in second is the same as coming in last.

This driving dedication can make a Saturn-subruled Virgo seem like a deadbeat when it comes to beating the bedposts. He or she views sex the same way they view everything else—as a battle that must be won. If you can manage to change Virgo's view on this you'll get someone great in the sack but someone who would still rather take than give. Your payoff? With Saturn jamming his or her airwaves, your babe will be badass in the business world and take the entire world by storm. They'll never leave you and they'll do everything in their power to make sure you're financially and sexually secure. How does this seemingly paradoxical situation strike? This type of Virgo will seek out a partner who's receptive. If this is all flying over your head, start taking notes now: You'll be constantly giving this earth sign head, getting fucked by 'em or fucking 'em (depending on what Virgo wants.) Virgo isn't a jerk in the bedroom, it's simply that his or her oh-so serious demeanor usually leaves them in the sexual driving seat. Some signs—especially Sagittarius—will feel extremely uncomfortable with this but other signs, like Cancer, Taurus, or even some Libras, will be happy beyond their wildest dreams.

Don't make the mistake of thinking this Virgo is an unconscientious lover either: Leave that to Leo. Virgo will work his ass off to keep you sexually satisfied but in a kind of CEO way instead of a flowers-and-candy approach. Be up front with this subsign about what you want because otherwise you're probably not going to get it. In the initial stages, he or she might ask, but make it to date number ten and your sexual agenda is set—so speak now or there'll be no forever holding his piece. Communication is vital so speak your mind but do so cautiously, because this sign has a way of taking things the wrong way. Exchange, "Your teeth fucking *hurt*," for "Mmmmm, could you use your lips a bit more?" and you're on the right track. This Virgo is all about reaching the top and if you choose him or her as your partner, get ready for a ride to all-new heights.

Venus: Virgo, the Vamp (September 13–September 21)

Team up the goddess of beauty and love with the head honcho of savvy moves and you get a brilliant combo. Venus tempers Mercury's maniacal streak with some much-needed calm and contentment. While Virgos born under the first two decanates can literally worry themselves to death (through ulcers or aneurysms), this isn't such a severe problem for this far more laid-back subsign.

This Virgo shares much in common with Libra: Both have an easy-going, affable charm and are usually big people pleasers. The difference is that Libra *must* be surrounded by a gaggle of admirers while Virgo picks his or her friends carefully. They must live up to certain criteria and if they don't, then they fail the test and are tossed back into the mix. This is the same approach this subsign takes to finding a mate: They might let you make a few mistakes—which the first two decanates would not—but if you screw up too many times, you'll be the one who gets screwed.

In the bedroom, this Virgo leaves the other two in the dust if you're looking for an active sexual exchange. Venus makes this subsign much more aware of what his or her sexual partner is seeking—and far more willing to comply. Venus curbs this Virgo's competitive and critical streaks so don't worry about getting a sexual critique when you're done doing the smutty samba.

Of the three subsigns, this is the only Virgo who can truly enjoy casual sex. While the other two might let you eat them out before sending you packing, this easier going earth sign will at least return the favor. One easy way to ensure a sexual score with this subsign is to snag a gift for them that not only stimulates the mind but is beautiful to boot. A beautifully illustrated book is a great example, but it better have *lots* of those lovely pics so Venus can keep looking while Mercury reads the fine print.

This subsign diminishes many of Virgo's worst traits but if you're aiming for a billionaire, keep in mind that the chances of your Virgo bringing in big bucks is diminished as well. This Virgo can be happy just enjoying life while the other two *must* produce. If you're looking for a savvy, social sex partner who'll stick by you even when the road gets rough, pick up the phone and dial their number.

Sexual Synergy

Aries and Virgo: Prim-and-proper Virgo is freaked out by Aries' free-wheeling attitude toward sex, so count on your first intercourse being extravagant. Later fornications won't be nearly so fantastic, however. Once Virgo gets used to Aries' M.O. of hump and dump, the sign of the virgin will start checking their watch.

Taurus and Virgo: The bodacious bull makes Virgo guys hard to handle and Virgo gals wet in all the right places. It's not merely a physical thing either, although Taurus is known for having the best pecs of any sign on the planet. It's the bulls straightforward approach to the sex act and his or her willingness to do whatever it takes to coax Virgos into all things sexual. You'll have to leave the bedroom eventually or face starvation—but when Virgo bumps the bull, neither will want to.

Gemini and Virgo: You'll have a lot more fun talking about sex than doing it. Since you're both ruled by Mercury you like to talk about almost anything and have almost too much in common. Once you bound into the bedroom you'll wonder if you're bumping uglies with your brother. Virgo needs hot, enduring passion; Gemini wants fun and games. Gem should go play Twister while Virgo continues their hedonistic hunt.

Cancer and Virgo: You'll have a fun affair if Cancer doesn't pull a *Fatal Attraction* and start stalking Virgo once things cool down. Sex will be sensational since Virgo knows all the right buttons to push to have Cancer climbing the walls. The crab's clingy nature will make Virgo feel somewhat claustrophobic, but in bed Cancer will willingly give Virgo everything he or she desires.

Leo and Virgo: Virgo thinks sex is an exchange of ideas, sensuality, and fun. Leo views it as a daily need somewhere up there with food and shelter. Leo's request for out-of-the-norm sex will likely draw laughter from down-to-earth Virgo. It's not that this earth sign isn't into wild-and-crazy sexual moves, it's simply that Leo's oh-so direct approach can sometimes come across as offensive. Virgo will eventually use sex as a weapon, like when she demands head from Leo but then falls asleep before returning the favor.

Libra and Virgo: Libra's easy sexuality turns Virgo on beyond belief. Virgo likes to posses his or her sexual liaisons and Libra is more than happy to acquiesce. Fun and games like oral affections and role-playing will occur later in the game for these two. For the first few rounds, Virgo will be intent on owning Libra, which equals lots and lots of face-to-face fucking.

Scorpio and Virgo: Sensual Scorpio releases Virgo's pent-up sexual frustrations, which is amazingly exciting for both signs. Virgo wants eyes only on him and Scorpio finds Virgo's trust and affection ultra-enticing. Usually Virgo likes to be in charge but he or she is willing to submit sexually to Scorpio: The sultriest sign in the zodiac will keep Virgo bedridden for days. Have pizza delivered because you won't be getting out of bed anytime soon.

Sagittarius and Virgo: The same moron who sent Jason Voorhees to New York for *Friday the 13th, Part 8* might think this ultra-odd couple stands a chance—but he's all alone in his foolishness. Virgo wants slow, passionate, eye-to-eye sex; Sagittarius wants three-ways, four-ways, silk scarves, and rubber body suits. They'll never make it as lovers and probably can't even stand each other as friends.

Capricorn and Virgo: Two hard workers who like to prove their love on a daily basis. When these two signs let their genitals get jiggy with it, you'll hear moans and groans for a block away. Normally, both are shy and reserved but when you combine the two you get sex that's so hot it burns the bedsheets. You'll have to be honest about sharing your fantasies, but once you do, get ready for some hellacious head, raunchy role-playing, and the most fabulous fucks you've ever faced.

Aquarius and Virgo: Since both of you are rather distant emotionally and find it difficult to come clean with what's on your minds, you might end up with an intellectual game of chess instead of the sweaty sex act for which you were hoping. Communication is very hard, which ensures nothing else will be. Cancel your schedule for sex and head for an art museum instead.

Pisces and Virgo: Put a virgin in bed with a fish and you get some of the most fantastic fornication anyone could dream up. Pisces' willingness to do *anything* holds awesome appeal for Virgo, whose super secret fantasy is to be a love 'em and leave 'em type. Pisces love to please and Virgos appreciate pleasure, so tell your fish to head south and get to work.

Exploring Their Erogenous Zone

Whether you're bedding a boy or girl, keep two Ts in mind when you're trying to release the vamp hidden in your Virgo. For guys, it's their treasure trails, and for the *chicas* think totally tummy. Virgos freak when you rub their stomachs—especially the region between their private parts and belly button. Virgos run the sexual gamut from prim and proper to peel me off the ceiling, but whatever your Virgo's bent is, start out by tickling their tummy.

Give your Virgo a soft kiss before slipping a hand underneath the sheet. Then, delicately rub your fingers down their chest—a playful maneuver that will throw them off guard when you go even lower. Then, as your kissing intensity increases accordingly, lightly rub their abdomen. If you're groping a guy, *gently* play with the hair that runs down from his belly button, occasionally wetting your fingers beforehand to increase the air of eroticism. If you face a female, take a more direct approach and take the old adage that her body is a temple to the extreme. Get on your knees and lightly lick up and down her abdominal region—from just below her breasts to just above her bush.

Once you've got your Virgo primed and ready, don't forget their fab factor just because intercourse is at hand. No matter what position you opt for you should be able to reach their six-pack and make use of it accordingly (okay, okay, for some of you *really* adventurous types this might not be a possibility.) Think about it though: Whether you're doing it doggy style or a simple 69, it's easy to manipulate a Virgo's moan zone. Whatever you do, don't get rough though: This erogenous region was meant to be titillated, *not* tortured.

When oral affections are your aim, always start off by making a beeline for his or her belly. Loving licks will get Virgo guys more rigid than Jesse Helms, while buzzing over your female's hot spot will turn her into your own personal water park. Then, while you're giving your hero or heroine that hedonistic head, make sure to play with their tummy while your mouth is otherwise occupied. They might come a bit sooner than the norm, but they'll be so happy, a blush will be as inevitable as *Die Hard 4*. Watch their face when you're done pleasing them and you'll see it's as red as their private parts were just moments before.

Come Again?

Virgo Man
Though your Virgo man might seem a bit prudish at times, keep in mind that as an earth sign his Pollyanna act is just that. Maybe he's not totally comfortable with his sexuality yet, but he is one of the most sexual signs in the zodiac. Aries wants to get off and Scorpio wants to get *you* off. Virgo is a two-way avenue, however, and given a name, it would be called Sexual Street. Make sure you're willing to

meet him on it and he'll make you glad you did. This shy guy has amazing recuperative powers so don't be surprised when Clark Kent goes for a Superman-style six or seven shots. Count on this: *You'll* tire out before he does.

That said, the best way to put the va-voom back into your Virgo is to get his ass into a bathtub big enough for two. If that's not possible, a shower will suffice, but a bathtub is always better for nervous Virgos. Why? Because the all-encompassing warmth forces your anxious earth sign to calm down a bit. Once you've got him in the tub, stand him up and soap him off, paying extraclose attention to his abs. Once you've soaped everything up, something will surely have popped up. At this point, odds are higher than Teri Hatcher's favorite mini that he'll be somewhat embarrassed about his body's betrayal, but that's all part of the fun. Your Virgo has always had a secret fantasy of being viewed as a sex object, so when you indulge his desire, he'll indulge yours as well.

Once your guy is clean as a whistle—and his whistle has bristled—turn around and ask him to soap *you* down. If there's one thing Virgo guys like as much as cleaning themselves it's lending a helping hand to others in their cleansing routine. "Accidentally" dropping the soap is a great idea if that's your bent but since soapy sex can be a bit painful, it's probably best to rinse off and slip into bed before beginning any serious banging. Once out of the tub, carefully dry each other off, paying as much attention to his toes as you do his testicles. This dude loves to come clean and if you delve into this delicious desire, cleanliness won't be the only thing that comes.

Virgo Woman

Virgo women get off on all things H_2O just like their masculine counterparts, but aim your *chica* toward the shower stall instead of the bathtub. While Virgo guys like extra emphasis on his six-pack and what hangs below, the Virgo woman likes all of her body to be stimulated at once and there's no better way to get that goal accomplished than to get her ass underneath a shower head. Slip her some vodka shots and ask her to begin her shower solo. Whether you're male or female you're sure to enjoy the show and your Virgo woman—though she might not admit it—will enjoy the attention. If embarrassment takes over, tell her you're not asking so *she* can get off, but simply because it's a private personal fantasy of yours. Taking the onus off her in this way will allow this shy schoolgirl type to have fun without thinking she's being filmed for the next *Penthouse* special.

Once she's slathered with soap, enter that shower stall to lend a helping hand. Gently wash her back, her hair, and anything else she might have trouble reaching. Showing your Virgo woman that you care makes her set to get wet for round two in seconds. Once you're done in the shower, wrap yourselves in one giant body towel—pressing your bod close to hers as the two of you use the same piece of cloth to dry off with. Look her in the eye while you're getting her dry, then lick off any wet spots that got missed. Be gentle, thorough, and forceful as you work through this process—whether you're male or female—to get the best response from a Virgo female. She wants someone who knows what they want, so if you want *her* let her know with every action you take and every word you utter. By this time, your Virgo woman should be ready to swing from a chandelier, so it's merely a question of finding your best spot for fornication. For a Virgo woman, it should be a clean, soft spot but that doesn't necessarily have to be your bed. Building a love nest in front of the TV set that is playing erotic—but not X-rated—vids is an awesome place to get her second best—and third, and fourth. Enjoy yourself.

But Will It Last?

Aries and Virgo: The first few times Aries tells Virgo what to do, the sign of the virgin will listen, but once the sixth sign realizes the ram usually leaps before looking, the virgin will blow off any future advice. This irritates Aries, who likes to view him or herself as an authority figure on almost anything. Translation? Your odds for success are lower than Mike Tyson's IQ.

Taurus and Virgo: Virgo likes to pick things apart in their oh-so analytical way. Taurus likes to conserve cash and protect the ones they love. Combine the two and you get such a strong—and long lasting—attraction, chances for a breakup are about as likely as Madonna going bankrupt. You'll find happiness with this coupling so lie back and enjoy!

Gemini and Virgo: So what the hell if you both love to talk? Just because you both share a gift for gab *doesn't* mean you're a match made in heaven. Gemini loves to gossip while Virgo's chat centers on reaching the next level in career or relationship. Virgo thinks Gem is a superficial loser, Gemini thinks Virgo is an asshole stick-in-the-mud. Kinda scary, huh?

Cancer and Virgo: A fun affair can lead to a fulfilling relationship since each of you supplies what the other desires. Cancer wants a strong partner who won't back down in the face of adversity, while Virgo lives to do the right thing. On the other hand, Virgo wants a lover who'll worship the sign of the virgin and when Cancer kneels to pray, that's when Virgo's smile widens. Awesome auguries.

Leo and Virgo: Leo thinks he or she is ruler of all they survey; Virgo thinks Leo is an idiot who's full of hot air. While Virgo might like to prick Leo's bubble—both figuratively and literally—once Virgo tries to prove his superiority, the fun and games end and World War III begins. This partnership is headed for disaster from day one.

Virgo and Virgo: You've found your mirror image, which has both a good side and a bad side. Since you both tend to be completely critical, you'll need to curb your lingual lashes if you want this partnership to last. On the upside, both of you will stand by each other when times get tough and you have a full understanding of the nervous temperament Virgos are famous for. Maybe there won't be many sparks here, but there *will* be some fire.

Libra and Virgo: Libra likes to socialize, party hearty, and spend loads of cash. Virgo thinks the ultimate evening is sex, followed by a flick on their DVD before heading to bed. Libra finds this scenario almost as entertaining as Elizabeth Berkely's acting in *Showgirls*. Virgo thinks Libra is flighty and full of shit. This coupling should avoid the institution of marriage and just head straight for an institution.

Scorpio and Virgo: Virgo thinks fooling around is for the birds and since cheating brings out the Michael Myers from *Halloween* in the sign of the scorpion, this union is outta this world. Scorpio makes Virgo feel protected and safe while Virgo's nonstop affection and gratitude make the sign of the scorpion glad to be alive. This is one of the best partnerships in the zodiac, so if you're faced with this option, *nab it.*

Sagittarius and Virgo: Imagine Hugh Hefner paired off with Mother Teresa and you've got a good idea of the chances these two have for success. Sagittarius is a modern day satyr, all about pleasuring himself and living in the moment. Virgos want to help the world, better themselves, and find a mate they can grow old with. Virgo wants the vital fantasy of real romance to come true; Sagi just wants to come. Singing in this duet will only cause despair.

Capricorn and Virgo: Capricorn is the kind of mate Virgo dreamed about when young. Driven, ambitious, and honest, Capricorn embodies traits that Virgos find extremely admirable. Maybe you won't get the scorched bedsheets of a Scorpio/Virgo combo, but the sex will still be scintillating and arguments will be absent (unlike the occasional mandatory row with Scorpio). When faced with Capricorn, Virgo should make a grab for the goat.

Aquarius and Virgo: When embarrassed Virgo says they'd like to give butt fucking a try, Aquarius will start talking about the rings around Uranus. While Virgo is firmly based in reality, Aquarius is all about theory. This enrages Virgo, who views sex as a duty, not an option as not-so-sexual Aquarius does. Fights will be fierce and sex will be scarce. Bad omens abound for this pointless pairing.

Pisces and Virgo: Once you get past the awesome sex, you'll find the fish and virgin have little else in common. Pisces' dreamy view of the world fills Virgo with insolence and irritation, while polar Virgo's black-and-white definition of all that surrounds him makes the fish frantic. Enjoy the sex for as long as it lasts—then hit the road *fast*.

Virgo Celebs: High-Strung Achievers

River Phoenix	August 23
Shelley Long	August 23
Barbara Eden	August 23
Cal Ripken, Jr	August 24
Claudia Schiffer	August 25
Gene Simmons	August 25
Sean Connery	August 25
Macaulay Culkin	August 26
Paul Reubens (Pee Wee Herman)	August 27
LeAnn Rimes	August 28
Shania Twain	August 28
Jason Priestley	August 28
Michael Jackson	August 29
Cameron Diaz	August 30
Deborah Gibson	August 31

Richard Gere	August 31
Gloria Estefan	September 1
Salma Hayek	September 2
Keanu Reeves	September 2
Charlie Sheen	September 3
Ione Skye	September 4
Dweezil Zappa	September 5
Freddie Mercury	September 5
Raquel Welch	September 5
Rosie Perez	September 6
Devon Sawa	September 7
Corbin Bernsen	September 7
Jonathan Taylor Thomas	September 8
David Arquette	September 8
Michelle Williams	September 9
Adam Sandler	September 9
Hugh Grant	September 9
Ryan Phillipe	September 10
Harry Connick, Jr	September 11
Kristy McNichol	September 11
Brain DePalma	September 11
Ben Savage	September 13
Fiona Apple	September 13
Dan Marino	September 15
Oliver Stone	September 15
Jennifer Tilly	September 16
David Copperfield	September 16
Jada Pinkett Smith	September 18
Sophia Loren	September 20
Ricki Lake	September 21
Faith Hill	September 21

Chapter 8

LIBRA
(September 22–October 22)

Sex Stats

Ruling planet: Venus, the planet in charge of beauty, love, peace, and stirring sensuality.

Signature symbol: The scales, since Libra is all about keeping things in balance. This means if you're strictly into servicing or being serviced, scoot past this sign.

Trademark color: Sky blue, a soft, easy color associated with serenity in the sack and a casual attitude toward love.

Favorite position: Any sex act that involves lying down, since this sign is from the old school of R&R.

Potent porn: *Blow Your Own Horn* will grab the gay guys, *Bangers* if you're a woman on a manhunt or vice versa, and *Erotic Exotics* for lovers from the isle of Lesbos.

Ultimate outfit (male): Comfortable hiking shorts paired with a top from Eddie Bauer.

Ultimate outfit (female): A high-class yet highly comfortable ensemble like a baby blue, scoop-neck dress from Saks.

Mattress mambo music: Old-school disco from the seventies.

Best sex toy: Joy jelly that will increase the sexual sensations speeding to your Libran lover's noggin', or Twister (play with the same rules you grew up with but leave your clothes behind).

After-fuck finger food: Caviar will please your air sign's over-the-top taste buds.

Do You Know What You're in For?

Libra is one of the sexiest signs in the zodiac. As a cardinal air sign ruled by Venus, Libras are easygoing, quick to take action, and ruled by an all-encompassing love of beauty. Beautiful objects, fabulous food, and allies who just happen to be easy on the eyes are always within arm's reach of a Libra. This love of the good life can get out of hand if you're saddled with an undisciplined Libra. If she can't get everything she wants from one lover, she'll opt for two, and if he can't make enough money to buy the hot wheels he's hot for, he'll find a way—whether legitimate or not—to get what he wants. Libra is blissfully unaware of this conflict, however. If you sat down the two Libras I just mentioned and forced them to confront their mistakes, you'd probably just see confusion on their faces.

"But I wasn't satisfied!" the cheating female Libra would explain, while the male who found sneaky ways to increase his income would say, "But you can't find Ralph Lauren sheets on sale!" Unless you're facing a mature Libra (and trust me, age is *no* indicator with Librans), you're in for some tough times. Adding to this confusing mix, Librans hate to cause a scene, so if they think their opinions or actions might cause a ruckus they'll simply neglect to mention them. Libra isn't so stupid to think life is perfect but by *pretending* it is, they get to gloss over so many distracting details. Libras are also notorious for holding their lovers to standards they themselves would never obey. A Libra can look you straight in the eye and say, "Never cheat on me because I'd never do it to you," even when they have a hot night of sex planned with someone else for that evening. Once indulging in their wickedness, Libra will file away that bit of info in a mental Rolodex under the heading "Never to be brought up again." Whether you ever discover this ruse depends on how long you last with Libra and whether or not he or she feels you can handle the information they're keeping contained.

Libras don't enjoy things that aren't pretty, so if you're intent on flossing your teeth in front of your mate, opt for a Virgo (who'll probably offer to help). On this note, keep a handle on burps, farts, and anything else your body might issue at an inopportune moment. Libra knows life isn't all about fun, games, and beauty but he or she would rather not dwell on the fact. If you're a driven type who wants someone to cool you down, Libra is almost the perfect prescription, but keep in mind that you may need a translator if you want to make your relationship last. If you're looking for a fun roll in the hay, realize that Libra is *exactly* what the doctor ordered. Built strictly as a pleasure model, Libras are happy to give off as much—or even more—than they receive.

Libra Man

Libra guys are unusually docile for the sex torqued with testosterone. Like a beautiful lake, this serenity disguises a myriad of actions beneath the surface. When you look at Libra, you see a guy with a gorgeous attitude, but keep in mind that his ruler Venus sometimes makes appearances very deceiving. Keeping the peace is Libra's objective in life, but this diplomacy can spell doom when it comes to dating. If your breath stinks or you're wearing high-waters to his favorite eating establishment, Sagittarius wouldn't give a shit while Virgo would carefully point out what you did wrong. Libra would say nothing, however. For one thing, the idea of hurting anyone's feelings on purpose is odious to this soft-spoken type. For another, purposely igniting an argument is against everything Libra believes in. The downside to this is that when Libra gets enough of the spooky scent emanating from your mouth and is fed up with your curdled clothing consciousness, he'll disappear without a trace, leaving you to wonder what went wrong. Getting a Libra to come clean with his feelings is about as simple as pegging why that lame eighties movie *Mannequin* was a big success. Some things in life simply can't be understood no matter how much you want to.

Libra guys usually have great bods, but if you're gunning for a stud who looks like he's on steroids you're better off with a hypermasculine Taurus or Capricorn. Libra's body is all about symmetry. Whether he's 180 pounds or 280, balding or bushy-haired, he'll be appealing as eye candy well into his eighties.

Libras are excellent as temporary lovers. If you're looking for lust on an occasional basis, that's cool with him. He sees making love as an exciting adventure and doesn't get bogged down with traditional ideas of romance and the dating game. He's willing to do out-of-the-norm activities in bed as long as he's assured you won't be sharing your erotic escapades with the world at large. Doing the dirty deed in wild scenarios like the bathroom stall of your favorite eating establishment holds extraspecial appeal for him. He likes being a bad boy—but only when he's certain he stands little risk of being caught. Libra is willing to entertain any fantasy you have, but whether or not you can also keep a tight hold on his heart remains to be seen.

Libra Woman

The only thing that separates Libra men and women is what's between their legs, so if you're expecting Libra women to have a softer approach to sex, you're all wrong. Libra women appear just as placid as Libra men and just like their brothers, there is much more to them than what meets the eye. Libras are all about partnerships, but while many astrologers think this always makes them ideal mates, I couldn't disagree more. Libra women are looking for a partner, yes, but whether this partnership equals momentary lust, long-term love, or somewhere in between is up to her. Figuring out exactly what she's aiming for can be extremely difficult. If a Libra woman thinks the truth stands between her and what she wants, she'll lie without a second thought. This isn't as devious or cold-hearted as it might appear on the surface, however. When a Scorpio or Virgo lies, they do it consciously and usually with a factor of revenge somewhere in the back of their minds. When Libra lies it's to avoid a scene or to make life easier. She's almost unconscious of this tendency, so don't take an occasional white lie too seriously. In time, she may try to force herself to say whatever weighs heavy on her heart but until you've been together for a few years, don't expect this to occur. Giving vent to negative thoughts is torture for this sign and she'll avoid it at all costs.

This can make figuring out her sexual hot spots harder than Jean-Claude Van Damme's abs, so plan on your first few sexual experiences to be hit-or-miss propositions. Don't force an answer out of Libra or you'll probably end up with bullshit. Instead, place your sexual focus entirely on her. When she groans that's a good thing, but establish eye contact to make sure she's not faking the big O. Work carefully with the Libra woman to establish her sexual idiosyncrasies: Once she becomes more comfortable with you and discovers you're willing to go the extra mile for her, she'll feel more at ease about coming clean with her sexual fantasies and desires. Many Libra women will fixate on pleasing their partner and whether this means some lesbian laps down under or hopping on your love pole to put a grin on your face, your first impulse will be to kick back and enjoy the ride. This couldn't be a bigger mistake. If you don't discover what it takes to satisfy your other half sexually, she'll keep on pleasing you—until she beats a speedy retreat. If you're lucky enough to finally establish open lines of communication with her, get ready because you've just found an amazing woman—whether she happens to be in a boardroom or your bedroom.

Five Surefire Ways to Break the Ice with Libra

Libra Man
1. Talk about a visually appealing movie that opened recently.
2. Discuss the verdict in virtually any famous court case.

3. Find out where he shops.
4. Ask which is the better brand of champagne.
5. Discover his advice for solving that age-old fight you had with a close friend.

Libra Woman

1. Find out what her favorite restaurant is, then tell her it's your treat (but be prepared to spend some big bucks with this bit of advice!).
2. Ask what vacation spot she'd recommend for some R&R.
3. Invite her over to see your cutting-edge widescreen TV or Dolby digital audio equipment.
4. Dress up, then ask her what tie or jewelry best accentuates your look.
5. Ask her about herself (Librans love to discuss their long-term plans).

Refining Your Sexual Strategy—The Subrulers

Venus: The Love That Looks (September 22—October 2)

With Venus both as their ruler and subruler, Librans born during this eleven-day period can make excellent lovers but not-so-great mates. Here's the problem: Venus isn't just headmistress of all things beautiful and serene, she's also got a major downside, since she isn't content with just one of anything. She likes to collect beautiful objects, ideas, and people, so if you're gunning to be the one and only of this subgenre of Libra, you'd better have one hell of a lot of charisma.

Guys and girls born under the double influence of Venus tend to see themselves through other people's eyes. If you're into playing games, it's easy to manipulate this Libra because they're usually very concerned with what other people think. Try this: "Gee, honey, everyone else before you *loved* to use my dick as a tonsil tickler." Before these words are barely out of your throat, this air sign will be deep throating *you* because this innate social response is almost impossible to get away from. Unless you're just aiming to get laid though, playing games with this sign is a one-way ticket to insuring a short-lived love affair. Libras are easily hurt and hate being manipulated (though they rarely recognize the manipulation until long after the fact, if ever.)

In the sack, this sign subspecies is best described as a cheerleader type. There is lots of passion but don't expect any Scorpio-style dominance or Virgo-ingrained leadership. Sex is very much a two-way street for this loving sign and if copulation isn't kept at an equitable level, they'll quickly set their sites on someone else. Putting it bluntly, the mattress mambo with this sign can be more fun than an all-expense paid trip to Disney World, but like the above mentioned analogy, you might get tired of the ride after a while. Style over substance isn't exactly the rule with these Libras but it *can* be their worst attribute, so look before leaping into anything long term with this sign.

Uranus: Independent Optimist (October 3–October 13)

Uranus, the planet whose powers include change and certain arenas of the intellect, lends power to flighty Venus, making this Libra a good option for long-term love. With wild-child Uranus flooding their forecast, they have a far more sexual side as well. This sign gets off on almost all things sexual, from spankings to smutty innuendo over din-din. While the other two varieties of Libra are extremely influenced by what others think, this sign is far more independent. He or she will take your opinion into account, but it won't rule their way of thinking.

Get ready for fantastic fun and games in the bedroom with this beauty-loving sign. Libra is centered on partnerships but is almost always focused on their feelings. If you find this concept confusing, imagine Libra as a giant mirror who reflects everything around them. This can make for weird sex: Libra is intent on pleasing you because it makes him or her feel better about themselves. This Libra, however, has more of an independent nature and won't be afraid to tell you what to do when you're doing the do. Although this Libra still loves to give others pleasure—in other words, get ready to kick back and enjoy yourself—this subspecies is less caught up in the head-game aspect. (Though you'll enjoy *many* head-games of a decidedly different nature with this ultra-affectionate sign.) This Libra is even into rough sex occasionally, so break out your leather boots and start ordering 'em around. As long as this Libra likes what he or she sees, almost anything is fair game and as an added bonus, this type will usually stick around when times get tough in a relationship. While all three types of Libra view sex as somewhat of a game they need to conquer, this type is less confused by the rules and more about having some awe-inspiring fun. You'll probably have to call the sexual shots, so if you've got a passive nature, move past this affectionate air sign. If you have a tendency to dominate though, and are looking for a lover you can lean on when your outlook is low, this is your final destination, so get onboard and then get off.

Mercury: Sexy and Savvy (October 14–October 22)

Smart-guy Mercury conspires with sex-kitten Venus to create a level-headed Libra who's harder to explain than why they made *Rocky V*. This Libra's looks are as delectably delicious as the other two subspecies, but mental Mercury can give an almost insidious twist to the mix. Even when this sign is head-over-heels in love with you, you might not be able to tell: If Libra wants to keep their feelings hidden, Mercury gives them more than enough mental energy to do so. This can make dating this subsign confusing and sex exponentially so—but your lovemaking will be ultra-exciting as well.

If Venus makes the sex appeal of Libra sizzle, Mercury adds some sunglasses to the mix. This can be lethal for your libido if you're trying to lasso a Libra sans conscience: With so much extra mental energy, you might get played like a fiddle as your Libra is off playing with someone else. The good news? You'll probably never find out.

Fornication is fascinating with this savvy sexual sign, who will always keep you guessing in the bedroom. One night it's by-the-numbers sex, the next you'll be going to—and coming at—a sex club in NYC. With Venus and Mercury so closely intertwined, this sign draws great power from his or her sexuality. Mercury can also deepen Venus' already potent sexual allure. Some might disagree, but Teri Hatcher wouldn't be so damn sexy if she were dumb and it's this beauty-and-brains combo that makes this sign so stellar at all things sexual. This Libra will cook up new sexual schemes when sex gets stale, so don't be surprised to come home to discover your carpet has been covered with Saran Wrap and your Libran answers the front door with a giant bottle of Wesson oil—and nothing else. This Libran is great at guessing your sexual needs but, like the other two, prefers a more passive approach to sexuality than most other signs. If you think this means you'll have to initiate everything from the initial stages of hanky-panky to hand jobs, think again: Libra loves to get the ball—or balls—rolling, but usually it's more important that *you* get off than he or she does. Depending on your attitude, this can be sensationally exciting or a major security destroyer. It might sound like a sexual match made in heaven to find a partner who is all intent on pleasing you but because of this same trait, it's hard to tell your Libra's true feelings. Concentrate on communication to make a go of it with this loving—and smart—sign.

Sexual Synergy

Aries and Libra: You'll probably fall in love—momentarily—seconds after your first fuck. Aries' forceful bedside manner leaves Libra feeling fantastic and Libra's easygoing attitude toward the smutty samba fuels Aries' tantalizing technique. Though Aries' fast-paced approach to lovemaking might leave Libra wanting a bit more, the first and second sexual sessions will leave both of you wide-eyed and begging for more.

Taurus and Libra: You're in tune sexually, but you'll probably end on a whimper instead of a bang. Taurus needs a partner who's more into give and take while Libra feels far more comfortable in a somewhat passive role. An okay role in the hay, but many signs will spell more sexual satisfaction for Libra.

Gemini and Libra: Grab that copy of the *Kama Sutra* you've got lying around in the back bedroom because the two of you are going to put it to immediate use. Nothing will be too extreme and even if kink like golden showers freaks you out, wait till you've downed a few shots of cinnamon schnapps and are locking lips. *Nothing* will be too extreme for the two of you.

Cancer and Libra: Sex between the enigmatic sign of the scales and the cautious crab will be almost as exciting as an edited version of *Last Tango in Paris*. See, just like the example I just illustrated, all the fun, dirty parts will be cut out between the two of you because neither is turned on by taking an overly active role in the sack. If you've got to sample sex with this combo, be sure to bring along a book: It'll help you pass the time once the boredom sets in.

Leo and Libra: Don't get embarrassed when Leo orders Libra around in the bedroom. The lion *isn't* trying to sabotage the sign of the scales' subconscious, it's just that Leos love to call the shots. Deep down, Libra wants someone who has rock-hard opinions—among other things—and taking direction is something for which this air sign secretly lives. Libras gettin' it from lions will soon be sighin', so get it while you can.

Virgo and Libra: Sex can be stellar between these two but only if Virgo is willing to free their fantasy of being master of the bedroom. Whether you're a male or female virginite, you'll need to bolster your butch side to keep your Libra loving. Call the between-the-sheets shots and Libra will make you shoot—again and again.

Libra and Libra: Both of you view sex as a game and there lies the problem. With no one to take charge, you can forget about forceful fucking or mind-blowing role-playing. Opt for positions like 69 instead, where both of you can please each other without having to take total charge of the situation. This may not lead to amazing orgasms, but put two loving Libras together and you're sure to get a wet spot.

Scorpio and Libra: The first few mountings will be magnificent, since Scorpio's passion equals Libra's in-bed intensity. Have a spare set of sheets handy because Scorpio will keep Libra locked in his or her arms for hours at a time. Libra's playful approach to horizontal hip-hop fascinates Scorpio—at least for a while. Have fun, because all too soon the good times will be gone for good.

Sagittarius and Libra: Since both of you are high-spirited free thinkers, discovering novel activities to engage in on the headboard-banging front will be an exciting adventure. Games are key to your sexual excitement, whether it's strip poker with the sexual spoils given to the winner or role-playing with you as the traffic cop and your other as the speeder willing to do *anything* to get out of that ticket.

Capricorn and Libra: Libra is initially drawn to Capricorn's forceful advances, but once the two enter the bedroom the equation changes considerably. Capricorn's dry sense of sexuality is wasted on ultra-explicit Libra and Cappy's distaste for sexual deviance strikes Libra as stodgy and dull. The good news? If you're having trouble sleeping, dreamland will be easy to enter when these two enter the sexual arena.

Aquarius and Libra: Aquarius' tendency toward flights of fancy is just the sex Rx the doctor prescribed for Libra. Fantasies—from impromptu stripteases to five back-to-back rounds of sperm swallowing—will be anticipated and indulged with these amiable air signs. Bump and grind is for more earthy types—the two of you view sex not only as a bodily function but something that can ultimately manipulate—and mold—your mind.

Pisces and Libra: Libras and Pisces have loads in common since both are affectionate, sentimental, and romantic. Problems pop up when Pisces realizes he or she wants a more dominating dame or dude to call their sexual shots. Libra isn't comfortable playing that role, so although you might enjoy some kisses and caresses don't count on anything too carnal.

Exploring Their Erogenous Zone

Livening up Libra's love zone is as easy as remembering LBA. Once you please their lower back and ass, they'll be ready to please you. So what's the best approach? First off, as your general M.O., you should please, squeeze, and pat your Libra's butt whenever you get a chance. I'm not taking about seedy sexual gropes like pinching your beau's ass hard or pulling your girlfriend's butt cheeks apart like you're kneading a loaf of bread. These signature sexual moves should instead be tokens of your affection. In other words, not every bump against your Libra's butt should be a prelude to a down-and-dirty bump and grind. Remember that Libra is the sign of partnerships—whether your lover is temporary or here to stay, and patting their ass lets them know they're yours. Even if this feeling is only temporary in your Libra's mind, it's a major turn-on to feel possessed by another.

Okay, now that you've had a crash course in everyday Libra logistics, let's get down and dirty. If you're wanting to liberate that famous Libra libido, next time you're swapping spit, reach under his or her shirt to stroke the lower part of their back: slow, sensual strokes that start in the middle-back region working down to just above the ass. Take your time doing this; whether male or female, Libra loves luxury and hates the idea of being rushed. Once you've put this air sign into back bliss, let your hands journey south to bubble-butt territory. Unloosen the jeans of your loved one—or one-night stand—and instead of going for an immediate genital grope, force your hands down through the back of their pants but still outside their underwear. Pull your Libran forcefully toward you (Libras love it when their girls or guys play the role of the big, bad sexual aggressor). Now grope that ass like it's a steak about to get tenderized. Again, don't let things get *too* out of control. You should come across as a strong-willed woman or man—not some horny adolescent. Don't push and pull their cheeks—*squeeze* 'em instead as you look deeply into their eyes. Whether you plan on spending a night or a lifetime with your bed buddy, you should always maintain eye contact—which is an ultra-important mode of communication for the very visual Libra.

If you really want to blow your Libra's mind and are pretty open to different modes of sexual expression, try licking your Libra's ass—kissing all around the area before going for the gold (special note to gay guys: Libras love to get fucked). Aiming for the anal area will drive your Libra so wild with desire, he or she will be willing to sign over their mortgage, first-born child, and anything else you might be wanting. Since the first two choices *probably* weren't what you were aiming for, I'll let you fill in the blank for number three. Get to work on your Libra and they'll get to work on *you*.

Come Again?

Libra Man

Libra guys are pretty hard to figure out when it comes to forging a second fuck. See, the problem is that although Libra is the sign of partnerships, ultimately Libra is more concerned with *his* side of the partnership. Once Libra knows you're warm for his form with that newly created wet spot, he won't be nearly as eager to please when it comes to a repeat performance. How do you escape this fornicational failure? There are many methods—whether you have to use one or all depends on the testosterone content of the dude at hand.

Never ask Libra man straight out, "Can we do it again?" You'll hear all of the standardized excuses from a 1950s female: "I'm too tired," "I don't feel good," and yes, even the ultimate excuse, "Not right now—I've got a headache." The key to priming your Libra for lovemaking round number two is to get him a) delirious with desire, and b) totally convinced that you couldn't care less whether you do it again or not.

If you're blessed with a bountiful bod, now is the time to show it off. Your best method for this is to take a shower as his sexual cylinders take a breather from their earlier workout. Cleanse yourself carefully and before you emerge from the shower, dry yourself completely and slip into casual but sexy underwear. For women, this might mean that although you'd opted for a red teddy in round one, this time slip into your cream-colored matching set of bra and panties. For guys, tidy whities or beautifully tailored boxers are by far your best bet. Libra loves good breeding and walking around in front of him with a dangling dick or your monkey exposed for all the world to see isn't exactly his idea of a class act.

As a very visual sign, he's probably turned on the TV set while you were showering. Turning it off will do the same for him, so attract his attention elsewhere with some "spontaneous" posing. For the ladies, this might mean checking your bod in a full-length mirror (making sure he sees everything you do). Don't even glance in his direction. Cup your breasts, view your face from various angles, and try some *Vogue*-style positioning that would put Madonna to shame. If he asks what you're up to, tell him you want to make sure you look good for work tomorrow—anything other than what you're aiming for—more action.

If you're a guy, follow a similar route. After you've showered and slipped into sexy underwear, throw a T-shirt on—just so you can pull it off again once you've re-entered the room Libra is lolling in. Yawn as you slowly haul your too-tight top off, as if you're about to fall asleep. Flex every important muscle group as you're doing this but the same advice that applies to females applies to you: Don't let your Libra know what's on your mind. Once you've been released from the shackles of your shirt, do a few artful digs as you rearrange the family jewels. I'm not talking about a *Married . . . With Children*—type move where it looks like you're digging around for a lost flashlight. Subtlety is key, so be meticulous as you move your merchandise about. At this point your Libra dude will be either asleep (not so hot, but with Libra guys sometimes this happens), or on his knees in which case you can finally dispense with the tidy whities and tell your guy it's time to loosen his lingual lash.

Libra Woman

Libra woman is just as hard to trick as her Libran brother but if you keep the same attitude in mind, your chances for success are higher than Hunter S. Thompson ever was. What attitude is that? Indifference. Not toward her but toward the sex act in general.

She's just as visual as her male counterpart, so all the tricks listed for men will also work for her: Slow, sensual stripteases where you basically act brain-dead are an awesome way to reenergize your lover's libido. Keep in mind that she's ruled by Venus, goddess of beauty and love, so you should do everything in your power to be seen as a sex object.

Special note to straight guys: If you think burping/farting or not brushing your teeth won't bother your Libra lover, put this book down now and go jerk off, because she'll *never* allow a round two with you. However, if you're from the Brad Pitt school of straightness, your equations for all things *amour* has just changed in a major way. Walk around with your shirt off—or casual shirt left unbuttoned—as you take a few swings at an imaginary opponent. Seeing you act all masculine will loosen up your Libra female for a ball-busting round two. If that seems to be floating her boat but she hasn't made a grab for your wang yet, do some push-ups. Working up a masculine sweat won't bother Libra females at all: It's nervous or work sweat—i.e., the stinky kind—that grosses her out. Ask her to spot you as you do a few bench presses or do an ab workout as she's watching TV and Tim Allen won't hold her attention for long as she eventually concentrates her tool time on *your* tool.

Okay, so let's flip the equation and say you're lesbian lovers who aren't all that into bench presses. (Supposing for a second that you are though, she'll be just as turned on by your butchness as her straight counterpart.) Suppose she's into lipstick lesbians—the types that always look like they fell out of *Cosmo* magazine. What's a girl to do? The female equivalent of her brother's made-up act—in other words, strut around showing off everything that makes you a female. Try on different kinds of lingerie, asking her which is her favorite. Just make sure as you're changing, you don't yank off that silver bodice—pull it off slowly instead so she can pay homage to your unveiling just like a newly released Italian sculpture. If she makes an early sexual move, ignore it but not in a mean way: She's testing the waters to see if you're playing a game and the last thing you want her to discover is that you are! Don't use any negative wordplay during this visual smorgasbord. "Do I look fat?" is a recipe for romantic disaster, so *enjoy* your image so she can do the same.

But Will It Last?

Aries and Libra: Libra likes life peaceful, passive, and quiet while Aries thinks arguing is a great way to pass the time. Although you might grow to love each other, communication will be harder than Gwen Stefani's abs. The difficulties only get worse over time. Popular opinion says men are from Mars and women are from Venus, but when Mars rules Aries and Venus rules Libra, whether you're male or female, what you get is a war to end all wars.

Taurus and Libra: Sex shines but when the cum shot is over you'll face a deluge of dilemmas. Taurus likes to veg at home while Libra likes to flit from person to person like a social butterfly. When tightwad Taurus sees Libra blowing cash, no one will get blown, which is just about the time you should make like a baby and head out of this nowhere relationship.

Gemini and Libra: If Libra and Gemini can keep their catty characteristics in check, this will be a pleasing partnership. Both of you are into beautiful things, ideas, and people, so you'll never get tired of discussing—and indulging in—pleasurable concepts. If both keep an eye on money and Gemini keeps his or her eyes solely on Libra, your bonding will be blissful. Enjoy.

Cancer and Libra: Cancer's introverted nature pisses off Libra, who fundamentally can't understand anyone who sulks to get their way. Libra would rather use charm, a characteristic that Cancer (mistakenly) finds cheap and dishonorable. Disagreements will pop up like weeds in an abandoned lot—if you even get that far in your relationship.

Leo and Libra: As long as Libra remains aware of Leo's somewhat fragile ego (an easy task for the diplomatic sign of the scales), this union will reach almost unimaginable heights of fun. When conflicts occur, Libra will probably have to back down, but Leo will make up for it by showering Libra with gifts, love, and affection. Libra's easy beauty combined with Leo's star quality make you a must-invite couple for any—and every—party.

Virgo and Libra: Libra's ultra-affectionate persona freaks out Virgo, who fears Libra has a hidden agenda. From the sign of the scales' point of view, Virgo's know-it-all prissiness is a major turn-off. Love—if it occurs at all—will have a very short season for these two.

Libra and Libra: You're both all about having fun, fun, fun. That might sound like it would make for blissful bonding, but it doesn't: Relationships take a hell of a lot of work and neither of you has what it takes to form a long-lasting commitment. You need someone who can ground your light-and-airy view of the world and another Libra *isn't* up to the task. Keep 'em around for when your right hand gets tired, but in the meanwhile keep looking for someone else.

Scorpio and Libra: Scorpio's smoldering intensity initially attracts Libra like a moth to a flame but get too close and that same Libra will get burned. Libras like to play and have fun while Scorpio thinks frivolity is for children and asylum inmates. A fabulous first fuck? Certainly—but if you're looking for someone who'll still be around a year from now, this *isn't* your cup of tea.

Sagittarius and Libra: Sagi's eager-beaver attitude toward adventure and all things outdoors stimulates and stirs Libra's love of beauty. Libra's casual attitude and laid-back approach to lovemaking keep Sagittarius hot and bothered 24/7. Libra will have to give Sagittarius a long leash in love and perhaps deal with a rare infidelity, but if you can handle a European-style romance, this contented coupling will be contagious.

Capricorn and Libra: Goats are materialistic, ambitious, and driven. Libras think life is to be enjoyed. Pairing the two is a bit like a moviemaker filming *The Godfather vs. Leatherface*. These two are simply too far apart in zodiacal terms to even come close to successful communication. You'll have trouble just trying to be comrades, but as a couple your odds for success are nil.

Aquarius and Libra: The two of you won't just be lovers. You'll be friends as well, which spells a union that can withstand the test of time. You both love to talk and exchanging ideas with each other will be easy, quick, and to the point. Sex, although an important part of your love liaison, will be important but so will communication and camaraderie. This is a great combo: Go for it.

Pisces and Libra: Your first few weeks together might be fine but as time passes, passions will cool quickly. Both of you need more extroverted partners and though sex will be somewhat entertaining, you'll both probably be thinking of others when you close your eyes. It's possible to make this relationship last but if you're not head over heels, why bother?

Libra Celebs: Balancing Acts

Scott Baio	September 22
Eric Stoltz	September 22
Jason Alexander	September 23
Catherine Zeta-Jones	September 25
Will Smith	September 25
Scottie Pippen	September 25
Heather Locklear	September 25
Christopher Reeve	September 25
Serena Williams	September 26
Linda Hamilton	September 26
Olivia Newton-John	September 26
Meat Loaf	September 27
Gwyneth Paltrow	September 28
Mira Sorvino	September 28
Janeane Garofalo	September 28
Bryant Gumbel	September 29

Martina Hingis	September 30
Jenna Elfman	September 30
Fran Drescher	September 30
Mark McGwire	October 1
Randy Quaid	October 1
Sting	October 2
Donna Karan	October 2
Neve Campbell	October 3
Rachel Leigh Cook	October 4
Alicia Silverstone	October 4
Anne Rice	October 4
Kate Winslet	October 5
Grant Hill	October 5
Elisabeth Shue	October 6
John Cougar Mellencamp	October 7
Matt Damon	October 8
Sigourney Weaver	October 8
Scott Bakula	October 9
Brett Favre	October 10
Mya	October 10
Luke Perry	October 11
Kirk Cameron	October 12
Nancy Kerrigan	October 13
Sammy Hagar	October 13
Usher	October 14
Ralph Lauren	October 14
Sarah Ferguson	October 15
Flea	October 16
Margot Kidder	October 17
Jean-Claude Van Damme	October 18
Martina Navratilova	October 18
Snoop Dogg	October 20
Tom Petty	October 20
Jeff Goldblum	October 22

Chapter 9

SCORPIO
(October 23–November 21)

Sex Stats

Ruling planet: Pluto, roman god of the dead, beginnings, and endings. This love of rebirth means Scorpio can't be beat when it comes to adding novel nuances to any relationship.

Signature symbol: A scorpion, poised and passionate but always ready to sting. In bed this translates into amazing action and staying power, but once you abandon the bedroom get ready for some arguments.

Trademark color: Crimson, the color of our life's blood and of passion.

Favorite position: Anything as long as it involves dominating your ass.

Potent porn: *Dead End Divas* for girls who grab girls, *Hunk Hunt* for gay guys, and *Hollywood Legs* for heteros.

Ultimate outfit (male): An appealing ensemble from Bergdorf Goodman, including a long-sleeved button-down shirt paired with sexy slacks and basic black boots.

Ultimate outfit (female): Scandalously slinky dresses that reveal as much as they conceal.

Mattress mambo music: From just your groans to thumping, classic eighties rock like Guns N' Roses.

Best sex toy: Ben wah balls for ladies and a riding crop for guys.

After-fuck finger food: Something filling and funky like roasted duck.

Do You Know What You're in For?

Scorpio is the sign of beginnings and endings, the sign of life and death, the sign of *extremes*. Scorpios run the gamut from bad ass business *chicas* to weak, clingy guys who'd be far better suited to Woody Allen flicks than real life. Why does Scorpio run such a wide gamut? Because while other signs tend to symbolize a few personality traits, Scorpio encompasses the entire spectrum. Scorpios are ruled by Pluto, which many people mistakenly believe is just in charge of death. Not so, since Pluto is also in charge of rebirth. Pluto is all about cycles and though the logical termination of every cycle here on earth is death, the ninth planet symbolizes far more than just the ending. In many ways this makes Scorpio the most unpredictable sign in the zodiac, but whether you're facing a strong Scorpio with a heart of gold or a conniving Scorpio who'd rather stab you in the back than suck you off, there are certain key traits all Scorpios have in common.

Scorpios tend to be very possessive and though many astro books point to this as a flaw, I disagree. Although some Scorpios are over the top about monitoring everything their mate does, many scorpions simply want what's theirs. They don't think flirting with other people is fair play once you're committed to someone. If you ever want to put this theory to the test, check out someone you find attractive while holding the hand of your Scorpio—even though you haven't said a word, merely *looked* at another person, your Scorpio's entire bod will immediately tense up as his or her hand clamps down on yours. If you're a sign who covets security like Cancer or Virgo, this will send a thrill up your spine. If you like playing the field or having a long leash like Gemini or Sagittarius, this show of ownership will instantly leave you feeling defensive, irritable, and harassed.

Knowing what a Scorpio is thinking is harder than trying to understand the lyrics to a Wu-Tang Clan album. Scorpio has a blank expression that can be adopted at a moment's notice, a mask that has been meticulously built over the years. For Scorpio, information is power, and they'll never release their agenda before its time. In fact, you might never know what your Scorpio is thinking. This would be the ultimate sadness because Scorpios can be the most passionate sign of them all. If you're stuck in a difficult situation and Gemini is too busy to help while Pisces pretends everything is A-okay, Scorpio will be the sign you can call on. A Scorpio who loves you will *never* let you down. Need a fun lunch date? Call Aquarius. Want a fun night out on the town? Set your sites on Sagittarius. Just murdered your worst enemy and looking for a place to bury the body? Make no mistake: Scorpio is the sign you want to accompany you on that Norman Bates–style ride.

Scorpio Man

Whether he's got a weak will or strong soul, the Scorpio guy you're after is probably 100 percent hottie. Scorpio males personify many of the masculine traits Hollywood has capitalized on with its heroes and villains for the past fifty years. Long, smoldering stares, take-charge personalities, and sexuality so strong it makes the viewer dizzy are all hallmarks of male Scorpios. While Aries is the jock who proves his masculinity on the playing field and Capricorn proves his in the boardroom, Scorpio reserves his strongest strokes for the bedroom. If you're lucky enough to be on the receiving end of a Scorpio's affections, bear one thing in mind: You'll walk away satisfied, *unless* he has a score to settle. His ultimate goal is to keep his bedmates' eyes just on him and unless you've done something to undermine his affections you'll be the sole benefactor of this bonding bliss.

So how do you piss off a Scorpio? It's easy: Betray his trust. Whether you've screwed around on his ass or just faked a few orgasms, be forewarned: Every mistake you make is filed away in a tiny mental Rolodex that Scorpio keeps handy. Although he may not call you on your flub (in fact, he might not point out *any* of your mistakes), he's keenly aware of them. Screw him over one too many times (and with Scorpio, one is too many) and he'll wreak his revenge. Vengeance is a strong part of this guy's character and if he feels justified in doing so, he'll play hellish head games with you in and out of the sack. To him, sex is sacred, but if you betray his trust he's more than willing to use it as a weapon.

So is the rumor that Scorpios are the most skilled at sex true? Well, just like the myth that all black guys have giant wangs, it's not entirely accurate, but there is certainly a seed of truth hidden beneath the fable. Scorpio guys have been to the slow-and-easy sex school and whatever your sexual bent is they're more than likely to indulge you in it. From tantric sex to three-ways, your Scorpio guy will happily oblige—*if* he knows you're head over heels for him and your attention is still firmly focused on him as that third party does their perilous pillaging on your privates. Scorpio will allow almost anything—as long as you're honest with him and keep him as the number one object of your affection. For Scorpio, coming in second is the same as coming in last and in either case, making *you* come will suddenly stop being a priority.

Scorpio Woman

The Scorpio woman can be just as vengeful as her brother but gettin' some from a female Scorpio is just as wildly exciting, too. This is the original femme fatale, a woman who can say more with one stare than other signs can say in a sentence. She might appear quiet but underneath the shy facade beats the heart of a wildly passionate woman. If you're going to break things off with a Scorpio woman, don't make the mistake of taking her to a fancy restaurant. While other signs might be afraid to vent their anger in such a public venue, Scorpio will simply rise to the occasion. Raising her voice the entire time, she might even break a few rare bits of china before she tosses her martini in your face and makes her exit—making *you* look like a total fool. For Scorpio, revenge is a dish best served cold and your best bet is to make sure you never get that dinner service.

She's a dynamo in the bedroom—a fact that might be hard to imagine when you see her dressed in a business suit behind the glasses she uses to shade her magnificent eyes. She's all woman, but she's uncomfortable letting someone know that unless she trusts them implicitly or is three-sheets-to-the-wind snockered. Wanna get blown till the cows come home? Scorpio is your gal. Is your secret fantasy to relive your high school days in a highly sexed state? She'll happily oblige. Keep in mind though, that for Scorpio, love is a two-way street. Although she might play service girl all night without a word, the next day she'll expect you to return the favor. She might even be embarrassed about acknowledging this fact, so when you're aiming to please a Scorpio woman never let her talk you out of it. While her masculine counterpart feels free to acknowledge his sexual needs, she often doesn't. If you can get her to come clean with her sexual side, watch out! Not only will she be eternally grateful, you'll have a much more calm and content scorpion at your side.

Playing head games with her by talking about other women or playing too hard to get is a major mistake. Although she doesn't like guys or girls who are crude or feel too free exposing their slutty side, withholding your affections when she's in the mood will only sabotage her sexuality. She'll remember that you used sex as a weapon and begin to do the same. Unless you happen to be a Scorpio also, this is a game of one-upsmanship that you will *never* win, so don't let it get started in the first place. Feel free to discuss whatever is on your mind—unless it involves a fantasy about someone else—because she's at ease in both the sexual worlds of fantasy and reality. Some final words of advice about dealing with a Scorpio's sexuality: If there's a taboo fantasy you can't stop thinking about—and not much is taboo for the Scorpio female—refer to it obliquely until she figures it out.

Chances are stronger than Bob Paris that if she instigates your idea she'll feel far more comfortable with it than if you just asked for it straight out. Dishonest? Definitely not. You're just letting her be the power player on an idea of which she's not fully enamored—yet.

Five Surefire Ways to Break the Ice with Scorpio

Scorpio Man

1. Listen carefully to and comment on everything he says: A major turn-on for male Scorpios.
2. Get his curiosity going by mentioning a wild time you had when you were younger.
3. Tell him he gets you weak in the knees: Stroking Scorpio's sexuality makes him ready for the real thing.
4. Ask him if he wants to go to the beach or lay out with you.
5. "Accidentally" brush up against him: He'll get the hint sooner than you think.

Scorpio Woman

1. Ask her about that bitch she can't stand (since it's a virtual guarantee she'll catfight with other *chicas*).
2. Tell her she seems mysterious—a not-so-secret turn-on for Scorpio females.
3. Find out what went wrong in her last relationship (you might not get the truth but getting her to vent will help you plot your next move).
4. Discuss how far you've gone to protect someone you love.
5. Talk about a power lunch you've been to recently.

Refining Your Sexual Strategy—The Subrulers

Pluto: Hail to the Chief, Baby (October 23–November 1)

Male or female, this is a very studly subspecies of Scorpio. Pluto gives added intensity to Scorpio's already hypnotic sexual allure (as if any more was needed)! This magnifies everything that makes Scorpio what he or she is. Before going any further, listen up: This Scorpio is the most possessive of them all, so if you're going to cheat get ready for *you* to get screwed in the end (and though Scorpio would be more than happy to do this in a literal sense, I'm talking figuratively, so get your mind out of the gutter). While other signs might believe in forgive and forget, this Scorpio's motto is "Fuck over, then forget." Toy with this sensitive sign's affections and they'll get you one way or another. Whether this entails throwing a martini in your face at your favorite eatery or grabbing an ice pick—a la *Basic Instinct*—depends on you and exactly what you did to screw your scorpion over.

Okay, now the warning is over so it's time to fixate on fun stuff. Yup, this sign is going to dominate you in bed, so if you have to call the sexual shots, wooing this water sign won't work out. Interestingly enough, even if you're a sign prone toward leadership—like Virgo or Capricorn—you probably won't mind letting this potent sign grab the reigns of raunch. In a word, this Scorpio's love-making prowess is *amazing*. With such a strong control of his or her bedroom skills, you needn't worry about Scorpio making mistakes in the mattress mambo—and if they do they will never make the same mistake twice.

Don't expect loads of debauchery from this supremely sexual sign though. Leave the golden showers to Gemini and the three-ways to Sagittarius. Scorpio is very fixated on whoever he or she is making love with or *in* love with. Sex will be stellar but only if you give this Scorpio 100 percent of your attention and sexual energy—99 percent won't do. Unless you're willing to give this relationship your all, you face an all-or-nothing equation and you can be sure Scorpio will leave you with nothing.

If you don't break the boundaries of your relationship, this sign will stick by your side no matter what happens. Scorpio will insist on making the rules but as long as you're willing to follow them, this scorpion will be an amazing protector and moneymaker for you. Be your best and be on your best behavior with this occasionally moody mover and shaker and you'll be glad you put forth the effort.

Neptune: The Intense Romantic (November 2– November 11)

Neptune lightens the load on this Scorpio lessening the all-out intensity of personality and raising the factor for romance. This scorpion will be the one who sends flowers and candy and will expect the same in return from you. Whether you're male or female, don't worry about ever having to open a door again: This subspecies is known for chivalry and sweet-natured sexuality. The bump and grind is extremely important to all Scorpios, but this particular type is equally concerned with kissing and smoldering stares. If you're the long-walks-in-the-moonlight type, this sign will deliver everything you need. From champagne to caviar, this sign is all about the finer things in life and with such strong money-making skills, they can certainly afford them.

Honesty is key—as it is with all Scorpios. While the first and third subrulers of

Scorpio insure they can keep the rules of romance in mind, this subruler guarantees your scorpion can get blindsided by *l'amour.* The other two are more driven toward revenge as well, while this scorpion will turn his or her pain inward. You'll certainly feel the Fred Krueger claws if you ever fuck over this sign, but revenge will fall by the wayside as they tend to the painful wounds you inflicted first.

This sign will court you as if we were still living in the 1800s. When Neptune and Pluto join forces it's as if you just won the lottery of love. Long-term commitment is ultimately what this sensual sign is all about and though he or she might be excellent as a temporary love affair, you'll soon find out whether or not this Scorpio plans on keeping you in the picture. If you fall into the first category, count on an amazing night followed by a handwritten note on your pillow the next morning: Without love, this Scorpio tends to be shy once he or she has shot their load. If you fall into the latter category, however, get ready for this scorpion to never leave your side. This might sound like pure peaches and cream but if you're an independent sign like Sagittarius or Aries, it will just make for ultimate dating disaster. This Scorpio is looking for a one and only and once he or she finds what they're looking for, they'll spend 24/7 with you, so be prepared for lots of quality time. Be careful what you say to this Scorpio as well, because Neptune tends to make them take out-of-context comments quite personally. Once this Scorpio has had his or her heart broken, they'll never be exactly the same, so if you're scoping out a Scorpio who is on the rebound from a marriage or commitment they weren't ready to end, you'll have a tough road in front of you. If you're lucky enough to find a Scorpio unsullied by someone who's lied in love though, you'll have an amazing future if romantic evenings by the fire are your idea of bonding bliss and an extremely long-lived love life.

The Moon: Rock and Roll (November 12–November 21)

The sexy Moon polishes Scorpio's already potent sex appeal as it also ups the mood swings, for which the earth's only satellite is famous. Scorpios born during these ten days are more direct than those born under other subrulers, but they're also far more prone to depression. These scorpions are a bit more shy than others, but the aura of mystery and melancholy that surrounds them only adds to their allure. All Scorpios are driven by a strong sense of justice and all-or-nothing personalities, and for this Scorpio those personality traits are emphasized by the seriousness of the Moon.

It's hard not to fall fast for this type of Scorpio because they tend to be less dominating than their stronger-willed counterparts. If you're looking for a Scorpio who *might* be willing to share their leadership role a bit—both in the bedroom and beyond—this water sign is the one for you.

Communication is difficult for this sign, for the Moon tends to obscure the facts and emotions. While the first two decanates of Scorpio are more direct than Jesse Ventura, this subspecies shares characteristics with the cautious sign of Cancer. This makes for a bedroom partner who is more willing to take the receptive role. Don't make the mistake of thinking this makes them less sexual than the first two versions of Scorpio—they're just less direct about their advances.

The Moon also shines their social skills, so expect Scorpios with the Moon as their subruler to be more extroverted when it comes to accumulating allies. Friendship is far more important for this subspecies than it is for the first two. While most Scorpios are happy as loners with life partners, this type needs a variety of friendships for keep its head above water. Friends help ease the depression this sign is prone toward, so encourage this sign to pursue a few relationships outside of your own. Don't expect this sign to be a social butterfly like Libra but keep in mind that you'll have to share the attentions of this scorpion with a few select others. This type of Scorpio is the quiet, sexy type who turns everyone's eyes when they walk into a room without saying a word. If you're a little more give than take and happy gadding about in the social scene once you win this water sign's affections, you'll be glad you did.

Sexual Synergy

Aries and Scorpio: Both of you are totally into power plays, so at least for the first few rounds of lovemaking you should both walk away with smiles on your face—and be *extremely* exhausted. Jealousy will rear its ugly head sooner rather than later, but making up should lead to some mind-bending sexual adventures—at least for a while.

Taurus and Scorpio: Whether female or male, Taurus has the balls to give Scorpio *everything* the scorpion needs in the bedroom. Sex between these smoldering signs will be awe-inspiring since Scorpio's inventive sexual side will always intrigue the bedroom-oriented bull. Beyond the bedroom, big problems will occur, so stick solely to sex for as long as you can.

Gemini and Scorpio: Gemini's sparkling wordplay and raunchy attitude toward all things sexual get Scorpio so excited, you'll probably end up walking a bit bow-legged after one of your extreme all-nighters. Gemini comes up with novel ideas to bump and grind and Scorpio happily puts those ideas into action.

Cancer and Scorpio: Cancers aren't quite as kinky as Scorpios would like, but except for that small sticking point the sex life between scorpions and crabs should be fly. Cancer will be embarrassed by some of Scorpio's more militant demands in the sexual arena, but deep down the sign of the crab loves both the attention and the eventual act.

Leo and Scorpio: Leo thinks he's the ultimate lover. Scorpio thinks the sign of the lion is a sad sack of shit. Put the two together and you create a competition Scorpio will win *every* time. Leo might be used to being the center of attention in the real world, but when it comes to the sexual realm, Scorpio has no equal. Beware of this brooding bond: It leads nowhere fast.

Virgo and Scorpio: Virgo is initially quite shy with Scorpio's bold sexual advances, but deep down the sign of the virgin finds scorpions to be the ultimate sex partner. Scorpio's take-charge attitude toward all things sexual makes Virgo feel like an innocent schoolgirl—or boy (a favorite fantasy for this oh-so innocent sign). Scorpio's strong possessiveness makes Virgo feels safe and protected and Scorpio will reap the rewards of this undying loyalty.

Libra and Scorpio: Sex will be so-so between these two signs with radically different life philosophies. For Scorpio, sex is all serious; for Libra, doing the bedroom bounce is all about fun and games. Scorpio might enjoy dominating Libra for a time, but when Libra says, "Hey, let's hurry up, because *Dharma and Greg* comes on at seven," Scorpio will withdraw from the relationship ASAP.

Scorpio and Scorpio: Remember that robot from *Lost in Space* whose only function seemed to be screaming, "Danger, Will Robinson!" Well, that robot might as well be talking about your relationship. When you combine two sexual sulkers known for jealousy, you get a positively dangerous relationship. Can we say, *Fatal Attraction*? Avoid sex shenanigans with another Scorpio *at all costs.*

Sagittarius and Scorpio: At first, Scorpio is tantalized by Sagi's brilliant mind and powerful people skills, while Scorpio's passionate attitude toward life intrigues flighty Sagittarius. Once the novelty wears off, sex begins a fast downward trek, so although the first few dates might rock—and get your rocks off—all too soon both will be looking for more suitable sex partners.

Capricorn and Scorpio: Both of these signs are superserious about everything from sexuality to career. You won't be indulging in wild Gemini pursuits like fucking in the backyard on a sunny day, but you will realize that the goat and scorpion are perfect foils each other in the bedroom. Capricorn's prim-and-proper attitude gets just the right tweak from supersexual Scorpio. Plan on l-o-n-g lovemaking sessions with an emphasis on quality over quantity.

Aquarius and Scorpio: Aquarius' head is stuck firmly in the clouds while the scorpion just wants to get some good head. This makes for a creepy combo: Aquarians live life in theory and want constant discussions about everything from bumping uglies to charting their career trek. Scorpio believes in action—not talk—and when the scorpion arranges a sexy candle-lit dinner only to hear Aquarius discuss the best way to help starving children in Africa, Scorpio will search for an easy escape.

Pisces and Scorpio: Strong-willed Scorpio is the perfect counterpart for somewhat passive Pisces. Scorpio likes playing the role of protector and that's exactly what the sign of the fish is searching for. Scorpio's wilder sexual fantasies excite the fish, who will do everything in his or her power to make the fantasies—and Scorpio—come true.

Exploring Their Erogenous Zone

Since Scorpio is the sign known for simmering sexuality, it only makes sense that their moan zone is the sex object sited between their legs. That's right; if you want to score with a scorpion, pumping their private parts is both an awesome beginning and end. Of course, unless you've taken a vow of celibacy, almost everyone enjoys their genitals jiggled, but with Scorpio there's much, much more to the picture.

While most astrological tomes suggest a Scorpio's privates are the only place to be, I disagree. They have an area that's equally erotic but it doesn't involve aiming for their little head—opt for the big one instead. A Scorpio's mind is just as potent a form of stimulation as their man-thing or monkey. Here's a crash course on giving Scorpio everything he or she wants and needs.

First, remember an all-important directive. You've got to be supersubtle to fully engage a Scorpio's awe-inspiring sexuality. In other words, jamming your fingers into your girlfriend before muttering, "Let's go, baby," isn't the way to win her emotions or affections. On a similar note, beating your guy's meat as you focus on his phallus will make your stud think you're a slut—*not* sexy. So think coy instead of being a girl or boy toy to make your Scorpio soar to new sexual heights.

Start with some scintillating eye contact—preferably from a distance. Letting your lover know you're having dirty thoughts is a perfect prelude to the real deal. Once your Scorpio has exchanged your stare, take things a step further by saying something flirtatious. "Wanna fuck?" might work occasionally, but probably, "Man, you sure look sexy/beautiful/babe-alicious," is a better bet. If your compliment is sincere, blood will start rushing to all their sexual spots, which is when you move in for the kill.

Stand close enough to your partner to touch but not so close that he or she can pull you into an embrace yet. Now is the time you can put your prim-and-proper persona aside and start releasing your raunchy side. S-l-o-w-l-y stroke the family jewels of your bed buddy before acting as if you've been seized by passion. Actually, you probably won't have to act at this point, since most Scorpios are too sexy for their own good anyway. As you're trailing your fingers up, down, and around the clothing covering their hot spot, start spewing ever-hotter sexual comments. This is the point where you can whisper, "God, I want your dick *so* bad," or "Why don't we try that move we saw on the Discovery Channel?" Scorpios have excellent senses of humor, so don't be afraid to mix in a little innuendo with your amour. Use a James Bond lexicon of love to please—and paralyze—your lover. "Aren't you the cunning linguist?" won't just crack your cutie up, it will also give him or her an idea of your plans for the evening.

At this point the object of your affection should be rock hard or wonderfully wet, depending on their personal plumbing. Cut out conversation at this point and move in another step, but don't wrap your arms around them just yet. Instead, unwrap their package, slowly and methodically as if you were opening an ultra-expensive gift that you're sure you don't want to damage. Pretend you're on a precipice as you remember this adage: *Don't look down*. Stroke their sex parts through their underwear instead to turn up the heat to an even hotter notch—as you keep your eyes locked on theirs the entire time. At this point every

Scorpio will grab your ass and head for bed, but if you're feeling unusually naughty tell 'em to put their hands behind their back until you're finished. Keep up the underwear stroking as you run feathery affections all over their other body parts—making sure one area gets lots of extra attention.

Now you're ready for the final step. Finally look down at their reproductive region—still encased in a teddy or tidy whities, as the case may be. Don't just take a passing glance though; stare at what they've got like it is the most expensive objet d'art you've ever seen. At this point your Scorpio will be close to passing out. Give one last *light* grab, then finally let out the object of their libido. Keeping your eyes locked on it as if it were the coolest thing since sliced bread, let out a long, low sigh of anticipation.

Then, as if you were bowing before the king and queen of England, lower yourself to your knees. Again, subtlety is key here: If you act like a whore, your scorpion will get off and get out. If you act fascinated by the sexual act, that same Scorpio will get *you* off again and again. Grab him or rub her *gently* and with lots of kisses surrounding their sexual spot. Now, your Scorpio won't be able to wait any longer. If oral affection is your goal, put your mouth where his or her money-maker is and get to work. With so much stimulation this water sign probably won't last over a minute. If rough and tumble love is your goal, however, trail your tongue back up to his or her mouth. Your Scorpio will be willing to do whatever you want at this point, so let your imagination be your guide as you lie back and enjoy what this oh-so sexy sign has to offer.

Come Again?

Scorpio Man

Getting a scorpion stud to gun for round two is easier than Microsoft making another million, since this sexual sign doesn't just want sex—he *needs* it. And if you're willing to knead him, third or even fourth big bangs aren't too much to hope for. The key is to remember what every blue-balled teenaged boy dreads: foreplay. Sweet, sensual kisses about his face and neck as you talk about how much fun you just had is an excellent start.

Then lie back as you talk about some of your tamer sexual fantasies. This is a touchy subject for Scorpios, so be careful about the carnal carnivals you're contemplating sharing. What's acceptable subject matter? Your desire to be drizzled in chocolate sauce before he licks it off of you. Your daydream about giving a table dance for one as she's dressed in her best business suit while your getup's a G-string. Basically, any situation that involves just the two of you with some raunchy addition from X-rated flicks to oil-covered eros will re-erect your scorpion's sexual appetite.

Mention *some* secret fantasies and you've entered into taboo territory for the eighth sign of the zodiac. Three-ways, orgies, and intimate illusions you've had that involve other guys or girls will give your guy an iffy stiffy instead of hardening your hunk. Discussing your desire for someone else is like slapping your Scorpio across the face. While Gemini might find this kind of talk titillating and Sagittarius would ask, "When do we get started?" Scorpio is very threatened—and irritated—by the thought that you might be thinking of another beau as you're bopping him. *Never* discuss how handsome you find someone else unless it's a matter of theory, as in, "Michelangelo's *David* is the ultimate hunk," or if the subject in question is dead: "That Cary Grant was such a cutie." Otherwise, your sweet-hearted Scorpio will turn sour with irritation and envy. Concentrate on kisses, caresses, and compliments instead to steer your stud toward all things carnal. Your coworkers might notice you galloping with a rather odd gait the morning after your evening of hedonistic horniness, but your wide smile will keep you from noticing.

Scorpio Woman

The same *chica* who'll inundate you with more mind games than Bill Clinton telling Hillary what he did last night isn't immune to her favorite M.O. Sex is a tricky pastime for Scorpio women, so unless you're willing to understand where she's coming from you won't be coming very often. In the world according to the Scorpio female, sex is a game with very definite rules and if you're not willing to abide by them, you're fucked—but only in a figurative sense. First, if you've lied to her about anything, all bets are off. Assuming you've followed the straight-and-narrow path, however, this stirringly sexual creature will do you again and again and again—*if* you can adapt to her playing field.

Okay, so let's assume your first screw of the evening was somewhere between blissful and not so bad (because if the sex sucked your chances of getting laid a second time are lower than Casper Van Dien's odds of winning an Oscar). Once you're done bumping uglies, forget about heading for the fridge to grab a brew. Pop something like champagne instead and your odds of popping again are raised exponentially. Sparkling wine or chilled zinfandel are fine ways to wet your whistle between bops—and sharing a glass is the best way to do it. The beverage you share doesn't even have to be alcoholic—just something classy, like shimmering white grape juice instead of a tired can of Pepsi. As you share sips, talk about sensuality, *not* just sex. Tell her about that embarrassing time you popped a bone in sixth-grade algebra and had to cover the evidence with a schoolbook to avoid showing your teacher a whole new side of yourself. If you're gay and looking for some lesbian laps Down Under (and I ain't talkin' Australia), tell your girlfriend all about that searingly sexual dream you had the other day about getting eaten out in a not-so-private place. As with Scorpio males, never discuss other sexual partners (whether real or imagined). Instead, discuss your own sexuality—what turns you on, off, and everything in between. Talk to her about her fantasies, too. At first, the Scorpio woman will be far too shy to tell her innermost sexual secrets, but once you've fessed up to your own fantasies she'll feel far more free to share hers.

Establish an intimacy with your Scorpio woman and sex will simply never stop. While Aquarius is idealistic and Virgo is all about improving themselves and the world around them, Scorpio is first and foremost sexual. When you learn to tap this hidden well of unending eroticism, it won't be a question of, "Will you get any?" but "How often do you want it?"

But Will It Last?

Aries and Scorpio: If you're aiming for a long-term relationship between the ram and the scorpion, you'd best buy some boxing gloves before moving in together. Why? Because there is going to be more fighting than all those *Rocky* flicks combined—with even more damage. Sex soars between the two of you but that's *all* you have in common, so unless you're only humping, head in opposite directions.

Taurus and Scorpio: When you put together the two signs notorious for being more hard-headed than Bruce Willis, you create a situation where vengeance and control become far more important than love and lovemaking. Unless both of you can learn to compromise—which is *highly* unlikely—this affair has a shorter life span than a mayfly's.

Gemini and Scorpio: You'll have an interesting time talking to each other since you're both fascinated with each other's differences, but eventually the same disparities that attracted you to one another spell doom. Gemini is flighty and fun while Scorpio finds Gemini's "What, me worry?" attitude churlish and childish.

Cancer and Scorpio: Cancers are quiet, calm, and sometimes clingy. Scorpio finds all three of these traits more exciting than a *Star Wars* sequel. Every excellent relationship needs the right balance of give and take and these two meet all the requirements. You'll both need to curb your critical streaks, but once you jump that hurdle, there's nothing but smooth sailing up ahead.

Leo and Scorpio: Leo thinks he or she is the ultimate shit, while Scorpio simply thinks the sign of the lion is a piece of shit. Two volatile personalities who couldn't have less in common, this pairing will result in more bloodshed than *Freddy vs. Jason*. Abandon all hope and get the *hell* out of this relationship.

Virgo and Scorpio: So what if Virgo is freaked out at first by Scorpio's scintillating sexuality. Over time, the sign of the virgin will be so fascinated with Scorpio's strength both in and out of the bedroom, the sixth sign will do almost anything to keep Scorpio smiling. Scorpio loves Virgo's shy side and strong dependability. A meticulous and moving match: Your love will last a lifetime.

Libra and Scorpio: Scorpio's wild side excites Libra until the scorpion's possessive power comes into play. Scorpio thinks Libra is fun but is all style and no substance. Although sex may be the glue that binds you together for a time, eventually you'll grow bored with the bump and grind. This not-so-delightful duet *won't* make beautiful music together for long.

Scorpio and Scorpio: For the first four or five days you'll fuck like rabbits, but once you get out of bed to wash the sheets trouble will start. You have everything in common and therein lies the problem. You're both controlling, love to sulk, and *have* to have your own way. Sound like a scarier picture than a nude David Spade? You got it—so aim for a one-night stand with this sign or nothing at all.

Sagittarius and Scorpio: Scorpio finds Sagi's easy way with luck and money fascinating but on a much deeper level, the sign of the scorpion thinks Sagittarius is irresponsible and somewhat out of his or her mind. Sagittarius thinks Scorpio is a hothead who wastes time worrying. This union will end with animosity, *not* admiration.

Capricorn and Scorpio: Scorpio's searing sexuality finds a welcome home with a goat guy or girl. Capricorn wants someone dependable who won't screw around and is always aiming for future goals. This describes Scorpio to a T. Scorpio will enjoy dominating Capricorn in the sack, which Capricorn, in turn, finds ultra-enjoyable. A great combo, as Capricorn and Scorpio supply exactly what the other needs.

Aquarius and Scorpio: Scorpio wants commitment; Aquarius covets conversation. Combining Scorpio's "Let's do it" with Aquarius' "Let's talk about it" leaves the sign of the scorpion feeling unloved and unappreciated. Sex will be as exciting as a *Police Academy* sequel. Abandon any thoughts of lasting love with this unbelievably bizarre blend.

Pisces and Scorpio: These water signs get along with each other swimmingly. Both are great at guessing what the other needs, both in and out of the bedroom, since water signs are naturally intuitive. Pisces' desire to be possessed thrills sexual Scorpio, so plan on an enduring emotional bond that's fortified with fabulous—and frequent—fornication.

Scorpio Celebs: Smolder and Sizzle

Michael Crichton	October 23
Monica	October 24
Kevin Kline	October 24
Tracy Nelson	October 25
Hillary Rodham Clinton	October 26
Jaclyn Smith	October 26
Cary Elwes	October 26
Julia Roberts	October 28
Bill Gates	October 28
Winona Ryder	October 29
Kate Jackson	October 29
Gavin Rossdale	October 30
Harry Hamlin	October 30
Dan Rather	October 31
Jenny McCarthy	November 1
Lyle Lovett	November 1
Larry Flynt	November 1

k.d. lang	November 2
Dolph Lundgren	November 3
Kate Capshaw	November 3
Roseanne	November 3
Sean "Puffy" Combs	November 4
Vivien Leigh	November 5
Bryan Adams	November 5
Ike Turner	November 5
Ethan Hawke	November 6
Sally Field	November 6
Jason and Jeremy London	November 7
Billy Graham	November 7
Parker Posey	November 8
Bonnie Raitt	November 8
Mackenzie Phillips	November 10
Sinbad	November 10
Roy Scheider	November 10
Leonardo DiCaprio	November 11
Demi Moore	November 11
Calista Flockhart	November 11
Tonya Harding	November 12
David Schwimmer	November 12
Grace Kelly	November 12
Whoopi Goldberg	November 13
Prince Charles	November 14
Sam Waterston	November 15
Oksana Baiul	November 16
Lisa Bonet	November 16
RuPaul	November 17
Lauren Hutton	November 17
Martin Scorsese	November 17
Rock Hudson	November 17
Linda Evans	November 18
Kerri Strug	November 19
Ted Turner	November 19
Larry King	November 19

Jodie Foster	November 19
Bo Derek	November 20
Veronica Hamel	November 20
Ken Griffey, Jr	November 21
Troy Aikman	November 21
Goldie Hawn	November 21
Marlo Thomas	November 21

Chapter 10

SAGITTARIUS
(November 22–December 20)

Sex Stats

Ruling planet: Jupiter, god of money, luck, and good times between the sheets.

Signature symbol: The archer, who is active, outdoorsy, and rarely misses the mark. Although this means Sagittarius will probably snag you if he or she is warm for your form, it doesn't translate into amazing headboard-banging prowess.

Trademark color: Purple, color of royalty and out-of-the-norm ambitions.

Favorite position: Sagi guys and girls are game for almost anything. Think quality *and* quantity.

Potent porn: *Dallas Does Hawaii* for dudes who find other dudes delicious. *Hard Ride* for heteros, and anything that involves three-ways or multiple partners for the lesbian set.

Ultimate outfit (male): Loose-fitting clam diggers paired with a comfortable tank top.

Ultimate outfit (female): A blousy dress or ensemble that doesn't constrict and is easy to yank off.

Mattress mambo music: Play playful, spirited songs by Culture Club or N'Sync to make your Sagi smile.

Best sex toy: Handwrite a sexual fantasy of yours and leave it on Sagi's pillow. You'll be surprised at what happens next.

After-fuck finger food: Something calorie-laden like Doritos or a milkshake in almost any flavor.

Do You Know What You're in For?

Remember when you were a kid and there was always one other rug rat you thought was the most fun to hang out with? Well, that kid symbolizes everything that's cool about Sagittarius. Playful, laid-back, and oh-so fun to party with, Sagittarians are the wildest characters you'll ever hope to meet. While Gemini goes through more personality morphing than Madonna and Leo plays the role of megastar, Sagittarians aren't playing a game to try to get noticed. They're just as wild as they appear, whether they've coopted their penchant for wild-child behavior into becoming the biggest, baddest businessman around or the most colorful drug dealer you'll ever meet. This be-as-wild-as-you-wanna-be mentality *definitely* has its downside though. Just like that kid you grew up with, Sagittarians are strong believers in bullshitting to raise their TVQ. Need to borrow some money? Want to lock down your career promotion? Sagittarius will promise you all these things and more, but whether or not Sagi actually delivers on these pledges is a different story altogether. I'll put it this way: When you hear, "The check is in the mail" from a Sagittarius, don't start spending money till you've actually cashed that bad boy. The odds are Schwarzenegger strong that a) you won't get it, and b) it'll bounce if you do. Am I saying Sagittarians make better friends than lovers? Not necessarily. If you've got an open mind and love to have fun, Sagi might make a good love match. If you're aiming for an awesome one-night stand, put your prudish side out to dry because whatever you end up doing, it'll be something that you've *never* done before.

Sagittarians are mutable, fire signs and what this means to you is that although the object of your affections has a fire within his or her belly just like fellow fire sign Aries, this willingness to take action is tempered by an ability to be flexible. Unlike Aries, a Sagittarius looks before leaping, which increases his or her skill in business-related ventures accordingly. Think of it this way: An Aries might start a company, make a million, but be bankrupt a year later because the business grew too fast. Sagittarius would start the same company but instead of beating it into the ground, it would be sold off to some giant conglomeration like Time Inc. to create more capital, which in turn could be used to create bigger, better businesses. It's not mere coincidence that the ninth sign in the zodiac is ruled by Jupiter, head honcho of money matters and luck. Not only are Sagittarians the luckiest people you'll ever bump heads with, they also realize that money *does* matter and probably have a large stash of it locked away somewhere.

For such glib, fun-loving souls it seems almost impossible that they would be hard to get to know, but that's exactly the case. Underneath the Clinton-esque charm there *is* a dark side to their personality, but unless you're caught in the throws of a difficult divorce or trying to untie the knot that binds in your cohabitation, you probably won't see it. Underneath the humor and charisma lies a far different personality that no one truly understands but the Sagittarian in question. Tread lightly when you're aiming for Sagittarius, be prepared to give him or her a *very* long leash, and always check their silver-tongued assessment of a situation against the facts.

Sagittarius Man

You know that overweight businessman who kinda looks like Buddha but is always surrounded by a bunch of hotties of either sex? In the words of Austin Powers, he's Sagittarian, baby, and although looking good has never been all that important to him, having fun *is*. That's why he's either a babe or man magnet: His fearless pursuit of happiness is a major turn-on for most other signs. This doesn't necessarily translate into bonding bliss if you hop in the sack with Sagittarius, however. Ultimately, he's all about fulfilling his needs, so if you take lots of stroking—whether figuratively or literally—between the sheets to enjoy yourself, count on frustration-filled nights as you stare at a snoring Sagittarius. This all-about-me attitude can have some major fringe benefits, however. Say you're a gay guy who's prone to top-man style fantasies and you encounter a Sagi with an oral fixation. He'll give you head 24/7 and though ultimately it's just because he likes to suck dick, *you'll* walk away the winner. On the other hand, say you're a woman blessed with a Shania Twain–style bod who bumps heads with a Sagittarius who can't get off till his mate has. Again, his sexuality borders on the semisociopathic, but who cares if you can't stop smiling?

There's one more important point to hit home about Sagittarian men and sex. He likes doing the wild thing just as much as he likes accumulating cash, so count on mattress mambo-ing *a lot*. You won't just be doing it on mattresses either. He'll have you dress as a Girl or Boy Scout depending on his tastes, swing from the chandeliers, and lick ice cream from your most erogenous zones. If sex starts to taper off, don't think your Sagittarian has discovered saltpeter. He's merely indulging his biggest vice: namely, cheating on your ass. Of all the signs and sexes, Sagittarian males are most prone to indulge in bedroom antics with someone other than their other. If you're not willing to indulge his fornicational fantasies, whether they happen to be three-ways, group sex, or golden showers, count on him finding someone who will.

Sagittarius Woman

Replace testosterone with estrogen and you get a much more subtle Sagittarius. While Sagi guys often let their little head do the thinking for their big one, Sagittarian women aren't ruled by their sexuality. They view sex as a game—just like their masculine counterparts—but they're far more willing to stick to the rules instead of breaking them. Am I saying Sagittarian women never stray? As if: Dissatisfy a Virgo or Cancer *chica* and you get a frustrated female on your hands. Skimp on pleasuring a Sagittarius and she'll still be smiling, since she'll have fulfilled her needs elsewhere. Again, note that this response is different from her masculine mirror image. While a Sagittarian male gets off on breaking society's rules, Sagittarius women usually only do so when the need arises. She's willing to think out of the box—but only if you force her to. This willingness to bend the rules makes her an excellent bed partner for many signs. Ask a shy Taurus to pleasure herself as a prelude to the real deal and you'll face a bull beaded with sweat who's none too pleased with your request. Sagittarian female offers a far different scenario. Maybe she'll get herself off in front of you because it's her number one fantasy, maybe she'll do it because it's new and different and she'll try anything once, maybe she'll just do it on the condition that you do the same. The point is, a Sagittarian woman will listen to your sexual request and won't let society's taboos scare her off. That said, can *you* handle her open-minded sexuality? If you mange to persuade a Pisces into husband swapping or a same-sex scenario that's against her basic nature, she'll make the best of it because she knows it turns you on. With Sagittarius, she's not going to do it unless she has fun in the process, so if you're the jealous type, make sure you know what you're up against before asking Sagittarius to indulge you in some of your wilder fantasies: When she has more fun than you do it might be a bitter pill to swallow.

In love, she's fun but detached: If your affair came to an abrupt end she wouldn't debate slitting her wrists like a single-minded Cancer or wreaking vengeance like a strong-willed Scorpio. She'd find another honey quickly instead, and with her keen analytical skills, you can bet that he or she won't have the hang-ups you do. The Sagittarian woman is pragmatic: If there's a problem, she'll find the solution. If there's no solution, she'll walk away without a second's thought. Although she'll hide her emotions from you, don't make the mistake of doing the same with her. She'll take it as a personal insult if you don't come clean with her about your thoughts and dreams. Each sign and each sex has their ultimate fantasy and for such a seemingly wild woman, a Sagittarian female's is relatively tame. She's looking for a mate she can trust 100 percent and though her untrusting nature will play havoc with reaching that goal, anything you can do to reinforce her faith in you will solidify your status as her suitor.

Five Surefire Ways to Break the Ice with Sagittarius

Sagittarius Man
1. Ask his advice on the best spot to go camping.
2. If you just want to hop into bed, detail a risqué fantasy: He'll make it—and you—come true.
3. Debate a current get-rich-quick scheme.
4. Invite him to Vegas.
5. Talk about a time you "bent" the rules, whether you traded insider info on stock at forty-five-years of age or used the five-finger discount at fifteen.

Sagittarius Woman
1. Make her laugh with your *best* joke.
2. Ask a riddle—the more complex, the better.
3. Challenge her to an outdoor sporting event like tennis or archery.
4. Invite her to a rustic, tree-surrounded cabin that overlooks a lake.
5. Make a bet on anything from a card game to tomorrow's weather.

Refining Your Sexual Strategy—The Subrulers

Jupiter: Party Hearty (November 22–December 1)
With anything-goes Jupiter playing first and second string, this Sagittarius will be strictly for fun and games. Although this guy or gal will make an awesome ally and scorching sexual liaison, they're looking for anything but the long term in a relationship. Amazingly lucky, this decanate of Sagittarius is the kind who seems to breeze through life, getting away with everything. This isn't entirely accurate, however: Jupiter is no dummy and since he's head honcho of adventure, travel, and luck it only makes sense that someone whose airwaves are rocked by his heady mix will get away with anything short of murder.

Jupiter is all about philosophy, and accordingly, this sign wants to see and experience everything life has to offer at least once. If you're sexually extreme this can be totally to your advantage. Wanna finally try that golden shower? Have you been wanting to film your fornicational exploits and send 'em over the Internet? Gotta fulfill that orgy fantasy? Stop in your tracks, because this particular brand of Sagittarius will give you all of that and more.

What *is* particularly hard for this subgenre to give is their full attention. When you're reading the paper over morning coffee, take note that Sagi's attention will drift from the paper, to the TV set, to the taste of the coffee, and finally—*maybe*—to what you're talking about. With a million ideas blasting through their brains—many of them money-makers btw, since Jupiter heads all things moola—it's hard for them to give 100 percent of their attention to anything. This applies to long-term love as well so if you're wanting to marry this Sagi who is oh-so prone to stray, make sure they're over the magic age of forty years old. By this time, their hormones have died down a bit and they've had the opportunity to have already indulged in many of their wilder ideas. If short-term sex is your goal, get going: Sex with this Sagittarius is strictly a no-strings affair (unless you insist on tying each other up).

Mars: The Sagi Who'll Stick by Your Side (December 2– December 11)

Mars is the only weight heavy enough to ground Jupiter and with the fourth planet's drive and direction to complement luck sent from the biggest planet in our solar system, you get a rare combination: A Sagittarius who doesn't think long-term love has to cancel out all the fun life has to offer. People born during these ten days are amazingly generous and influential. While the other two decanates are geared toward having a good time—and nothing but—active Mars adds drive and determination to the mix.

You'll still need to give this Sagittarius a long leash, however. Sagittarians can be just as stubborn as Virgoans but with a completely different underlying psychology. Sagittarius wants to see the world. If you share this dream on both a literal and figurative level, you will be the perfect partner for this ultra-extroverted type. If staying at home is more your style, however, like Cancers and Taurus are prone to, you'll irritate Sagittarius faster than the powers that be can crank out another *Batman* flick. While irritation leads to rage from Scorpio, Sagittarius hates feeling angry. He or she will walk away from a relationship long before things start to get too rocky, so if arguing is one of your favorite M.O.'s, aim for a few days with this fun-loving sign instead of a lifetime.

A few days can be utterly fabulous, since this sign works well in the short term. Expect lots of laughter from this practical joker type. Though Mars brings Jupiter down to earth, he can't steal all of his thunderbolts. Jupiter makes humor the best method for your Sagittarius to work through most issues, so if he or she cracks a joke when you bring up a serious subject, don't take it to heart: it's this fire sign's way of dealing with the dark side of life.

Mars can lend a distant quality to love and lovemaking from this sign, so don't assume the Sagittarius of your dreams isn't falling for you because they just might be. Love is a touch-and-go equation with any Sagittarius but with this one, forever can be just as likely as a one-time fantastic fuck.

Speaking of fucking, Sagittarians with Mars pulling some strings have a more determined in-the-sack style than other types. While the other two decanates view various sexual activities as equal, this type hails more from the basic down-and-dirty sex school. This isn't to say your Sagittarius won't eat you out in the bathroom of an airplane, it just means they'll also want some by-the-numbers nether-knocking occasionally.

If you've got a forceful personality and like to call the shots sexually or else-where, this Sagittarius isn't for you—even for the short term. If you view life as a roller-coaster ride, however, this type of Sagittarius can be your guide. The even better part about this particular strain of Sagittarius is that she or he will still be sitting by your side once the ride is over.

The Sun: Charisma Counts (December 12–December 20)

The Sun is in charge of all things ego and animation and combining these two traits with everything lucky Jupiter has to offer creates quite a heady mix. Whether they're five foot five with two or three hairy warts on their chin or a David Hasselhoff/Denise Richards lookalike, this sign has so much damn charisma hanging around him or her it's like being on a presidential campaign. While Scorpio turns heads with smoldering sexuality and Gemini does the same with sparkling wordplay, for Sagittarians born during this decanate, such strong charisma is simply a basic building block of their personality.

Obviously, if you're the jealous type this won't result in much romantic rev-elry. This subsign is particularly prone toward cheating, so count on having fun but don't count on this type when things get tough. Sagittarius will be happy to lend—or give—you moola and won't mind helping you build that outdoors deck but when your relationship starts to kick into overdrive, this strain of Sagi will start looking for the exit door. If you're looking for the perfect emergency booty call, however, you can stop worrying because noncommittal sex is a specialty of this witty fire sign. One interesting thing that sets this sub-Sagittarius apart from the other two is that they crush and crush *hard*. Often, Sagittarius will mistake this crush for love. This is a major mistake on Sagi's part because their emotions are anything but. If there is one thing this Sagittarius truly adores it's the hunt. While wooing a handsome man or sexy woman, Sagittarius will do anything in their power to make that sex object their own. Once they've attained it, however, the crush quickly loses appeal, so before you say "I do" to a Sagittarius, realize you might end up being one of many instead of their one and only.

So much Clinton-style charm makes this sign excellent in anything from politics to an even more public, celebrity-style persona. Fall in love with this star in the making and you'll be sorry. Screwing their brains out before saying adios will leave you smiling, however, so unzip your pants and go to work.

Sexual Synergy

Aries and Sagittarius: Sagi blows Aries on the stairs, Aries devours Sagittarius on the dinner table and then you'll *really* start to cook. What am I trying to say? Sex between these two fabulous fire signs will be a never-ending event. You've both got supersexual streaks, so when you opt for a five-minute quickie at a friend's dinner party, just make sure you lock the bedroom door, okay?

Taurus and Sagittarius: If you're debating doing the do with this sign, why not consider a card game instead, since it'll be a lot more exciting than a bull locking horns with the sign of Sagittarius. Taurus likes to be in charge; Sagi likes to have fun. When Sagittarius drips Wesson oil down the bull's bod, Taurus will likely hop out of bed for a quick shower. A lethal love connection if there ever was one.

Gemini and Sagittarius: When Gemini starts the raunchy talk for which this air sign is famous, sexy Sagittarius will think heaven is at hand. This gut instinct is right on target: Both Gems and Sagis are known for being talkative, fun, and loving to live in the moment. Role-playing, forbidden sex-club antics, and everything you'd be far too ashamed to mention to Mom will be available between this contemplative couple. No matter who dreams up what, you'll both be willing to put your ideas into immediate action.

Cancer and Sagittarius: The first few times the crab and archer head for bed you'll both emerge with smiles on your faces. Sagi's playful approach to pumping leaves the sign of the crab feeling naughty and nice—an awesome combo for hard-to-please Cancer. Although communication between these very different signs will be more perplexing than Wes Craven's decision to direct *Music from the Heart,* the universal language of love is something they both completely understand.

Leo and Sagittarius: Both of you have the balls to say exactly what's on your mind, so Leo's natural tendency to intimidate those he or she loves won't be a problem. Sex won't just be great—it will be an awe-inspiring event between these two vocal signs who believe in asking for exactly what they want. There'll be some playful competition but nothing so severe it silences the sexual aspect of your relationship. Just make sure to have a pillow handy to muffle your moans, since both of you have *loud* libidos.

Virgo and Sagittarius: Sagittarius thinks Virgo is a stuck-up prude; Virgo thinks Sagittarius is the ultimate big-time bullshitter. This doesn't exactly make for stellar sex—in fact, you'll be lucky to reach the unzipping stage before you start arguing. Sex will be bad, boring, and bland. Perhaps you'll be allies but just say no to amour.

Libra and Sagittarius: Sagittarius is thrilled by Libra's laid-back ways and love of beauty. Libra is intrigued by Sagi's easy sexuality and experimental attitude toward all things sexual. Combine the two and you get more sexual positions than *The Joy of Sex* ever depicted. Have fun exploring each other since, for the two of you, sex holds *no* stop signs.

Scorpio and Sagittarius: Scorpio wants to control Sagittarius in the sack but Sagittarius lets *no one* call the sexual shots. While Sagi likes to play, Scorpio likes to pump and Sagittarius thinks this earthy approach to sex is just a bit too much by the numbers. Fights will be frequent, frightening, and severe. This is a worse combo than Sylvester Stallone and Dolly Parton in that piece o' crap known as *Rhinestone.*

Sagittarius and Sagittarius: Start that strip Monopoly game, grab the peppermint-flavored lube, and get to work on this scintillating sexual union. You're both paramount players and up for *anything*. From entering the mile-high club to bumping uglies in your backyard on a sunny day, the sky is your sexual limit, so lose your clothes along with your inhibitions and *get busy*.

Capricorn and Sagittarius: Capricorns go for gloom and doom when faced with the eternal optimism of Sagittarius. It's not that goat guys and girls are perennial pessimists, it's just that they can't stand Sagi's view of life as one giant joke. Sex will suck harder than your average Hoover, since Capricorn finds Sagi's easy sexuality more akin to sluttiness. Sagi thinks Capricorn spells boredom in the bedroom. An alliance full of enmity that won't last even as long as Carmen Electra's career.

Aquarius and Sagittarius: Both of you are constantly examining the future and don't think sex is all about just making babies. Aquarius' free thinking is the perfect complement to Sagittarius' idealism. Initial sexual liaisons might leave a bit to be desired since you operate from somewhat different philosophical perspectives, but don't worry: Practice makes perfect.

Pisces and Sagittarius: Expect an immediate, almost overwhelming sexual attraction between the archer and the sign of the fish. Pisces finds the Sagittarian view of sex as a circus all-exciting, so Sagis should plan on introducing the fish to the wide, wonderful world of sex through a variety of methods. From dildos to delirious rounds of late-night lovemaking, this combo is up for anything and everything sexual, which equals bliss in the bedroom.

Exploring Their Erogenous Zone

When it comes to your secret sexual strategy for getting off your archer, the thighs have it. Hips and thighs are extremely sensual for Sagittarius so pay attention to the area below the pelvis if you want to please your partner. Tact isn't a turn-on for the ninth sign in the zodiac, so forget about tracing circles on their inner legs or letting your fingers do the walking around their middle. Sagittarius views sex as a rough-and-tumble game, so if you're the prim-and-proper type, count on being pumped once and passed aside. Get gutsy instead. Whether you're male or female and whether you're viewing his va-voom or her vagina, the same method applies. Grab your Sagittarius the same way you'd grab a bear and *don't let go*.

A strong massage around the upper-leg area will get your Sagittarius salivating. Speaking of spit, you can use your own oral elixir to give the perfect rubdown or use an over-the-counter flavored oil. Forget flicking your fingers or playfully teasing your archer's erogenous zone: You're not dealing with a cautious Cancer or high-spirited Aquarius, so use a forceful approach, going over their entire thigh area as methodically as a butcher would tenderize a piece of meat. Although softening isn't a measure of success in this particular situation, methodically pulling and pushing your paramour will bring their private parts into play quickly. Tell your Sagittarius, "Not so fast" though: Your sex games aren't over yet.

Once you've given a thorough massage to everything between the kneecap and their nether region, give your Sagi a strong, open-mouthed kiss as you keep constant pressure on their inner thighs. There's a fine line between tickling and titillation here, so make sure you're doing it the way your lover likes it. The best way to find out what a Sagittarius is thinking is to ask, so between kisses discover your Sagi's secrets by being direct. "Is this too rough?," "Do you like it lower?," and "Should I try my tongue instead of my finger?" are all questions this fire sign will be happy to answer. Once you've figured out the sexual secrets of your Sagittarius, sexual nirvana is only a grope away. One more bit of info: If you *really* want to blow your Sagi's mind, do the thigh-grope thang in a public place. Your Sagittarius will be scouting out a more secretive spot to return your affection within seconds.

Come Again?

Sagittarius Man

If you can understand sex the same way your Sagi guy sees it, getting him to go for a second blastoff is a strong possibility. But if you're aiming for more than that, look for another lover. After all, sex is a game to Sagittarius, and the sign of the archer thinks *any* diversion loses its draw eventually. So let's assume you've wiped up the wet spot and are ogling your other as you yearn for more of the same. First off, *don't* pour on the pressure. Ask a Sagittarius for something and he'll likely oblige, but demand your dude do the same and you'll get *anything* except what you asked for.

An important prelude to a second sex act is letting your Sagi guy cool down for a few. Tell some jokes, flip on a flick (but no Leno or other types of typical TV), or just chat about anything interesting on your mind since Sagittarians love to talk. Of course, relating the saga of Fido's untimely death from a choking fit probably isn't a numero uno subject for discussion, so try to keep your topics relegated to fun subjects that interest your Sagittarius. Three M's are always acceptable bedroom banter: movies, magazines, and money. Once you've talked for a few minutes, grab his ass for an impromptu wrestling match. If he thinks lust isn't your aim and you're just playing a game, you've just gotten through hurdle number one. In the midst of your bedroom battle, your activities can take a turn for the carnal. "Accidentally" brush up against his dick as you're trying to pin his arms down. Kiss your way up his treasure trail as you're innocently tickling him and his best friend will turn to attention.

The whole key to keeping sexuality fun and spirited with the Sagittarius male is to keep it from getting too serious. Don't demand declarations of love. Don't tell him about all the kids you want to have with him. Don't say that all the other gay guys on the block are going to be jealous because you're the one who got him. Keep a spirited sense of fun in all things sexual and your Sagittarius will keep you content—but weigh him down with questions or catty comments and he'll find another bedroom to bop in before you fall asleep.

Sagittarius Woman
The Sagittarian woman is one of the most fascinating combinations in the zodiac. She has all the sexual chutzpah of her male counterpart but the turned-down testosterone level makes her less likely to stray. This makes your opps for scoring a second time stellar. The same sexual strategies that work for her male parallel apply to her—but with a Sagittarius woman you have even more options from which to choose.

If you're aiming to appeal to her playful side, start a pillow fight. She doesn't need as much time to recharge her sexual batteries as Sagittarius man, so as soon as she's hit her big O you can take your first shot. Grab a king-size pillow and lob it at her and she'll likely come after you with a vengeance. Forget throwing on any underwear before the bedroom battle either: Sagittarians are naturally not so shy, so if you feel the need to cover your private parts you'll likely stifle some of her renewing desire. Hide-and-seek in the buff is another boffo way to get this girl going. Just make sure she's the one who hides first because with her practical joker side, if you run to hide, she might just leave you there.

Another way to attune her to the Mommy/Daddy dance is by regressing to third-grade level and initiating a food fight. Though throwing a cantaloupe her way probably isn't a brilliant brainstorm, wiping chocolate ice cream between her breasts will excite her as you do it—plus you get the added bonus of being able to lick off the evidence yourself.

If all else fails, issue Sagittarius woman a challenge. You can be fair or unfair about this but if you choose the unfair route, you'll always win. What do I mean? Suppose it's Halloween night and you get into a debate over which Jamie Lee Curtis sequel will be on the tube at any given moment. Unbeknownst to your babe, you've looked the flick up in *TV Guide* already so when you say, "If it's *Halloween 2,* we can go to sleep but if it's *Halloween 5,* I get a blow job," you can count on getting a great view of the back of her head bobbing up and down. Even if she finds out you've cheated to get your way, she'll probably crack up instead of getting pissed: Sagittarius lives for fun and games and as long as no one gets hurt, all's fair in love and lust.

But Will It Last?

Aries and Sagittarius: Here's the downside: You're going to argue a hell of a lot and power plays will be an almost daily problem. Now for the good news: You both love to argue and your constant quest to gain control will equal a spicy sex life that never fails to please. Both of you are volatile fire signs, which means that although there might never be a moment's peace, your love and affection can still last for the long haul.

Taurus and Sagittarius: Sagittarius is a risk taker, willing to gamble on almost anything. Taurus hoards his or her dinero and thinks the Sagittarian trait of shooting for the moon is stupid and simplistic. You couldn't have less in common and you'll drive each other crazy sooner instead of later. Look elsewhere.

Gemini and Sagittarius: Since both of you are always up for something new, you'll never experience boredom in the bedroom or beyond. The sticky point is your shared fly-by-night nature. When neither sign is willing to contemplate commitment, affairs are short lived instead of long lasting. Share some fun fucks, then find someone else.

Cancer and Sagittarius: Cancers are cautious and love to stay at home. Sagittarius is a born risk taker who'd much rather be on a round-the-world vacation than tending to the backyard's flower patch. Arguments may not occur as often as they might in an Aries-Sagi combo, but Cancer will feel loads of simmering resentment at the Sagittarian freewheeling philosophy—and when Sagi gives in to his tendency to stray sexually, Cancer will terminate this rocky romance.

Leo and Sagittarius: When the archer aims for the sign of the lion, this couple will discover that the world is their oyster. Two more fun-loving signs never existed and when you pair this completely confident combo you get a brilliant, sparkling mating that all your friends will envy. Plan lots of parties because everyone will want to hang with the two of you.

Virgo and Sagittarius: You'll be lucky to form a conversation between these decidedly different signs—much less a long-term commitment. Virgo is simply far too serious for playful Sagi, while Virgo can't understand the Sagittarian trait of "What the hell?" While Virgo plots and plans, Sagi acts without a second thought. This unamicable union will turn into torture before you know it.

Libra and Sagittarius: If any sign can keep Sagittarius from his trademarked tendency toward sexual straying, it's fun-loving Libra. While other signs might make the mistake of lecturing or questioning Sagittarius' motives, Libra is content to kick back and enjoy life. Sagi finds this so attractive, he or she won't feel the need to look for love or lust outside the boundaries of the relationship. A glorious mating.

Scorpio and Sagittarius: Outspoken Sagittarius is anathema to brooding Scorpio. Scorpio wants loyalty and unending attention from their other half while Sagittarius wants to explore the world and all it has to offer. Understanding each other will be impossible since you operate from totally different mental plains. Forget forging a fornicational alliance with this odd couple: You'll be lucky if you can even make it as friends.

Sagittarius and Sagittarius: Yup, the sex is so hot you'll never need to run the heater again, but once you leave the bounds of your bedroom, problems will pop up just as often as sexual desire does. Neither of you is into being tied down and both of you view commitment as claustrophobic. You're excellent sex partners but don't have what it takes to make an enduring alliance. Keep in touch for when your horniness gets out of hand, but don't make the mistake of heading for the big M.

Capricorn and Sagittarius: Sagittarius could give a shit what other people think while Capricorn carefully assimilates the opinions of those near and dear. Sagi is free and easy with spending while goat guys and girls hoard their cash as if an economic recession is just around the corner. You'll irritate each other in bed and enrage each other beyond it. All signals say no, so set your sights on someone else.

Aquarius and Sagittarius: Aquarius is willing to give the long sexual leash Sagittarius needs, while Sagi's witty wordplay keeps a smile on any Aqua woman or man's face. With so much shared imagination, you'll dream up positions the Kinsey Report never listed, so aim for the long term before heading for the bed-room.

Pisces and Sagittarius: Sex will be the tie that binds the two of you together—at least for a while. Once bedroom high jinks draw to a close you'll have more problems than Donald Trump on tax day though: Pisces wants a lover who won't look at another while Sagittarius has to play around every once in a while. Over time, Pisces will become withdrawn and unhappy and that's where the affair will end.

Sagittarius Celebs: When Life Is a Game

Mariel Hemingway	November 22
Billie Jean King	November 22
Jamie Lee Curtis	November 22
Rodney Dangerfield	November 22
Harpo Marx	November 23
Christina Applegate	November 25
Amy Grant	November 25
John F. Kennedy, Jr	November 25
Ricardo Montalban	November 25
Tina Turner	November 26
Charles Schultz	November 26
Robin Givens	November 27

Jimi Hendrix	November 27
Bruce Lee	November 27
Anna Nicole Smith	November 28
Judd Nelson	November 28
Jeff Fahey	November 29
Diane Ladd	November 29
Ben Stiller	November 30
Billy Idol	November 30
Robert Guillaume	November 30
Dick Clark	November 30
Better Midler	December 1
Richard Pryor	December 1
Woody Allen	December 1
Britney Spears	December 2
Lucy Liu	December 2
Gianni Versace	December 2
Brendan Fraser	December 3
Ozzy Osbourne	December 3
Holly Marie Combs	December 3
Tyra Banks	December 4
Fred Durst	December 4
Jeff Bridges	December 4
Little Richard	December 5
Walt Disney	December 5
Tom Hulce	December 6
C. Thomas Howell	December 7
Larry Bird	December 7
Sinead O'Connor	December 8
Kim Basinger	December 8
Teri Hatcher	December 8
Jakob Dylan	December 9
Kenneth Branagh	December 10
Susan Dey	December 10
Jermaine Jackson	December 11
Donna Mills	December 11
Teri Garr	December 11

Mayim Bialik	December 12
Sheila E	December 12
Dionne Warwick	December 12
Bob Barker	December 12
Frank Sinatra	December 12
Ted Nugent	December 13
Christopher Plummer	December 13
Patty Duke	December 14
Lee Remick	December 14
Don Johnson	December 15
Steven Bochco	December 16
Leslie Stahl	December 16
Bob Guccione	December 17
Steve Austin	December 18
Steven Spielberg	December 18
Brad Pitt	December 18
Katie Holmes	December 18
Christina Aguilera	December 18
Cicely Tyson	December 19
Tim Reid	December 19
Jennifer Beals	December 19

Chapter 11

CAPRICORN

(December 21–January 19)

Sex Stats

Ruling planet: Saturn, the god who oversees time, discipline, and dedication. Translated, this means your Capricorn can go the distance—with major staying power—in bed and beyond.

Signature symbol: The goat, surefooted and smart, knows just where to go to reach the top. Whether this pinnacle results in sexual success, however, largely depends on you.

Trademark color: Forest green and russet brown, two earthy colors straight from nature that reflect Cappy's affection for the Mommy/Daddy dance.

Favorite position: Spoon fashion as you lay side by side. Goat guys and girls love to take and/or be taken from behind.

Potent porn: *The Legend of Joey Stefano* for boys buoyed by boys, *Buttwatch* for the straight—but not narrow—segment of society, and *Decadent Divas* for girls who get it on with girls.

Ultimate outfit (male): A business suit from an upscale designer like Armani.

Ultimate outfit (female): An ultra-expensive, decadently dressy ensemble from Ellen Tracy.

Mattress mambo music: Basic twang by Reba McIntyre or retro rock from Kansas or Asia.

Best sex toy: An office desk to bedroom bond on—merging Cappy's ambition with eros will get your goat randy fast, or a XXX video is a great way to loosen up any goat guy, but opt instead for more erotic-type NC-17 material with your goat girl.

After-fuck finger food: Pressed finger sandwiches made with the best cuts of beef available.

Do You Know What You're in For?

The famous scene in *The Shining* where Shelley Duvall discovers Jack Nicholson's catch phrase "All work and no play make Jack a dull boy" is a great representation of everything that's wrong with Capricorn. The zodiac sign best suited for business, Capricorn is all about making money, achieving goals, and getting there *first*. When this ambitious streak spins out of control Capricorn can become ruthless, manic, and consumed with whatever goal the goat happens to be after. If this sounds a bit like Virgo, you're right, but while Virgo can be happy with a career in social work, acting, or gardening, Capricorn has narrower sights. While an aging Virgo might look back on her life and wonder, "Was I the best I could be?" a Capricorn facing death would shorten the question to, "Was I the best?" While Virgo takes life's detours with a grain of salt, the sign of the goat jumps over them. As a cardinal sign, Capricorn believes in taking charge of a situation before it takes charge of him. Enterprising and never willing to take no for an answer, Capricorn *will* achieve whatever goal he or she sets out to achieve—or die trying.

This take-no-prisoners attitude can make sex with a Capricorn toe-clenching fun or mind-numbingly boring, depending on your attitude and what you're looking for in a mate. If you're looking for a wild life with your lover you're far better off settling with Sagittarius, or if you're jonesing for someone who'll call those between-the-sheets shots, Aries is the sign for you. If you're looking for a stable, steady bed partner who's full of quiet determination, Capricorn's soulful quest for success will ensure your sex is stellar. You'll have to scratch the surface of your Capricorn to reach the gold underneath, but ultimately you'll find the journey was worth it.

If you're getting the feeling that goat guys and girls are just about accumulating wealth, think again. As earth signs, they're intimately in touch with their physical needs although they might not like to admit it. Often, they can appear cold and detached as they gun for their goals but nine times out of ten, this is all part of an elaborate defense system designed to keep people out of their inner sanctum: They believe that if they don't fall in love, they won't feel vulnerable. If you're unlucky enough to end up with that one in ten who has become so enthralled in the rat race he or she has forgotten his/her humanity, don't just be afraid, be *very* afraid: Whichever sex your mate happens to be, you've just hooked up with the moral equivalent of J. R. Ewing from *Dallas*. Cut bait now or wait a few years for a big-ass divorce settlement; whatever you choose, you'll feel cold and used if you opt for a Capricorn sans conscience.

Capricorn Man

Capricorn man is far more militant than his goat-girl sisters. He feels that proving himself in the business world proves his masculinity and until you can break him of this concept—or accept it yourself—he'll probably be more interested in accumulating cash than commandeering you. Often, Capricorn men will come to this realization on their own but the process takes time, so if you're aiming for a goat guy under forty years of age, keep in mind that his career will be your strongest competition.

You won't need to worry about him getting sex on the side unless the terms of your relationship are ill defined. When he makes a commitment, he believes in sticking to it, but while Scorpio would do the right thing out of guilt, Capricorn *believes* in contracts. If he's only as good as his word, he'll make sure he sticks to what he says.

One-night stands with goat guys can be almost as exciting as watching paint dry or grass grow, so unless you're planning on tossing back some shots before sex be prepared for a rather dry, detached experience. In other words, he probably won't decline your offer of sex, but when he indulges it will be solely for his gratification—not yours. Since imagination isn't a strong suit for Capricorn, first times usually aren't very fab.

Date a Capricorn guy—or better yet, make him fall for you—and you face an entirely different equation. If he plans on keeping you around, he'll do everything in his power to keep you happy. If you think life is a contest to see who can accumulate the most stuff, Capricorn man will play into this delusion, plying you with more and more material items as he accumulates more and more cash. But you'll never see his true self, which is a crying shame: Capricorn men are some of the most trustworthy, masculine men in the world, but *only* if they know you love them—not their wallets.

That said, if you're looking for a shy stud that can truly rock your world Capricorn is certainly a sign to steer for. Concentrate on communication, as in, "Lick me there, nibble me here, *now* stick it in," and he'll pay close attention. This is the guy who sat in the front row of algebra class and got an A on every test. Now that he's facing the real world, he's ready to take even more detailed notes, but only if you're willing to provide them. Capricorn isn't a mind reader so if you're looking for someone who'll know your every wish without your having to say a word, Capricorn isn't a sign you should consider.

Capricorn Woman

A Capricorn female is usually more loving than her masculine counterpart. She has internalized society's messages that love is an important part of being a woman. She's taken this memo to heart even though she'll never be the type of girl who's willing to be used as a doormat. She's ultrarealistic about matters of the heart but at least she is happy with the fact that ultimately she's a creature that needs love—something Capricorn men often have a major problem with until late in their lives.

She's not into games so abandon your fantasies now about making X-rated home movies or having an orgy in the back bedroom of your house. If she's ever willing to take a walk on the wild side it will be some variant of a power play, whether she's headmistress to your naughty schoolboy or CEO to your mailroom girl. Like male Cappys, she's all about power but unlike her brother signs she's far more at ease when it comes to playing around with the concept of give and take, so don't be surprised when she decides to try out the school/mailroom girl role once in a while.

Like Beverly Hills real estate agents, Capricorn women are all about "location, location, location." So what if her favorite sexual position is the basic missionary style? She's ready to go for it in a variety of venues, from an Italian villa in Venice to a cozy cabin in the winter wonderland of Chamonix. Travel is an awesome way to stimulate her sexuality: It brings out her adventurous side and forces home the idea that she's allowed to take a break from the ruthless pressure she places upon herself. When she's trapped without a break in her home environment she's constantly being reminded of unachieved goals. She *needs* to snag that promotion. She's *got* to buy into that tech stock before it jumps another fifty cents. She *can't* buy that new dress because she'd feel so much more responsible if she locked it away in her savings account. Reminding your Capricorn woman that there's a bigger picture at hand through travel or travels through her sexuality will keep her sane and sanguine. She'll appreciate the favor and when you become beneficiary to all she has to offer, you'll thank God you gunned for this goat.

Five Surefire Ways to Break the Ice with Capricorn

Capricorn Man
1. Ask how he's diversified his stock portfolio.
2. Talk about a recent shift in the economy.
3. Find out what his long-term goals are.
4. Tell him he has striking facial features: Capricorns are known for their awesome bone structure—a fact of which they're quite proud.
5. Discuss a company's marketing strategy, whether it's Apple's brilliant introduction of the I-Mac or Sony's domination of the electronics field.

Capricorn Woman
1. Chat about a woman who dominates her field of choice, whether it's Penny Marshall or Sarah Michelle Gellar.
2. Ask which is the better investment for your savings—stocks, CDs, or money markets.
3. Talk about a movie franchise (from the *Nightmare on Elm Street* flicks to *Jurassic Park*) and how much easy money they bring in.
4. Compliment her cheekbones or other *specific* body part: "Gosh, darn, you sure are pretty" won't go over well with Capricorn woman.
5. Ask if you can buy her lunch (she loves to save money.)

Refining Your Sexual Strategy—The Subrulers

Saturn: The Ultimate Hard Worker (December 21– December 31)
Saturn is the planet that directs our discipline and when Capricorn gets a double dose, sometimes a "doom-and-gloom" attitude is the result. This Capricorn will break their back to reach the finish line but even after they've crossed it and won first place they'll still think about the one or two missteps they took along the way. They're all about being precise and orderly, so don't dare make the fatal mistake of placing their pencils where their pens belong in their incredibly organized office.

This all-encompassing perfectionism extends to the bedroom as well, but for many signs, mugging with the chairman of the board won't be nearly as exciting as it sounds. This sign is all about getting the job done and while that approach might get you off in the bedroom, don't make the mistake of thinking you'll wake up the next morning to find roses. Sex is a responsibility and a job for this sign associated with achievement and if that doesn't sound like your idea of romance, then it probably isn't. Get promoted, feed the cat, fuck my mate, balance the business budget. It's all in a day's work for this Capricorn who can sometimes come across as cold and calculating.

Saturn is a serious taskmaster though, and if he directs the Capricorn in question toward a lifelong commitment, you needn't worry about this sign screwing around on you. The question becomes, Will you screw around on *them?* It's hard to be put in the same class with business, a cat, and a promotion but for Capricorn all of these things must be done and they all fall into the same "must-do" boat. If you're patient and passionate you might be able to raise this Capricorn's temperature to a solid 98.6, but in the long run you might just end up asking yourself, Was it worth it?

If you're looking for a rock-solid survivor, this kind of Capricorn is your woman or man but if you're needing more emotion and less businesslike behavior in the bedroom, get this goat out of your boudoir *now.*

Venus: Beauty Bonds with Business (January 1–January 10)

Venus is the beauty in love with love and when she softens slave-driving Saturn's hold you get a far more gracious goat. Men and women born during this ten-day period are far more peaceful and serene than the other two kinds of Capricorn. She gives the goat in question an increased appreciation and appetite for love, affection, and sexuality. Just like Virgo, Capricorn is all about achievement but unlike the other two decanates this Capricorn knows when the business day is done and it's time to get down and dirty.

Though sexually reserved at first, in time this Capricorn will open his or her eyes to wilder forms of lovemaking. If you're wondering if this acceptance will eventually become all-encompassing as your Capricorn yields to three-ways and other shocking sex games, stop wondering because it *ain't gonna happen*. Capricorn, like Scorpio, is looking for a partner who only has eyes for him or her. If your eyes are on someone else, you'll be written off as a bad business investment and forgotten. This isn't to say your goat gal or guy won't feel like shit that you were interested in someone else—it's simply that they'll *never* let you see their emotions once they've decided you're not *the one.*

This subsign is extremely devoted, whether to his or her job, a mate, a favorite pet, or to their future. If you find one focused on anything other than yourself, realize from the very beginning that you'll probably not be able to take out your competition—whatever it is. Capricorn is all about focus and though Venus brings beauty to the view, she doesn't shade the picture. This devoted goat is all that, *if* you happen to be what he or she is looking for. If you're not, don't worry: You'll know soon enough.

Mercury: Streamlined Strategy (January 11–January 19)

Mercury, big cheese of reasoning and analyzation, gives brilliance to Saturn's dedication and drive. As the Lone Ranger of logic, Mercury doesn't exactly add affection to the mix, so keep in mind that this kind of Capricorn can be just as cold and calculating as the first decanate. Mercury does change the mix as far as goals go though: While Capricorns subruled by Saturn are all about reaching the top, mental Mercury reminds Capricorn that an easier way might be to just accumulate a whole helluva lot of money. While money is important to any Capricorn, it gains an all-new aura of respect with Capricorns subruled by Mercury. This might seem odd since Jupiter is the god of cold, hard cash but when you combine the M.O.s of Saturn and Mercury, all the puzzle pieces fall into place. Saturn is all about reaching the top and Mercury is always looking for a shortcut. When you put the two together you find the ultimate realist: A person who innately understands that money equals power in our society, so to get one you've got to go full force after the other.

Capricorns of this kind can be odd and unassuming in relationships. At times, you might get the feeling that you're interchangeable and that your Cappy in question might have been just as happy with someone else. Though there aren't any hard and fast rules in astrology, this guess is probably closer to the target than you'd like to imagine: Capricorns are all about putting everything into place and sometimes that rationale dictates that some of the pieces must be occasionally rearranged. If this kind of Capricorn totally falls for you, which is possible but rare, they'll try to loosen up their badass business attitude, but if you find your Capricorn staring at you like a possession, you might want to rethink your relationship. If you're looking for no-strings sex, meanwhile, this sign is a supermistake unless you're the type who gets off on all give and no take: Capricorn might let you blow him or eat her out but when you're done it's doubtful that they'll even give you a kiss good night. A brusque "thank you" and a speedy slide to the nearest exit is far more likely.

Sexual Synergy

Aries and Capricorn: Love and lust go hand in hand for the goat and the ram. Both of you are totally headstrong and more than willing to ask for exactly what you need from your bedroom buddy, so count on explosive sex. Neither of you is overly experimental, so nix those handcuffs and body paints but head-to-head sex will be an aerobic workout that will leave both of you breathless—and begging for more.

Taurus and Capricorn: Stick a bull with a goat and you get unbelievable endurance in all things erotic. Capricorns tend to be somewhat distant emotionally but stalwart Taurus can help unleash their solid sexuality without saying a word. Capricorn needs an affectionate, *dependable* lover and that's exactly what the bull brings. Capricorn's staying power, meanwhile, will keep the bull beaming and when the cum shot finally hits, you'll both fall asleep with smiles on your face.

Gemini and Capricorn: Though this could be an exciting fling, sex between the twins and the goat is an odd experience. While many signs see Gemini's witty wordplay and relish for raunchiness as exciting, Capricorn is secretly intimidated by this rough-and-tumble approach to sensuality. Gemini thinks Capricorn is a fuddy-duddy and unless Gem has a secret fantasy about father figures, the sex won't be sleazy or scintillating—just so-so.

Cancer and Capricorn: Sexual fireworks make for a big bang instead of a whimper between these two sexual sophisticates. Although Capricorn's big-shot attitude toward headboard banging grates on quiet Cancer's nerves, ultimately the crab is fascinated with the goat's constant sexual advances.

Leo and Capricorn: Leo loves to be worshipped while Capricorn thinks the big-headed lion is a big-time bore. While Leo likes opulence and leisurely lovemaking, Capricorn is from the far more basic bump-and-grind school of getting it on. Leo thinks love should read like a romance novel, while Capricorn sees love as a business spreadsheet. 'Nuff said.

Virgo and Capricorn: Although Capricorn might need to give Virgo's prudishness a push to get everything the sign of the virgin has to offer, if Capricorn is willing to up the sexual ante, sex will be stupendous. Strong-willed Virgo meets the perfect match in ballsy Capricorn and if the two can find a way to abandon their inhibitions, happiness won't be the only thing that comes.

Libra and Capricorn: Capricorn's smoldering sexuality gets all hot and bothered by Libra's charm and charisma. Libra, meanwhile, finds Capricorn's blatant approach to bumping uglies ultra-exciting. Once you leave the sanctity of your love nest more problems will pop up than in Clinton's terms in office, but as long as you bury yourselves in the bedroom, your sex lives will be a cause for celebration.

Scorpio and Capricorn: Whether you leave the lights on or decide to do it in the dark, sexual symbiosis between the scorpion and goat will scorch the sheets, sofa, or wherever you plan on doing your very adult dance. Since both of you are extremely sexual animals, plan on doing everything you've seen on the Discovery Channel and a hell of a lot more. Doggie style will seem dead and role-playing retro for you two extreme sexual adventurers. Take the phone off the hook and get it on *now.*

Sagittarius and Capricorn: Sagi's fun approach to all things fornicational is just what prim and proper Capricorn needs to get the ball—or balls—rolling to an excellent start. Fun and games will be your bread and butter as you indulge in activities other signs only dream about. Things cool off quick once you vacate your pleasure pit though, so once you get off you'll probably want to get out.

Capricorn and Capricorn: When you combine two signs known for their dependability and durability you end up with another D-word: dull. Both of you need sexual spouses who are geared toward the new and different, but since Cappys love the same ol', same ol', get ready to do the missionary position once a week for the rest of your life. It's not that the sex will suck exactly, but it'll be an awesome way to ensure sleep.

Aquarius and Capricorn: Capricorn thinks Aquarius is like an antiquated sixties love child; Aquarius thinks Capricorn is a boring business type. Hedonistic pleasures like oral affection or playful spanking won't be an option for this extremely odd couple—in fact, you'll be lucky if you can even make it into the bedroom without starting an argument.

Pisces and Capricorn: What might seem like a sexual match made in hell isn't: Pisces' dreamy quality is exactly what goat girls and guys need to release some of their hidden fantasies. Sweet Pisces makes compliment-coveting Capricorn feel like a million bucks while Cappy's forceful mode of fornication makes the fish feel fabulous. Capricorn loves to call the shots between the sheets and willing Pisces will do whatever it takes to keep their Capricorn content.

Exploring Their Erogenous Zone

Goat gals and guys are among the most anal signs in the zodiac so they need plenty of buttering up. He's worried about that stock transaction. She's worried about her maybe/maybe not promotion. With so much going on in your goat's gray matter you'll be lucky to liberate their locked-up libidos, so bear in mind that releasing your Capricorn's carnality will involve some work from your end. So what exactly is your goat's hot spot?

Whether knobby or noble, the erotic zone you're aiming for are the knees. You're not just stuck with this four-inch area, however. Feel free to trail feathery strokes down the front and back of your goat's legs, paying careful concentration to the knee region. Massaging this area is cool but don't get too rough: Goats like light stimulation not bump-and-grind ballistics. Lick around the entire region, kissing the kneecaps of your lover lightly before edging into nips and nibbles. Trailing your hands up and down your paramour's form as you get down and dirty with their knees sounds like a crazier idea than teaming Sly Stallone with Kurt Russell, but if Hollywood can do it, why not you?

For the more adventurous types, when you're on top during the carnal carnival with your goat, face the opposite direction and play with his or her knees while you're bumping uglies. This is a magical method for ensuring that your lover gets off. Capricorn is often disturbed by performance anxiety and by stimulating your goat guy or girl in more than one way at the same time, they can't concentrate on what might go wrong because they're too enthralled with how damn good they feel. It sounds weird on paper but give it a try: Your Capricorn will thank you in the morning.

Come Again?

Capricorn Man

Appeal to your goat guy's overachieving attitude to get him ready for a second rumble. While you'd emphasize an Aries' manhood, as in "Wow, you're such a stud," and trick Sagittarius with "If the penny comes up heads, will you give me some?," Capricorn is a much tougher customer to deal with. Totally to the point, the Capricorn man can't be won over with false praise or banter that borders on begging. Though he hates to admit it, love is very important to a Capricorn male. If he loves you, he'll see it as his duty to keep you as sexually satisfied as he can.

Suppose you're still in the dating game or just want to get your money's worth from that hotel room. How do you do it? Tell Capricorn what he was good at. Whether his forte was balls-to-the-wall missionary-style sex, celebratory 69, or just some excellent finger fucking, let him know what you liked and *why* you liked it. The why part is all-important with Capricorn man because it's his proof that you're not filling him full of bull. It also shows you were totally titillated by some of his earthier activities. While Leo needs after-fuck flattery to inflate his over-abundant ego, Capricorn wants to know he did the job right. Once you let him know he has, look him in the eyes and say you'd like some more. Be prepared though: If you're not his type or he's viewing you as something to be used and abused, he won't have any qualms at saying, "No way," so you should have some inkling of his feelings before you put yourself in this very vulnerable position. However, if he likes you, loves your bod, or foresees a future with you, this goat guy will do virtually *anything* to get your groove on, so gear up for more fun from his love gun.

While we're palavering about penises, realize that once this guy gets a hard-on he's got to do something with it. Get a Libra erect and he might just as well opt for a game of checkers, turn a Cancer's connector to concrete and he might just as well start an argument as oral affection. But give a goat guy a bone and he'll use it on you, so as a last resort, gently play with his private parts the same way you'd wrestle your stuffed animals when you were a kid. Pay attention without present-ing pressure and your Capricorn can rise to almost *any* occasion.

Capricorn Woman

Capricorn women are cool characters. If you're the type who can't help but act like an adolescent hornball when you're scouting out a second round, get ready to pleasure yourself in the bathroom solo once she's fallen asleep. If you're a skillful lover, however, who can keep your emotions in check as you let your desire be known, the Capricorn woman will be more than happy to pleasure you and herself. Just as she's addicted to business deals and money maneuvers, for goat girls once is never enough—as long as she enjoys herself during the process.

Capricorn women want a guy with charm and finesse, so if you're some grease monkey she picked up for a fun fling count on getting booted from her Lexus seconds after your booty call. Easy sophistication holds major appeal for this etiquette-loving female, so try to release your inner Cary Grant as you maneuver her mind for more bedroom behavior. Heartfelt compliments mean the world to this woman, but if you lie or lay on too much bullshit you've just shot your sexual strategy in the foot. Translation? "You've got the most beautiful green eyes I've ever seen" is a fly forerunner to fuck number two but, "You're the most beautiful woman I've ever seen" will make her grimace with irritation before she ejects you from her bed. She wants the truth—and if you're not willing to give it you're certainly not going to get any. Muscles hold great appeal for goat girls so if you're built like Brad Pitt, lay back so she can get an awesome look at your abs. If you're a female aiming to emulate the same equation, casually walk around in the nude. *Don't* make the mistake of being obvious, because if there is one thing a Capricorn woman can't stand it's someone who can't control themselves.

What if you look more like Chris Farley than Christopher Reeve or the Wicked Witch than Wonder Woman? Talk about your accomplishments: Achievement is a major muff wetter for Capricorn females and if you can discuss your skills in business it will only serve to increase the action you'll get in the bedroom. Don't exaggerate your success unless a one-night stand is your only goal, because if your Capricorn woman ever discovers your dereliction to tell the truth, your position as girlfriend, boyfriend, or just plain old sex partner will be thrown out with yesterday's stock quotes.

But Will It Last?

Aries and Capricorn: Sex soars between the two of you, but when all you have in common is a penchant for penetration problems pop up faster than another Will Smith album. Since neither of you will give an inch on anything from deciding who gets to mow the lawn to which James Bond flick you're going to slip into your DVD player, your union is better suited to the WWF instead of the Wonderful World of Sex. Though you might last a few rounds, you'll ultimately end with a knockout.

Taurus and Capricorn: Capricorn loves creating capital; Taurus loves to hoard that cash away. Two such similar mind-sets make for a great coupling—as long as you don't let your materialistic sides get the better of you. Concentrate on loving each other instead of trying to keep up with the Joneses and your love lives will last a long time.

Gemini and Capricorn: Capricorn likes life orderly and plays life by the numbers. Gemini thinks rules are made to be broken and is given to flights of fancy that Capricorn finds incomprehensible and unforgivable. This love match is anything but, so unless you're a glutton for incessant arguments do the right thing and diss dates between these two totally different sun signs.

Cancer and Capricorn: You both totally enjoy doing the nasty with each other but once you abandon bump and grind for the real world you'll be as bizarre a match as Julia Roberts and Lyle Lovett. Capricorn isn't the most affectionate sign in the zodiac (to say the least) and Cancer needs constant reassurance and round-the-clock attention. Fights might be infrequent since neither of you like confrontations, but eventually resentment will build, breaking your relationship to bits.

Leo and Capricorn: By-the-numbers Capricorn thinks Leo belongs in a mental institution for the narcissistically insane. Leo, meanwhile, thinks Capricorn is almost as exciting as Al Gore in a muzzle. Don't worry about an explosive argument at the breakup since you'll be lucky to even make it through a first date.

Virgo and Capricorn: Stop the presses, because you've just found a copulation combo sent straight from the heavens. Capricorn loves Virgo's strong sense of right and wrong and excellent work ethic. Capricorn's studly ways in business, boardrooms, and bed pull usually cautious Virgo into an entirely new sexual stratosphere. Both of you have a tendency to shut down emotionally when you're in pain. Fight this inclination and life between the goat and the virgin can be as pleasing—or perverse—as you want to make it.

Libra and Capricorn: Libra's laid-back approach to love gives Capricorn the creeps since goat guys and girls aren't really all that into romance. Capricorn sees love as a binding contract; Libra sees it as flowers, champagne, and fancy dinners. When you mate this radically rational realist with an eternal optimist you get anger not eros, which will butcher your bonds faster than you can say "crappy couple."

Scorpio and Capricorn: Scorpio's sexual eccentricities find a happy home with goat gals and guys. Since Capricorn is naturally a bit of an introvert, Scorpio's over-the-top sex drive is the perfect prescription to loosen the goat's loving libido. Two such strong personalities *must* occasionally argue, so be careful not to hit below the belt when you're hashing out your differences. Except for that one downside, all omens point toward a lengthy, loving relationship.

Sagittarius and Capricorn: Optimistic Sagittarius brightens dour Capricorn's mood—but only for the short term. All too soon, Sagi's noncommittal attitude grates on the goat's nerves. Capricorn wants truth, attachment, and bonds so strong nothing can break them while Sagittarius cannot be tied down because the archer was sent here to explore the world. A heartbreak waiting to happen.

Capricorn and Capricorn: You've met your match when you lock horns with another goat guy or girl. The sticking point is that you're both so damn serious about everything your lives will resemble a documentary on the BBC. Expect little laughter and lowered lovemaking expectations. You like each other a lot but you need someone who'll loosen you up—*not* a mirror image of yourself.

Aquarius and Capricorn: Even Aquarius has no idea what he or she will do next until its done. Capricorn finds this lack of planning infuriating and can't understand someone who doesn't plan their life out years in advance. Aquarius thinks Capricorn is a pompous paramour—someone who believes in all work and no play. That couldn't be any further from the Aquarian style, which means all bets are off for this relationship.

Pisces and Capricorn: Realistic Capricorn finds a welcome respite from the dull and dreary in Pisces' fascinating dreamworld. Compare this merger with a mortal and you get this: Pisces is the head that dreams of better days, while Cappy is the feet that move the body in that direction. A marvelous match for eroticism, entertainment, and affection.

Capricorn Celebs: Gotta Have It All

Ray Romano	December 21
Chris Evert	December 21
Florence Griffith Joyner	December 21
Jane Fonda	December 21
Maurice and Robin Gibb	December 22
Diane Sawyer	December 22
Corey Haim	December 23
Susan Lucci	December 23
Ricky Martin	December 24
Annie Lennox	December 25
Jimmy Buffett	December 25
Sissy Spacek	December 25
Gerard Depardieu	December 27
John Amos	December 27
Denzel Washington	December 28
Jude Law	December 29
Jon Voight	December 29
Mary Tyler Moore	December 29
Tiger Woods	December 30
Tracey Ullman	December 30
Matt Lauer	December 30
Val Kilmer	December 31
Donna Summer	December 31
Christy Turlington	January 2
Tia Carrere	January 2
Cuba Gooding, Jr	January 2
Mel Gibson	January 3
Victoria Principal	January 3
Michael Stipe	January 4
Dyan Cannon	January 4
Marilyn Manson	January 5
Pamela Sue Martin	January 5
Diane Keaton	January 5
Joey Lauren Adams	January 6

Nancy Lopez	January 6
Nicolas Cage	January 7
Katie Couric	January 7
Ami Dolenz	January 8
Elvis Presley	January 8
Stephen Hawking	January 8
Dave Matthews	January 9
Pat Benatar	January 10
George Foreman	January 10
Naomi Judd	January 11
Kirstie Alley	January 12
Howard Stern	January 12
Julia Louis-Dreyfus	January 13
Gwen Verdon	January 13
Jason Bateman	January 14
Faye Dunaway	January 14
Martin Luther King, Jr	January 15
Aaliyah	January 16
Debbie Allen	January 16
John Carpenter	January 16
Kate Moss	January 16
Jim Carrey	January 17
Susanna Hoffs	January 17
Eartha Kitt	January 17
Betty White	January 17
Cary Grant	January 18
Dolly Parton	January 19

Chapter 12

AQUARIUS
(January 20–February 17)

Sex Stats

Ruling planet: Uranus, the god of unexpected sexual twists and turns.

Signature symbol: The water bearer, who dispenses his or her sexual knowledge and prowess freely.

Trademark color: Neon blue, the color that adds an electrical charge to the sex act.

Favorite position: Mutual masturbation as a prelude to completely carnal copulation.

Potent porn: *Hollywood Legs* for humans hunting for the opposite sex, *Flex TV* for gay guys, and *Real Female Masturbation* for girls who like girls.

Ultimate outfit (male): Bell-bottom jeans paired with a basic black T-shirt.

Ultimate outfit (female): Seventies style, complete with platform shoes, baggy pants, and a top with a vinyl picture emblazoned on it.

Mattress mambo music: Eclectic funk like Sly and the Family Stone or Aretha Franklin.

Best sex toy: A dildo: whether you're gunning for gay, straight, male, or female, Aquarius will have some fun with this.

After-fuck finger food: Vittles from any country your Aquarius isn't a native of, from Tandoori chicken to mu shu pork.

Do You Know What You're in For?

Aquarius is all about having the balls to march to your own drumbeat. This is the man who wasn't afraid to be a computer nerd or out-of-the-closet gay guy in high school or the strong-minded feminist female who grew up in a small-minded, redneck town. Aquarius is the sign of the future, of theories, and invention. In some seriously mistaken astro tomes you'll read that Aquarius has to do with water but this couldn't be more off base. Aquarius is an air sign and *always* has his or her head firmly trapped in the clouds. This can make for an odd combo of personality traits if you decide to date—or do—the sign of water bearer, but if you gun for an Aqua woman or man, count on one thing: you'll never meet anyone else quite like 'em.

The first thing you'll notice when you talk to an Aquarius is their tendency to talk about life in the abstract. People *shouldn't* be bigots. It's wrong to lie. Do the right thing. If you point out to this same Aquarius that he or she doesn't like short people, just bullshitted her mom on some off-the-wall subject, and cheated on her taxes, don't expect a mass retraction of everything she just said. Just because an Aquarius doesn't practice everything he or she preaches doesn't mean they're going to change their opinion. Aquarius is a fixed sign ruled by Uranus and although it seems contradictory to have a sign who's unwilling to change their mind ruled by the god of change, it really isn't. Aquarius operates on two levels: the stark reality of the here and now (which holds little attraction) and theory. Aquarius loves to get caught up in conjecture, even if it holds little bearing to his or her personal existence. In some instances this translates into so-so sex. If you're after an Aquarius who'd rather talk about sex than experience it, get ready for a crash course in pleasuring yourself solo since you won't be indulging in an active exchange very often. If you're lucky enough to find an Aquarian who views sex as one of the few experiences in life where reality and theory can merge, you just might have found paradise. Expect the unusual no matter what. In the world according to Sagittarius, sexual rules were meant to be broken, while Cancer follows society's rules to a T. Aquarius *sets* his own rules, which can make for a totally confusing—and totally exciting—adventure. If you want to decipher an Aquarian's love laws, finding out is simple since he or she loves to talk but get ready for a lengthy explanation. Dating (or simply screwing) an Aquarian is like trying to learn a new language: It can be a real bitch but if you're up to the task you'll reap major rewards.

Aquarius Man

The first thing you'll notice about an Aqua man is that he's a hell of a lot of fun to talk to. While Gemini has a quicksilver wit and Virgo loves to play with words, Aquarius is more interested in the true meaning of the point he's trying to get across. In other words, while other signs get caught up in their particular modus operandi for messaging, for Aquarius it's all about the message itself. He's open and always quick to offer his comment on any given subject and while you should never trust a Sagittarius or Pisces right off the bat, the same doesn't hold true for Aquarius. If he says he's going to call you tomorrow, he will—and if he doesn't, whatever you do, don't make the mistake of calling him. He's obviously *not* interested.

This guy has amazing staying power in the sack. He can keep at it without losing his load for as long as it takes to get you off—and whether that's once or five times depends on your preference and his. Keep in mind that he's supercerebral though, and views sex more as a merging of the minds than a biological act. Crude behavior like Gemini's penchant for dirty talk *isn't* cool—unless you let him know up front that you're playing a game. Once he's in on the fun almost anything is cool, from role-playing to S&M to posing nude in your backyard at five A.M. Some areas that *are* off-limits include three-ways, partner swapping, or open relationships. Although an Aquarius man certainly has indulged in these practices, he won't participate when the love of his life is involved—and if he does, he'll regret it. What am I saying? Simply put, if you and your Aqua man are bumping uglies with someone other than *each* other, then you're his Mr. or Ms. Right Now—not his Mr. or Ms. Right.

He's way more private than an over-the-top Aries or earthy Taurus, so make sure you always shut the door before using the bathroom. The reason for this isn't exactly what you'd expect: While Libra likes his other half to be pleasing to the eyes, ears, and nose and Virgo likes to pretend his mate doesn't take a dump, Aquarius doesn't like the reminder that we're tied to this planet by our own needs. His secret fantasy is not to be tied down by the here and now, whether that happens to be a job, a mortgage, or bowing to our biology. Fueling his fantasy by constantly stimulating his intellect as you downplay the more mortal parts of our existence will keep him coming back for more.

Aquarius Woman

With almost all the signs you get some major changes when you move from male to female within each sign. As mentioned earlier, often these changes aren't rooted in basic differences between the sexes—instead, their origins lie in the way the different sexes are treated by our society. A female Aries has to tone her balls-to-the-wall behavior down or the world at large views her as a bitch. A prim-and-proper Virgo male has to let loose with the requisite number of burps and farts when he's hanging with his guy friends or he'll get called a sissy. But society's view of intellect in males and females is relatively balanced, which means that Aquarian women and men have almost everything in common. For Aquarian women, growing up before the feminist movement must have been similar to water torture, but with the increased opportunities available to women all that's changed.

Like her male flipside, she's not into fooling around. She's looking for a lover who'll be up-front with her about everything but until she finds him she'll be willing to make do with whatever—or whoever—happens to be available. She's actually even more detached than Aquarian males when it comes to love and sex. She's got a typical American guy attitude about the whole thing, so don't be surprised by the fact that dating around doesn't make her antsy. What *does* freak her out? Love. Those four simple letters totally blow the mind of this supercerebral sign. In fact, love is one of the few things that frighten an Aquarius woman. Like Virgo, she likes keeping her emotions under tight control and although this might come across as seeming cold, she's not thinking about hurting you; she's obsessed with protecting herself. Some Aquarian women make the mistake of committing to someone they're not in love with because they feel they'll be able to retain control if they keep themselves distanced emotionally. Thinking like this backfires, however. It's the same conundrum all Aquarians face. Live life in theory and you never run the risk of getting hurt. Touch down in the here and now and you might find love—or a hell of a lot of pain.

Five Surefire Ways to Break the Ice with Aquarius

Aquarius Man

1. Ask his opinion on virtually anything.
2. Chat about a crooked politician.
3. Debate a song or movie that's been remade. Whether *Psycho* or *American Pie*, Aquarius will *only* like the original.
4. Talk about the cutting edge in communication from cable modem connections to the latest model Palm Pilot.
5. Discuss a bud you have in common: Friendship is all-important to Aquarius.

Aquarius Woman

1. Talk about the latest horrible atrocity some bigot has perpetrated on a minority.
2. Debate the merits of your favorite Parker Posey flick.
3. Let her know about any charity work you're accomplished.
4. Discuss a recent—and cool—innovation or invention.
5. Find out where she stands on drug legalization: a hot topic about which she's sure to have a strong opinion.

Refining Your Sexual Strategy—The Subrulers

Uranus: Ready for Almost Anything? (January 20– January 29)

This Einstein-like sign was born to think out of the box: With wild-card Uranus as ruler and subruler, the tried-and-true path is simply for dweebs who couldn't find a faster mode of transportation. A brilliantly progressive thinker, this sign was the type who fought against slavery in the past and fights for the women's movement or gay rights today. Always about ten steps ahead of the rest of society, this Aqua woman or man feels weighted down by societal constraints. Who ever said black people had to sit on the back of the bus? Why can't gay guys get married? What moron said all Asians look the same? Certainly not Aquarius, that much is sure.

In the bedroom this wildly inventive behavior might translate into lying in a sex swing one evening only to be followed by a romantic dinner for two the next. The only thing you can count on with this kind of Aquarius is that you won't be getting what you counted on. The one area where this maxim doesn't hold true is love: Once you've won the heart of this air sign, you'll have to go the extra mile to break it. If anyone can understand and forgive the tendency to stray, other than Sagittarius, it's this forward thinker. While Sagittarius understands screwing around because he or she is probably guilty of it themselves, Aquarius isn't the type to fuck around. Sleeping around simply holds little interest for this understanding air sign.

This almost-freakish level of acceptance can be very confusing in relationships. Many signs accuse Aquarius of being cold and distant. Though this might appear to be the case it couldn't be further from the truth: Aquarius is simply all about figuring things out and, to do so, *must* approach life in a logical fashion. Virgo does the same but in a one, two, three kind of thinking; Aquarius takes intuitive leaps that would leave Virgo with vertigo. One leads to five that in turn leads to twenty-five. While Virgo must have all the pieces to assemble the puzzle at hand, Aquarius excels at theories and guesses. If you want to know which degree to go for in college, ask Virgo; if you want to know if you should consider blowing college off entirely and head for Hollywood instead, ask Aquarius. This sign is the forefront of humanity, leading the way for the rest of us, but all the progressive thinking this kind of Aquarius is known for might leave you feeling as if they'd rather live life in theory than reality. The truth is that they would: Theory is far less lethal than reality and when you make a mistake in your mind you can always take it back.

Mercury: Mind Over Matter (January 30—February 8)

Aquarians born under this decanate get Mercury's lively way with words added to their mental mix, which insures a fiercer wit than the other two types. While any Aquarius will speak his or her mind, this kind's tongue is a virtual lingual lash and if they feel like slashing you to shreds, all it will take is a few carefully calculated words from their end. This will rarely happen unless you push Aquarius to his or her limits. Basically a happy camper, this kind of Aquarius will only attack when cornered or confronted with a bigot or other similarly small-minded moron.

In sex and love, this sign has a secret fantasy about being swept off their feet. In reality, however, caution and carefully curbed emotions keep this from happening. Everything must first be approved in theory before it can be put into practice and by the time the practice part comes around, emotions have already cooled. Though Aquarius would rather not admit it, keeping cool about all things emotional keeps them feeling safe and in control. Though you might be able to embroil Aquarius in a raging debate about romance, getting the eleventh sign similarly enraged about the real deal is next to impossible. Thinking takes precedence over action because in action things can go wrong while keeping everything intellectual keeps it all a comforting distance away.

If your feelings are easily hurt, don't dare date this sign. "Jeez, you're *terrible* when it comes to swapping spit" would be acceptable dinner conversation to this ultra-open sign. Unless you have a thick skin—or can fully realize that there is no malicious intent behind the negative things Aquarius says—just say no to that first Aqua date.

Casual sex is another affair entirely. This sign, although certainly not the most sexual in the zodiac, will sometimes indulge in off-the-wall, totally spontaneous sex. The weird part will be after the fact: While another sign would spark a cigarette, Aquarius will want to discuss the event in all its glorious detail—from that awesome first kiss to that horribly embarrassing fart you let out halfway through the act. Nothing is taboo to Aquarius so if there are subjects you tend to shy away from, opt for someone other than this subspecies.

Venus: Finally, the People Pleaser (February 9– February 17)

As the lady in charge of love, Venus loosens the bug that Uranus stuck up Aquarius' ass. Theory still reigns supreme, but beneath the analysis more emotions are at the ready. While the first two decanates tend to be distant in relationships, this sign has the strongest ability of the three to form long-lasting, loving relationships.

Instead of just thinking things through, this sign likes to get out there and *do* things. Travel is important to people born during these ten days and this willingness to go around the world reaches to the bedroom as well. Venus ups the raunch factor in usually detached Aquarius. Sex is more consuming, more passionate— and a hell of a lot more often for you. While the first two subspecies of Aquarius view sex as more of a mental exchange, this kind gets off on the physical aspect as well. It's as if Venus added extra nerves in the dick of your dude or the tits of your temptress: What would make another Aquarian smile will make this one *scream*.

Even the bedroom itself will look far different when this Aquarian is the one who happens to be the one designing it. While the first two decanates aim for a utilitarian look (too much stuff muddies the mind), this sort will probably have piles of pillows on a king-size bed. Venus also tempers the tongue of this Aquarius, so instead of having to hear "God, you're *terrible* at giving head," you'll more likely listen to "When you're going down, would you mind stroking me with your tongue instead of wiggling it back and forth like a tadpole?" In other words, don't expect total diplomacy, but at least your dick won't nose-dive or your pubic region dry up when you hear their from-the-heart request. This Aquarian is also far more prone to please you, so tell them what you have in mind and they'll more than likely oblige.

Sexual Synergy

Aries and Aquarius: This couple has mixed sexual signals. Aries likes the Aquarian traits of imagination and originality but Aquarius has problems with the ram's requirement to constantly dominate all things sexual. If Aries can force him or herself to an occasional compromise, you'll give the bedsprings a run for their money but if the ram gets too bossy, Aquarius will immediately look for an easy way out.

Taurus and Aquarius: Aquarius' slack view of sexuality berates the bull's brain, who sees bumping uglies as an all-important part of any loving relationship. Aquarius thinks sex is important too, but that the relationship comes first. For Taurus, these two ideas are interchangeable. Sex will be dull, dry, and dreary, leaving Aquarius wondering, "Are we done yet?" and the bull wishing he'd opted for the television set instead of not-so-tantalizing sex.

Gemini and Aquarius: Both of you love to talk and when Gemini turns the conversation carnal something is *sure* to pop up. Neither of you are into arguing and aren't overly possessive, which makes for a very positive partnership. Nothing will be too wild for the two of you, so bring on the three-ways, five-hour fucks, and whatever else you two ultra-intelligent air signs can dream up.

Cancer and Aquarius: Aquarius can't stand Cancer's clingy attitude toward sexuality. Although the first foray into fornication may be totally titillating, once Aquarius forgets to call Cancer the next morning with an undying declaration of love, things can get uglier than Rush Limbaugh's ass *fast*. Cancer, meanwhile, thinks Aquarius is careless, cruel, and cold-hearted. This is strictly one-night-stand material only.

Leo and Aquarius: The sign of the lion loves Aquarius' freewheeling sexual style. Aquarius gets off on Leo's sensual skills and love of the high life. Fuck like rabbits while you can because out of the bedroom your amity will soon turn to enmity. As long as you're locked behind bedroom doors, however, getting down and dirty will be a delight for both of you.

Virgo and Aquarius: You're both intelligent and tend to use rational reasoning instead of being ruled by emotions, but your similarities end there. Aquarius is basically an optimistic free spirit while Virgo has a darker sexual side better suited to someone like Scorpio or Capricorn. Aquarius would rather not delve into this sulky sexual spirit. You'll make fascinating friends but aim for toe-clenching coitus and you'll be left a loser.

Libra and Aquarius: Fun-loving Libra turns up the heat for open-minded Aquarius. Trash that "better sex" book stuck beneath your bed because the two of you will come up with more than enough earth-shaking sexual positions on your own. Anything will be fair game as you forge new sexual ground, so grab your video camera, drop your clothes, and yell, "Action!"

Scorpio and Aquarius: You might not be able to stand each other outside of the bedroom but once you're in it you're virtual sex magnets for each other. Think *9 1/2 Weeks* (if you make it that far) as you explore every sexual scenario you could possibly imagination. There's lots of potential for pain in this profound pairing, so tread carefully and after an eight-hour lovemaking bout, make sure you've devised a good excuse for your friends to explain why you're walking funny.

Sagittarius and Aquarius: You've found another imaginative partner for carnal copulation, but there isn't as much potential for pain as the Aquarius/Scorpio combo. Sagittarius wants fucks that are fun and fabulous, with no strings attached and while Aquarius is not quite as emotionally detached, they can always view sex as a fun way to pass the time instead of something sacred. Relish the ravishing close at hand with this coupling: You're a delightful—and dramatic—duet.

Capricorn and Aquarius: Capricorn thinks Aquarius is a brain-dead idiot while Aqua women and men think the sign of the goat has a stick up his ass a mile long. Sound like romantic rapture? Not exactly: If the two of you can even make it to a bedroom you'll end up arguing about the wallpaper before indulging in the dance mammals made famous. Sex between goats and water bearers won't flick your Bic—but it might make you sick.

Aquarius and Aquarius: You've just found a sexual soul mate who is as open to exposing his or herself to the new and different as you are. Boring stuff like 69 can be left to the more earthy signs like Virgo and Scorpio. The two of you see sex as an almost mental experience, so get ready for free-flowing thoughts and sexual fantasies that would put *Penthouse* to shame. There's no room for embarrassment here, so say what you want—and *get* it.

Pisces and Aquarius: Aquarius thinks Pisces' old-fashioned, romantic style is fun—at first anyway. Pisces, meanwhile, likes the Aquarian trademark of inventiveness, so prepare for Aqua man or woman to take the sign of the fish to new heights of sexual pleasure. Unfortunately, sex will begin an almost imperceptible slide as the two of you get to know each other. The solution? Screw while it's still exciting—at which point Aquarius will be more than ready to walk away. Pisces will have a few problems at the parting but will get over 'em fast.

Exploring Their Erogenous Zone

Finding an Aquarian's secret sex spot is easy if the object of your affection is wearing shorts. Trapped by slacks, you'd never be able to contact their calves and ankles: The two hot spots that drive the sign of the water bearer wild. But grabbing the object of your affection's ankles is easier said than done unless you happen to be a Russian gymnast. You've got to make your moves carefree and *seemingly* absentminded.

Set the stage by lazing side by side in what would be termed the 69 position if oral affections were your aim. Since waxing the bean pole and muff diving aren't your aim, however, it doesn't matter if your Aquarian is wearing next to nothing or almost fully clothed—as long as you have complete and easy access to their lower leg region, electrifying the eros of your Aquarius is within easy reach.

Titillate this open-minded air sign with tickles and teases that run from their ankles around their inner calf and then trails along the outer side of their leg. It sounds crazy—and if you make your erotic moves too obvious—you'll get giggles instead of groans from your Aquarius. You've got to make the whole erotic escapade seem somehow unplanned. *You* might know the ultimate objective but it's best to keep Aquarius in the dark for as long as you can. Once you've tickled and teased the calves, forget your fingertips and put your tongue to the same task. Lick up, down, and all around—anywhere above the foot and below the knee is fair game for your Aqua man or woman. Lightly nip the ankle of your Aquarian. This might result in laughter but this laughter isn't the kind detailed above. It's a release of tension that most definitely *will* lead to lovemaking, so keep it up.

Once you're trapped in the throes of passion with an Aquarius, a great way to encourage an awesome orgasm on their part is to return to the original scene of your crime. Let's say you're a woman on top of your Aqua dude. Face away from him while he's inside you as you rub, tease, and vex his secret sex spot. Ride his love lance while you're having fun within the area above his feet and he'll be anything but a Johnny-come-lately. More likely, he'll come way more than the norm, and emerge from beneath you with a smile wider than Julia Roberts's.

Change the scenario a bit by imagining two gay guys or lesbian lovers and you're still left with the same libido-loosening technique. As you're bumping uglies or riding the wild pony, face *away* from your Aquarius so you can devote extra special attention to his or her love zone. They might end up so exhausted from all the erotic affection they'll fall straight to sleep, but don't worry: They'll thank you in the morning.

Come Again?

Aquarius Man

To get an Aqua man ready for round two, you must keep his basic psychology in mind. Aquarius *isn't* an overly sexual sign like Scorpio or Sagittarius, so to him love is more of a concept than a carnal creation. Therefore, yanking his yang will leave you feeling foolish when you're still faced with an iffy stiffy after five minutes of pulling. Instead, you've got to stimulate his sexuality from the psychological sideline: To force additional hedonism from your hunk you've got to manipulate his *mind*. How do you do this? After you're done with lovemaking round number one, give him time to cool off by discussing almost anything, since this garrulous guy loves to talk. Obviously, some topics—namely death and taxes—probably won't serve as perfect preludes to lovemaking so chat about Jennifer Love Hewitt's latest flick instead of your grandma's untimely death. Once your conversation is light, airy, and theoretical—analytical Aquarius' fave place to be—turn the topic toward something more titillating. Female? Tell him about your fantasy of being eaten out by a million different guys. Gay guy lookin' to get some? Let him know you have this secret fantasy about being tied up and made to do whatever his bidding is. If you keep this sexual banter relegated to the mental region for at least the first few minutes, you'll be recharging your Aquarian's sexual batteries whether he's aware you're doing so or not.

At some point, theory must be turned into reality, so keep an eye on his cock to decide when his interest level is, um . . . peaking. Once he's standing at attention, you've got your marching orders: Keep up the sexual speech as you begin manually manipulating his member. Make the whole scene seem somewhat carefree and innocent to increase your odds of an awesome bonus bang. When he's ready for the real deal, he'll let you know and at this point, you can either drop the dirty talk or keep it up, depending on your sexual bent. Some words of warning before signing off: Aquarius man isn't into truck-driver talk like Gemini. "Give me that monster cock now, you motherfucker" might drive Gemini wild but it will leave your Aquarius feeling embarrassed and offended. So what's cool for conversation? "I've always fantasized about dropping the soap and you taking me from behind in the shower," "I jerk off thinking about you being with another woman," and "I'd love to kiss you while some hunky guy is going down on you," are all acceptable sexual starters. Think classy sexual banter instead of strictly sexual street talk and you'll have your Aqua babe begging for more.

Aquarius Woman

Aquarius woman has a lot in common with her brother sign but not everything. If his head's in the clouds, hers is somewhere in the stratosphere, so don't feel shy about exchanging fantasies that could never happen in the real world. Share some ice-cold vodka shots before you tell her how you'd love to jump out of an airplane and fuck her on the way down. Excite her by mentioning that your other gay girlfriends would love to take turns with her (actually exploring this with Aquarius is a major no-no, however).

Telling her about your hopes and dreams may not seem like an understandable approach to getting a woman wet, but Aquarian women are all about communication and if you let her know your attributes and aspirations, you'll warm her form for yours. Watch your negativity (Virgos and Cancers, listen up!) because talking about the not-so-fine aspects of life can leave your daydreamer depressed. She wants to save the world, so talking about all the starving babies in Africa *couldn't* be a worse idea. Talk about ideals, action, and inspiration and you'll warm up this ultra-analytical sign.

Once you've got her gabbing, follow the same M.O. you'd use with Aquarius man. In other words, start playing with her—gently—whether you're talking about sex or *Scream 3*. Rub her breasts affectionately—and absentmindedly—as you discuss the pros and cons of Microsoft's breakup. Then, let your hands move south as you change the subject to something a bit more sexual. Go for teasing, light strokes: If there's one thing Aquarian women can't stand it's feeling like they've been treated like a piece of meat.

The last, somewhat cheesy option is only available to some. If you love her, let her know. For Aquarian woman, love is the union of your physical and spiritual sides—a never-ending quest for the sign whose buzzword is *knowledge*. She wants to educate herself and if you can convince her that sex is spiritual in addition to being stimulation, you'll find she'll be hot for your bod more often than not. Aquarian women are difficult to understand but if you make the extra effort, you'll find a loving woman—who, although she finds showing affection somewhat difficult—will go the extra mile to make you smile.

But Will It Last?

Aries and Aquarius: Aquarius isn't a take-charge type, since the eleventh sign of the zodiac is all about equality. Aries wants to be in charge round the clock, however, which can create more problems than Anita Bryant at a gay fund-raiser. If Aries can tone down his or her basic need to manipulate, Aquarius will stick around for the long haul but if the ram's rambunctious side won't take a breather, Aquarius will be outta there *fast*.

Taurus and Aquarius: Pairing an Aquarius with a Taurus is like making a movie with Jim Carrey and Meryl Streep: What looks like a bad idea on paper is even worse in the real world. Open-minded Aquarians like to wander through life while Taurus just wonders why Aquarians are so damn out of the norm. Aquarius marches to a very different drummer and staid-and-stable Taurus finds that disturbing. Can we say, "No fucking way"?

Gemini and Aquarius: Both of you are a hell of a lot of fun to be around. Talkative, funny, and sexually inventive, you make an awesome mental and physical match for each other. You'll have lots of parties (to which everyone would kill for an invite) and when the party's over you'll create a sexual soiree à deux.

Cancer and Aquarius: Aquarius will strike up a conversation with anyone from your next door neighbor to that seventy-five-year-old meter maid. Cancer finds this extremely threatening. Although Aquarius is merely trying to expand his or her social circle, the sign of the crab sees this as staking out a second sex partner. Breakups will be big-time bad news, so don't let this relationship go too far before pulling the plug.

Leo and Aquarius: You'll unleash lots of sexual energy together but once you unlock your bods from the act of love, problems pop up faster than zits on a teenager. Aquarius wants to explore the world while Leo is all-intent on creating a comfortable kingdom. These far-flung philosophical differences spell dating doom, so concentrate on creating a carnal carnival before moving on to a merger that's more manageable.

Virgo and Aquarius: Virgo's a homebody who basically can't stand anyone outside his or her circle of friends. Aquarius is supersocial, aching for exposure to a variety of lifestyles, people, and places. Virgo wants to work, while Aquarius is intent on intellectual exploration. You might make this unemotional attachment work for a while but eventually you'll head in separate directions.

Libra and Aquarius: Quite often, Aquarians' biggest problem in relationships is their unwillingness to give in on almost anything—from where to head for dinner to who's on top in bed on any given evening. Luckily, Libra is a master of diplomacy, so if anyone can maneuver headstrong Aquarius into a more manageable position it's this ultra-accepting air sign. The tough part will occur when you aim for the long term. Neither of you are very forceful, so you'll need to work extra hard to make this amusing merger last for long.

Scorpio and Aquarius: You'll be so addicted to sex with each other, breaking up will be harder than your private parts but you'll have to part ways sooner or later. Aquarius' freewheeling spirit enrages stick-by-me Scorpio and Aqua women and men see the scorpion's penchant for possessiveness as pubescently preposterous. Cut things off—figuratively speaking, of course—before sex cools down too much or your breakup will mirror the Donald and Ivana's: a vendetta of vengeance and a plethora of pain.

Sagittarius and Aquarius: Screw that song by Wings: the two of you would much rather live and let live. You both share totally optimistic views of the world that mesh extremely well together. Traveling is a bag you're both into and meeting new people floats both of your boats. Prepare for penetrating philosophical discussions because you're both forward thinkers and are fascinated by the oddities our Earth has to offer.

Capricorn and Aquarius: You have such different views of the world your odds for long-term loving are lower than Tonya Harding's TVQ. Capricorn wants to rule the world; Aquarius wants to understand it. A few interesting intellectual exchanges might occur initially, but when Capricorn tries calling the shots, Aquarius will yell adios.

Aquarius and Aquarius: You're both happy giving each other a long leash and even cooler, neither of you is into cheating, so you needn't worry when one jets off to Paris while the other stays home to finish their novel. Your love is almost otherworldly, you're such forward thinkers. Open relationships are an option for this open-minded merger (although I wouldn't recommend them).

Pisces and Aquarius: Initial meetings might be merry but eventually your union will end in dating disaster. Pisces needs constant reaffirmations of love—something unemotional Aquarius is *totally* not into. This partnership *can* work if Pisces can realize Aquarius' love is for real: It's just that Aqua men and women aren't into daily declarations of undying affection. A star-crossed combo probably headed nowhere fast.

Aquarius Celebs: Ahead of Their Time

David Lynch	January 20
Emma Lee Bunton	January 21
Geena Davis	January 21
Diane Lane	January 22
Michael Hutchence	January 22
Linda Blair	January 22
Tiffani-Amber Thiessen	January 23
Tatyana Ali	January 24
Nastasia Kinski	January 24
John Belushi	January 24
Wayne Gretzky	January 26
Ellen DeGeneres	January 26
Eddie Van Halen	January 26
Bridget Fonda	January 27
Elijah Wood	January 28
Sarah MacLachlan	January 28
Andrew Keegan	January 29
Greg Louganis	January 29
Oprah Winfrey	January 29
Heather Graham	January 29
John Forsythe	January 29

Brett Butler	January 30
Phil Collins	January 30
Minnie Driver	January 31
Suzanne Pleshette	January 31
Lisa Marie Presley	February 1
Brandon Lee	February 1
Sherman Helmsley	February 1
Garrett Morris	February 1
Christie Brinkley	February 2
Farrah Fawcett	February 2
Michael T. Weiss	February 2
Morgan Fairchild	February 3
Fran Tarkenton	February 3
Oscar De La Hoya	February 4
Alice Cooper	February 4
Rosa Parks	February 4
Jennifer Jason Leigh	February 5
H. R. Giger	February 5
Barbara Hershey	February 5
Axl Rose	February 6
Natalie Cole	February 6
Garth Brooks	February 7
Chris Rock	February 7
Seth Green	February 8
Gary Coleman	February 8
Charles Shaughnessy	February 9
Mia Farrow	February 9
Laura Dern	February 10
George Stephanopoulos	February 10
Matt Lawrence	February 11
Brandy Norwood	February 11
Jennifer Aniston	February 11
Sheryl Crow	February 11
Christina Ricci	February 12
Arsenio Hall	February 12
Judy Blume	February 12

George Segal	February 13
Drew Bledsoe	February 14
Meg Tilly	February 14
Chris Farley	February 15
Matt Groening	February 15
Jane Seymour	February 15
John McEnroe	February 16
Ice-T	February 16
Joseph Gordon-Levitt	February 17
Denise Richards	February 17
Bryan White	February 17
Rene Russo	February 17

Chapter 13

PISCES
(February 18–March 19)

Sex Stats

Ruling planet: Neptune, the god in charge of delicious dreams, dangerous deceptions, and sexual fantasies.

Signature symbol: Two fish linked together, portraying Pisces' uneasy alliance between this world and the next.

Trademark color: Sea green and black, sensual shades associated with the ocean and cutting-edge sexual adventures.

Favorite position: Between your legs, since Pisces is all about oral affections.

Potent porn: *Czech, Please* for lesbian lovers, *Pheremones* for guys who gun for guys, and *Vagina Beach* for the straight set.

Ultimate outfit (male): A turn-of-the-century–type look with a billowy white shirt unbuttoned to the midchest paired with black parachute pants.

Ultimate outfit (female): Virtually anything from Prada.

Mattress mambo music: Soulful jazz by McCoy Tyner or anything techno.

Best sex toy: A copy of the *Kama Sutra,* since your fish is into almost anything.

After-fuck finger food: Spicy shrimp cocktails to keep your water sign in the swim.

Do You Know What You're in For?

Ruled by Neptune, god of illusion, deception, and wishes, Pisces quite often are odd little fishes. Represented by a fish, this symbol is all-accurate for Pisces. As mutable water signs, Pisces are often ruled by gut instinct, which often works quite well for them. While Capricorn must know the facts and Gemini must identify all the key players in any given drama, Pisceans are governed by intuition and a sixth sense most other signs don't share. This accurate third-eye vision can be easily blurred with drugs or drinking though, a major problem for most people born under the sign of the fish. Pisces can be dreamy and almost surreal in the sex act, but once your fishy has headed for home, double-check your medicine cabinet to make sure none of your Dilaudid tablets have been pilfered. Pisces is the sign that stands between the portals of the here and now and the great hereafter, and many of the rules that govern the rest of us simply don't apply to Pisces. A Sagittarius might bullshit another to foster his version of reality while Libra lies to keep the boat she's in from rocking too much. When a Pisces lies however, it's hard to know what their objective is. Only a thin line separates dreams from reality in the world according to fish and when that line gets erased, Pisces might be totally unaware that what he or she is speaking couldn't be further from the truth.

Pisces are prone to a multitude of sins, from stealing to unsafe sex to sugar-coating the truth, but don't make the mistake of thinking Pisces is malicious or evil since the sign of the fish is anything but. Pisces simply cannot—and will not—adapt to all of society's rules. If a dictate works for Pisces, she'll follow it to the letter but when she encounters directions she doesn't agree with, she'll conveniently forget whatever she was told.

Without a doubt, Pisces is the wildest sex partner you'll ever encounter. Nothing is taboo for this sign, and if you're into wilder aspects of sexuality (from kink to golden showers to slow, sensual spankings), you could do a lot worse than hooking up with the fish. Pisces runs the intellectual gamut from being majorly obsessed with the occult to thinking every conspiracy theory has roots in fact. Whether the Pisces in question thinks the Richard Gere/gerbil story is the gospel or *The X-Files* are actually top-secret government documents, convincing him or her otherwise is about as likely as an *Ishtar Part 2*.

In spite—or because of—these rather bizarre character traits, Pisces can be a bombastic bed partner who will always keep you guessing. If you want by-the-numbers sex with the lights out by ten, fishies aren't so fabulous, but if you're looking for someone who will go the extra mile to discover all of your secret moan zones, then the last sign in the zodiac is the one for you. Bed bonding with a Pisces will allow you to enter their dreamworld, a fascinating place that rivals anything Freddy Krueger could come up with.

Pisces Man

Pisces guys are full of surprises. From intuitively knowing all your inner fantasies to exposing you to the latest sexual disease, fully understanding your Pi guy will be harder than his dick when you do the do. Along those lines, Pisces makes an excellent lover. He's from the old school that sex should be an almost out-of-body experience and if you're the lucky one he's showering his attentions on, count on one thing: You're in for one hell of a good time. No fantasy is too bizarre for him, no act too extreme. He's a master at reading other people's emotions as well, so when he asks, "Wanna join the mile-high club?," make sure you answer honestly since any lies instantly register on his radar.

Equally comfortable with long-term love or a wham-bam-thank-you-ma'am (or Sam, if he's a gay fish), this dude is an expert in the field of love making. No Taurus-type hang-ups or Scorpio-style domination is necessary for this sign. His only equal in experiencing physical love with no distracting side effects is Libra, but while Libra men tend to be focused on themselves and their response to a mate in a relationship, Pisces is quite happy focusing on *you*. He thinks sex should be a mind-melding experience, which quite often equals stellar sensuality. For him, sex isn't just about physical pleasure, although that's certainly an important part. Mattress mambos are all about exploring himself and his other and he won't feel scared to say or do whatever pops into his mind.

If you're looking for safety and security in a mate, Pisces won't come close to filling the bill, but if you're searching for a sensual sexual partner who isn't afraid to show all of his different aspects, whether they're freaky, feminine, or just fun, then this dreamy man is everything you're looking for. Life, love, or lust with a Piscean stud will be wild, crazy, sexy, and cool but it will never be dull or predictable. The Pisces man thinks life is a dream and if you enjoy sharing his view of the world, you'll never have regrets about hooking this fish.

Pisces Woman

If anything, Piscean women are even more intuitive than their masculine counterparts, so before that first date, fabulous fete, or fantastic fuck, realize that trying to bullshit this girl is a major mistake. A lie won't exactly ruin your credibility since she loves to stretch the truth as well, but there's simply no point in tall tales as she'll see through them faster than Superman can fly. Pisces *chicas* are often attracted to bad boys, fractious females, or both. This fascination with the dark side of life doesn't always rule her world, however, and even when it does, many females will grow out of their "Oooh, I'm so naughty" phase rather quickly.

The same artistic bent that increases her odds of success in the worlds of drama, music, and writing increase your odds for scintillating sex. She's never satisfied with doing the same ol', same ol' when she knows there are more exciting options at hand. Want to pretend you're the captain and she's the *Titanic* about to go down on your ass? She's game. Have you lost sleepless nights fixated on the idea of making love in a public place? She has, too. Whatever you're wanting to try, Pisces will willingly oblige—on the condition that she doesn't feel like your objective for her is humiliation or degradation. Some Piscean females will even do that for you and if you find a Pisces bent on her own destruction, adding fuel to her fire is easy if you happen to be sans conscience.

If real, enduring romance is your objective, Pisces is also your gal. While Gemini would momentarily coo over fresh roses and Cancer would appreciate the gesture as solidifying your relationship, Pisces would be bowled over by the beauty of the bouquet and your gesture in presenting her with it. She's a strong believer in true love and once she feels the ties that bind she'll do anything in her power to protect you. Her devotion can confuse other signs, however, since, in many ways she's somewhat confused by all the rules and regulations our universe has. She'll probably never be a brainiac in the business world or a master with finances but her love for you will be so strong, you'll feel almost transcendental. This isn't mere coincidence either: Pisces has one foot here and one foot in the world beyond and if she loves you, you'll get to experience the benefits of both.

Five Surefire Ways to Break the Ice with Pisces

Pisces Man
1. Ask him out for a drink.
2. Get his take on Marilyn Manson or any other occult-oriented band.
3. Find out if he's ever meditated.
4. Discover where he partied last weekend.
5. Talk about weird coincidences in your life or flashes of intuition you've received.

Pisces Woman

1. Tell her about a weird dream you had.
2. Talk about *The X-Files* or some other conspiracy-theory–oriented TV show.
3. Discuss reincarnation or ideas concerning life after death.
4. Let her know about any poetry or writing at which you've tried your hand.
5. Ask what her favorite artwork is.

Refining Your Sexual Strategy—The Subrulers

Neptune: The Party That Never Ends (February 18– February 29)

Neptune is the dude who clouds our vision, who gives us wet dreams of people we'll never even meet, and makes us think we're up to tasks we can never complete. When you double this guy's forces you're faced with a fishy who's so prone to drugs and drinking you might need your own pharmacological stash just to get through the first evening. That's the bad news. So what's the upside? This particular Pisces is the ultimate romantic—no other sign in the zodiac is his or her equal. Love is extremely important to this drama-prone fish head, so though you might journey up a rocky road you'll enjoy the bumps and grinds along the way.

Sexually speaking, this Pisces is putty in your hands. Anything you want—*anything*—is only a question away, which makes the only question "Are you woman or man enough to tell this fish exactly what you want from fornication?" Don't let embarrassment be your guide. With one foot in this world and one foot in the spiritual realm, Pisces doesn't waste time beating around the bush (whether literal or figurative), so neither should you. From S&M to even wilder forms of kink, nothing is too extreme for this over-the-top tempter or temptress, so loosen up your libido before loosening your tongue.

Pisces is almost predatory, he or she is so sexual in the sack. While Scorpio likes to play top dawg, Pisces will adopt any role you require, so tell her to slip into that French maid outfit or tell him to slip into that thong that shows his ass off to maximum appeal.

Arguments are a must from this fiesty fish. When he or she goes through the downward spirals that are part and parcel of every Pisces' life, get ready to make war not love. The good news is that making up will be sublime and though your fish may lash out in the heat of the moment, ultimately he or she probably didn't mean what she said. Life is somewhat of a dream to this surreal sign and if you can handle being part of a Picasso painting, then go for this guy or girl with no holds barred.

One-night stands are sublime with this strain of fish because you get all of the fun with none of the next-morning BS. If you want to get into the pants of an un-attached Pisces and they're equally attracted to you, hitting the sheets is proba-bly only a question away. "Wanna fuck?" might not slide off your tongue easily, but when Pisces slides down on you, you'll be glad you asked.

The Moon: The Psychic Fishy's Network (March 1– March 10)

We've all heard of seeing-eye dogs but have you ever heard of seeing-eye fish? People born under these ten days are amazingly intuitive, so get ready for your fishy friend to know what you want in and out of bed without having to say a word. Whether you'll *get* what you're wanting is another question entirely, however: With the Moon added to their mix, people born under this decanate are more moody than a Hollywood starlet. If you happen to catch them on a good day, you'll get almost anything you ask for but catch this fish on a bad day and you'll catch hell.

If you're the type to screw around, like Sagittarius, be up front about your bedroom-bopping behavior from the start: Pisces may be one of the few signs who doesn't mind. If you let Pisces find out you've been straying outside the rules you've set for your relationship get ready for soap-opera–style shenanigans that would put Tori Spelling to shame. When pissed off, this Pisces will do almost any-thing to wreak revenge, so unless that Lorena Bobbitt tale about the cut cock ap-peals to you, try to stay on the good side of this dreamy denizen of the deep.

When the Moon is happy, this fish is, too, and when you're locked behind closed doors you'll wonder why you've been wasting time with less passionate signs. Anything is fair game as long as it's discussed first and sometimes even if it's not: It's that psychic power coming into play again that lets your fishy know the best way to make *you* come. You'll get odd sexual requests, so if you're from the old school of romance like Cancer, just say no to sex with this type. If you're into domination, however, and are wanting someone exciting who doesn't mind stepping beyond society's sexual boundaries whenever you want to, this fish is for you.

Long-term relationships hold little appeal to this strain of fish except the the-oretical kind. You'll often hear Pisces born during this decanate talk about finding the love of their lives only to change their mind two weeks later. Pisces' emotions are like the ocean's tides—and what comes up must eventually come back down as well. If you're looking for a fabulous fuck go for it, but if the big M or other similar long-term commitment is your objective, you'll be sorry that you caught this fish.

Pluto: Deep-Sea Fishing (March 11—March 20)

Pluto is the ultrapowerful god in charge of beginnings, endings, death, and life and with his potent power added to the Pisces mix, he gives gravity and depth to Neptune's clueless behavior. Of the three decanates, this is the most drawn toward spirituality and/or the occult. Pluto reminds Pisces that death is inevitable and this knowledge keeps this kind of fish from becoming as entangled in drugs or drink. Pluto forces the fish to consider the fact that when we die, we look back on our life as a spreadsheet—a series of pluses and minuses. This fish wants to insure he or she comes out on the positive end of things and that results in a less dramatic personality, but one with far more depth.

Just as sexual as the other two decanates, this sign doesn't delude itself about the end results like the other two do. While the other two might say they've fallen in love on the first date, this sign will hold back until they're more sure of their affection. Pluto adds imagination to the illusion Neptune provides and when you combine the two, you find someone who can make an awesome actor, screenwriter, or other Hollywood-type hot job.

One thing sets this fish apart from the other two. This particular Pisces must go through occasional solitary periods to readjust their mind to the changing framework life presents. If this brings out your insecure side, pass by this Pisces but if you're able to allow your Pisces solo time without feeling weird about it, don't worry: This last decanate of Pisces has the power to stick by you even when the fishing line gets a little taut. This sign is extremely affectionate and far more adult when it comes to expressing all that emotion than the other two types.

Curious and intellectual, this type will seek out new sexual adventures—but only if you want them to. Nothing is too extreme and with this type of fish you won't get anger the next morning. Unlike the other two types, this Pisces thinks out his or her moves in advance—a rare trait for the sign of the fish. All Pisces are ruled by emotion but with this subspecies, intellect has an important voice. Whether years of romance or an evening of eroticism is your goal, you'll get what you're looking for when you net this fantastic fish.

Sexual Synergy

Aries and Pisces: Pisces is intrigued with Aries' action-oriented attitude while the rambunctious ram loves dominating the sign of the fish between the sheets. Pisces imagination will keep Aries' sexual juices flowing while Aries knows all the right moves to keep this fish feeling fly. All sex signals are go, so all you need to do is get together to ultimately get down and dirty.

Taurus and Pisces: Bulls are rock-hard romantic partners and that's exactly what fishies need. Taurus falls immediately in love with Pisces' passion for all things sexual and can't get enough of Pisces' sweet-natured affection and admiration. Maybe you won't be trying on leather chaps or rubber bodysuits any time soon but this is definitely a romance novel waiting to happen.

Gemini and Pisces: Gemini likes Pisces' enigmatic nature for the first few bedroom bops, but by the time Gem realizes Pisces' attitude isn't a game but real life, sexual shenanigans begin a fast downward spiral. Gem's rapier wit wounds Pisces' gentle side, which doesn't exactly equal scintillating sex. Aim for one or two rounds of romance, then set your sights on someone else.

Cancer and Pisces: You'll need to install a fridge in your bedroom because you'll be staying between the sheets so long they'll get sticky. Sensitive Pisces gets everything he or she desires from caring Cancer. These two water signs are all wet—but when it comes to sensual, slippery sex, getting wet is your best bet.

Leo and Pisces: Though Leo might enjoy dominating the fish in fornication, it will only be as a prelude to dumping his or her ass. Leo mistakes Pisces' dreamy attitude for weakness (even though it isn't), while Pisces thinks Leo couldn't be more full of shit (debatable—depending on the lion at hand). Any way you look at it, sexual satisfaction is highly unlikely between these two. Combine a water sign with fire and you merely douse the flames.

Virgo and Pisces: At first, Virgo thinks Pisces' ultra-affectionate ways are quite a compliment, so count on quality coupling for at least the first few rounds. Over time though, Virgo's critical ways will wound the fish, who, in turn, will begin to use sex as a weapon. This won't fly with Virgo, who will up the ante by playing severe sexual mind games. All this eventually leads to yawn-inspiring sex.

Libra and Pisces: If you're comfortable separating sex from love, coupling between the sign of the scales and the visionary fish can be quite a trip. From around the world to sex acts that last hours instead of minutes, the two of you will find quite a variety of intimacies in which to indulge. Let your imagination run riot and you'll discover all the enigmas sex holds secret.

Scorpio and Pisces: Pisces is looking for a deep well in which to explore their sexuality and Scorpio provides the perfect receptacle. Penetrating, possessive Scorpio does anything and everything Pisces needs to feel satisfied sexually, while Pisces' undeniable attraction to the sign of the scorpion makes Scorpio feel lewd with lust. Scorpio will enjoy forcing the fish to bow to his or her will and Pisces' overly active sexual imagination will never leave Scorpio looking for lust from another. Sexually, you're a perfect match, so forge your bond so you can get to banging.

Sagittarius and Pisces: When passionate Pisces pairs off with anything-goes Sagittarius, it's time to rewrite all the sexual rules. From gender-bending antics to loving but lethal deep-throat action, *nothing* will be taboo in your bedroom. These sexual high jinks will lose some luster as time goes on but while the getting is good, *go for it.*

Capricorn and Pisces: Although you couldn't be more different intellectually, sexually goats get along great with fishies. What Pisces needs Capricorn happily supplies. Although you're not going to shake each other's world sexually, this is a happy, comfortable union that can sizzle if Capricorn is willing to let loose from the goat's notorious prim-and-proper persona.

Aquarius and Pisces: At first glance you appear to have everything in common sexually: You're both open-minded, easygoing, and ready for almost anything. The problem is that neither of you likes to initiate the act, so although you might share loads of titillating talk you'll rarely get down to the real deal. Skip sex and go watch *The X-Files* together instead: You'll have more fun sharing ideas than bodily fluids.

Pisces and Pisces: You're both creatures born for the bedroom but you accentuate all the wrong points in each other. Sex will seem similar to screwing a sibling as the two of you compete for the Sulker of the Year Award. Since both of you like to play games when it comes to gettin' it, neither of you will get *anything* very often.

Exploring Their Erogenous Zone

Penetrating Pisces' private passion patch is an ultra-easy feat: Just aim for your fishy's toes and work your way up to the base of his or her ankles. Yup, you guessed it: Pisces' zesty zone *is* their feet. How do you put this info to use when it comes to bonding in the bedroom? If you follow these directions, your fish will think he or she has floated from the top of the fish bowl straight to heaven, so read on.

If you want to make Pisces your love slave, start out with a warm—preferably scented—footbath. Forget that Mr. Bubble crap: You need something heavy with sea salt that will relax and enhance your fishy's aching feet. The water should be very warm to the touch but not scalding (unless you're aiming for a fight from your fish instead of a fuck). Once you've dipped their tootsies into this pleasure pit for feet, let 'em soak their for ten minutes. Then, with your Pisces sitting in a chair, sit cross-legged in front of them and rub their feet through the water. Your water sign will be turned on by seeing you take this subservient role even if the role pulls a 180 when sex gets started. An important note to remember is that although other signs might like their meat massaged gently, with Pisces this rule doesn't apply. Use forceful, kneading motions that run from their ankles to the tips of their toes. After you've indulged your fish's foot fetish for at least five minutes, get a scrub brush and clean their tootsies off with lots of TLC (you'd better be sure you do this or you'll be completely grossed out when you reach my final bit of advice). Now that your Pisces' feet are nice and clean, take them out of the salt bath and dry them off carefully, paying extraclose attention to the between-the-toes area (Pisces *really* gets off on this).

Next, grab some peppermint oil—you can snag this at specialty food stores or some drug store chains—and lightly massage it all over their feet. Keep massaging until the oil has soaked in completely. It might make your hands feel odd—kinda cold, is all—and if this bugs you, wash your hands before you reach the next and final step.

If your fish has a dick, he should already be throwing a major bone and if you're gracing your girlfriend with this foot favor, she should be squirming in delight (and though her feet might not be wet any longer, something else should be). All right, here's the final chapter, and if you're a prim-and-proper sign like Cancer or Virgo, get ready, because you might not like what you're about to read. Gently lift your Pisces' feet to your mouth and kiss each toe one by one. Once you've accomplished this simple task let your tongue take over where your mouth left off and begin licking in and around your Pisces' toes. Massaging the balls of the feet while you make lingual love to the toes will send your Pisces into a passionate peak. Finish off your mission by sticking your tongue back where it belongs and kissing all over the area you've just gotten wet. By this time your willing water sign will be a pile of mush and more than happy to trade their feet fetish for another F-word that's a hell of a lot more fun.

Come Again?

Pisces Man

When renewed amour is your goal with Pisces man, you need to have done a little prep work in advance. First, you'll need some kind of chilled alcoholic beverage in the fridge. Champagne is fine for luxury-loving Taurus but a Pisces can pass on all those tiny bubbles. He's probably more into ice-cold Skyy vodka, Cuba libres, or peppermint schnapps so cold that it's damn close to being frozen. Your second prerequisite is some smut. Although X-rated videos hold appeal for almost any red-blooded male they hold special powers over Pisces. All right; now that you've done your homework, let's put all your hard work into practice.

Scenario: You've just fucked and it was fabulous. Your Pisces has rolled over in bed to smoke his mandatory cig (Pisces have a problem about overindulging in drugs, whether they happen to be nicotine, cocaine, and/or anything in between). This is the point you head for your secret stash of spirits and present him with an icy-cold shot of whatever's at hand. Make sure he stops at two though, or you might come face to face with an iffy stiffy. Before clinking glasses in a toast to your recent romance moves, slipping in that XXX flick will immediately start to stiffen his dick. Now slam the shots—and, if personally you can't stand drinking, throw yours in a potted plant when Pisces isn't looking—and start checking out the on-screen eroticism. Comment on the action and engage Pisces in an oral exchange that might not be exactly what you're hoping for—*yet*.

Once Pisces has become sexually stirred by the footage at hand, start stirring his foot-long with *your* hand. So this is where you're supposed to go down on him, eh? Not so fast: Pisces love to please, so turn the tables by ordering him to make like the Taco Bell Chihuahua and cross *your* border. Not only is Pisces' favorite passion pleasing his partner, he also loves to get ordered around, so free your inner dominatrix—or dominator—to get your fishy friend to do whatever the hell you want him to do. While he's down there, giving you a salivated shower of oral affections, bark out commands at him like you're a drill sergeant and he's the newest marine on the block. "Harder, faster, slower, stronger" are all things you should be belting out between clenched teeth as he's getting busy. The more you command, the harder he'll work, so be a diva or a decidedly determined dude. By getting what *you* want, you'll be giving Pisces what *he* needs.

Pisces Woman

The Pisces woman needs a lot more tender loving care than her male counterpart. To get her sexual rocks rolling again, you need to tune in to her wavelength by stepping into her dreamscape. This isn't as difficult as it sounds as long as communication is something you're pretty adept with. After your first round of lovemaking, romance should be your first objective. Take her outside to stare at the stars or Moon (a favorite pastime of Pisces females). Well-chilled wine is another cool opp but more as a prop than a sexual stimulant.

Your true key to getting inside her again is to get inside her mind. Try free association as you kick back with her. To a Pisces female, life is a dream, so don't feel weird about saying anything and everything that pops into your mind. Tell her about your childhood, share sexual fantasies (just the romantic ones for now), or brainstorm new ideas you've been thinking about. While you're talking, concentrate on all the mushy stuff romance novels are made of, with a seriously sexual twist. In other words, hold her hand as you step into the backyard to see the sky but once you're back indoors, run your hands slowly up and down her body as you exchange that bedroom banter. Don't act like a rowdy adolescent but don't be too coy either: Whether you're male or female, keep in mind that the Pisces woman wants someone strong to give weight to her fantasy world, so play the role of protector in any way you can. You can take this advice literally, by wrapping your arms around her to give her a strong sense of protection, or figuratively, by letting her know about any power plays you were recently involved in or any out-of-the-norm courageous acts. Remember that your Pisces woman is very impressed by action, since she tends to have a problem making moves on her own, so telling her about that recent merger your company made can excite her. Don't make the mistake of relating boring business stories though. Once you've made your point, move on; getting bogged down with numbers or tiny details will be an awesome way to put your fishy to sleep.

After just fifteen to thirty minutes of this romance-oriented dialogue, the Pisces woman should be ready to go at it again—*as long* as you haven't forgotten to keep your hands moving in all the right directions. The cool part is, with a Pisces woman you probably won't have to make any overt sexual moves. Once she realizes you're interested with all the hand activity, she'll probably do it for you. And if she doesn't? Concentrate on kissing her as your hands move into overtime. This will prove too much for your Pisces woman and whether she wants to or not, she'll find herself getting wet all over again.

But Will It Last?

Aries and Pisces: This is the ultimate dynamic duo if Aries can learn to curb the big mouth for which rams are famous. Pisces is the perfect partner: sensitive, sweet, and dependent. These are all properties rams find pleasing but if Aries gives in to their tendency to attack at a moment's notice, trouble begins to brew. Work will make this willing combo consummate but without some subtlety from Aries all will be for naught.

Taurus and Pisces: Bulls and fish can form storybook romances since their differences make them the perfect partners. Though bulls can be Pisces' Prince or Princess Charming, dilemmas surface from Taurus' all-important practicality. If Taurus can loosen up a bit and dare to delve into his or her subconscious and Pisces is more realistic about money matters and getting the job done, this sexy partnership has everything else going for it.

Gemini and Pisces: You're drawn to each other like a hard rocker to Heather Locklear but once you get off, you'll be dying to get out of each other's sight. Gemini can't abide Pisces' saccharine sweetness while Pisces thinks Gemini's tendency to say whatever's on his or her mind is downright rude. Confrontations will be combative and constant. Go for this union if you groove on the *Mortal Kombat* video game, otherwise find a suitor who's more suitable.

Cancer and Pisces: Okay, so since the fucking's fab there's got to be a downside, right? Think again, because this complementary combo is great both in the bedroom and out of it. You both prize security and faithfulness and love staying at home but don't worry: You'll find plenty of activities to keep you busy on the homefront.

Leo and Pisces: If you're aiming for an instant enemy this is the ultimate alliance. Pisces likes private fantasies, dreamy love duets, and ideas; Leo loves public forays, dancing on tables, and action, action, *action*. If you make it as friends, count yourself lucky, but if you make it into bed break out the boxing gloves because all hell is about to break loose.

Virgo and Pisces: Virgo wants to reach the heights of material success; Pisces is searching for the perfect dream lover. Pisces' dependency frightens unemotional Virgo, while the sign of the virgin's tendency to criticize at the drop of a hat makes the fish feel unloved and unwanted. Merge an eternal pessimist with a procrastinating dreamer and you get a union predestined for doom and gloom.

Libra and Pisces: This fun-filled affair has everything it takes to make many months' worth of enjoyment but if you're wanting to spend a lifetime together, you'll have a rough road in front of you. You both love luxury and spending money, but neither of you is driven enough to be very realistic about getting it. Money matters and debt will be the biggest woes you face, but if you can work around these problems, this alliance might have a long shelf life.

Scorpio and Pisces: Since both of you are water signs, you can intuitively read each other's emotions as easily as other signs can read a book. Scorpio will go the extra mile to make sure Pisces feels protected, while the fish will invent new and novel ways to stimulate the scorpion's sexual side. Going from good to better, both of you think cheating is better reserved for the sleazy signs. Translation? You're well suited for each other sexually *and* spiritually.

Sagittarius and Pisces: Screwing is sublime between these fire and water signs, but when faced with life away from the bedroom your union goes from sexual to sour. Sagittarians want to explore the world and feel tied down when yoked to just one sexual partner. Pisces wants someone who'll hang around for the long haul and doesn't allow their eyes to rove. Use this union strictly for emergency sex. Anything else is begging for trouble.

Capricorn and Pisces: The two of you go together like peanut butter and jelly: Capricorn is the meat of the matter while Pisces adds light and sweetness to the mix. Capricorn's natural tendency toward pessimism and darkness is lightened up by Pisces' passionate love of life. You're total opposites but in this instance opposites *attract*.

Aquarius and Pisces: Sex between the two of you, while interesting, won't be a strong-enough glue to bind your bond eternally. You're far better off as friends, since on many intellectual issues you see eye to eye. It's your basic philosophies that are too different to allow an easy union. Aquarius is outgoing, loves to travel, and is always looking for new friendships. Pisces is a homebody and sticks by those he or she loves, not wanting to add more to the mix. Awesome allies but aim for life partnering and you'll be fighting a losing battle.

Pisces and Pisces: You're both so damn good in bed it's a shame you can't get along once you're out of it. You simply share too much in common and bring out the worst in each other. Sulking competitions, the silent treatment, and irritated glances will be your M.O. in this meandering merger. You're aiming for a partnership that goes nowhere and sooner or later you'll break the ties that bind.

Pisces Celebs: In the Swim

Molly Ringwald	February 18
Matt Dillon	February 18
John Travolta	February 18
Helen Gurley Brown	February 18
Justine Bateman	February 19
Seal	February 19
Kurt Cobain	February 20
Andrew Shue	February 20
Cindy Crawford	February 20
Jennifer Love Hewitt	February 21
Kelsey Grammer	February 21
David Geffen	February 21
Rue Mclanahan	February 21
Julius Erving	February 22

Drew Barrymore	February 22
Peter Fonda	February 23
Billy Zane	February 24
Justin Jeffre	February 25
George Harrison	February 25
Johnny Cash	February 26
Michael Bolton	February 26
Rozonda "Chilli" Thomas	February 27
Elizabeth Taylor	February 27
Bernadette Peters	February 28
Mario Andretti	February 28
Antonio Sabato, Jr	February 29
Jensen Ackles	March 1
Mark-Paul Gosselaar	March 1
Ron Howard	March 1
Jon Bon Jovi	March 2
Dr. Seuss	March 2
Jackie Joyner-Kersee	March 3
Herschel Walker	March 3
Chastity Bono	March 4
Patsy Kensit	March 4
Niki Taylor	March 5
Andy Gibb	March 5
Tom Arnold	March 6
Ivan Lendl	March 7
James Van Der Beek	March 8
Freddie Prinze, Jr	March 8
Kathy Ireland	March 8
Emmanuel Lewis	March 9
Jasmine Guy	March 10
Sharon Stone	March 10
Thora Birch	March 11
Darryl Strawberry	March 12
Liza Minelli	March 12
Dana Delany	March 13
L. Ron Hubbard	March 13

Taylor Hanson	March 14
Billy Crystal	March 14
Fabio	March 15
Sly Stone	March 15
Erik Estrada	March 16
Rob Lowe	March 17
Gary Sinise	March 17
Kurt Russell	March 17
Queen Latifah	March 18
Bonnie Blair	March 18
Vanessa Williams	March 18
Bruce Willis	March 19
Glenn Close	March 19